THE RELIGION OF TH
Anglican Essays in Commer

THE RELIGION
OF THE
INCARNATION

Anglican Essays in Commemoration of *Lux Mundi*

Edited by Robert Morgan

Published by Bristol Classical Press

Printed in Great Britain

First published in 1989 by
Bristol Classical Press,
226 North Street, Bedminster,
Bristol BS3 1JD

©Bristol Classical Press, 1989

British Library Cataloguing in Publication Data

The Religion of the Incarnation: Anglican Essays in
  Commemoration of Lux Mundi
  1. Anglican communion. Christian doctrine
  I. Morgan, Robert, *1940-*
230'.3

ISBN 1-85399-063-9
ISBN 1-85399-064-7 pbk

CONTENTS

CONTRIBUTORS

Rev. J. Barton, DPhil, DLitt, read Theology and was research student at Keble, was research fellow and junior chaplain at Merton, and has been University Lecturer in Old Testament studies and Fellow and Chaplain of St Cross since 1974. He was a member of the Doctrine Commission of the Church of England 1978-85, secretary of the Faculty, 1985-8, and Bampton Lecturer in 1988. His publications include *Amos' Oracles against the Nations* (1980), *Reading the Old Testament* (1984), *Oracles of God* (1986), *People of the Book? The Authority of Scripture in Christianity* (1988).

Rev. D.W. Brown, DPhil, read Philosophy and Theology as Alexander Campbell Fraser scholar at Oriel, where he has been Fellow, Tutor and Chaplain since 1976. His publications include *Choices* (1983), *The Divine Trinity* (1986), *Continental Philosophy and Modern Theology* (1987).

Rev. T. Gorringe read Theology at St Edmund Hall, was Chaplain at Wadham (1975-9) and since 1986 has been Fellow, Tutor and Chaplain at St John's. His publications include *Redeeming Time* (1986).

Rev. P.B. Hinchliff, DD, read Theology at Trinity, has been Fellow and Tutor of Balliol since 1972, was Chaplain 1972-86 and Bampton Lecturer in 1984. He has been Canon of Grahamstown since 1964 and Canon theologian of Coventry since 1972. He now represents the University on the General Synod. His publications include *John William Colenso* (1964), *Cyprian of Carthage and the Unity of the Christian Church* (1974), *Holiness and Politics* (1982), *Benjamin Jowett and the Christian Religion* (1987).

Rev. A. Louth read Theology at Cambridge, was Fellow, Tutor and Chaplain at Worcester College 1970-85 since when he has been Senior Lecturer in Religious Studies at Goldsmith's College, University of London. His publications include *The Origins of the Christian Mystical Tradition* (1981), *Discerning the Mystery* (1983), *Denys the Areopagite* (1989).

Rev. A. McGrath, DPhil, was an undergraduate at Wadham, research student at Linacre and senior scholar at Merton where he also read Theology. He has been tutor at Wycliffe Hall since 1984 and is Bampton Lecturer-elect for 1990. His publications include *Luther's Theology of the Cross* (1985), *Justitia Dei* (1986), *The Making of Modern German Christology* (1986), *The Intellectual Origins of the European Reformation* (1987).

Rev. R. Morgan read Theology at Cambridge and has been University Lecturer in New Testament theology and Fellow of Linacre since 1976. He was secretary of the Faculty 1978-85 and has been priest-in-charge at Sandford-on-Thames since 1987. His publications include *The Nature of New Testament Theology* (1973), (with Michael Pye) *Ernst Troeltsch: Writings on Theology and Religion* (1977), (with John Barton) *Biblical Interpretation* (1988).

Rev. J. Muddiman, DPhil, read Theology at Keble, was Research Fellow and Assistant Chaplain at New College (1972-6), Vice-Principal at St Stephen's House (1976-83). He has been Lecturer in Theology at the University of Nottingham since 1983. His publications include *The Bible: Fount and Well of Truth* (1983).

Rev. D. Nicholls, PhD, was Fellow, Tutor and Chaplain of Exeter College (1973-8) and has been Vicar of Littlemore since 1978. His publications include *Three Varieties of Pluralism* (1974), *The Pluralist State* (1975), *From Dessalines to Duvalier* (1979), *Haiti in Caribbean Context* (1975), *Deity and Domination* (1989).

Rev. D.G. Rowell, DPhil, read Theology at Cambridge, was Research Fellow and Assitant Chaplain at New College 1968-72 and has been Fellow, Tutor and Chaplain at Keble since 1972, a member of the Liturgical Commission since 1981, and Canon and Prebendary of Chichester since 1981. His publications include *Hell and the Victorians* (1974), *The Liturgy of Christian Burial* (1977), *The Vision Glorious* (1983).

Rev. Prof. M.F. Wiles, FBA, DD, read Philosophy and Theology at Cambridge, and has been Regius Professor of Divinity and Canon of Christ Church since 1970. He was Bampton Lecturer in 1986 and a member of the Doctrine Commission of the Church of England 1968-76, chairman 1973-6. His many books include *The Making of Christian Doctrine* (1967), *The Remaking of Christian Doctrine* (1974), *Working Papers in Doctrine* (1976), *What is Theology?* (1976), *Explorations in*

Theology (1979), *Faith and the Mystery of God* (1982), *God's Action in the World* (1986).

Rev. Prof. R.D. Williams, DPhil, read Theology at Cambridge, was a research student at Wadham and Christ Church (1971-5), has been Canon theologian of Leicester since 1981, Lady Margaret Professor of Divinity and Canon of Christ Church since 1986 and a member of the Doctrine Commission of the Church of England since 1986. His publications include *The Wound of Knowledge* (1979), *Resurrection* (1982), *The Truce of God* (1983), *Arius: Heresy and Tradition* (1987).

Rev. T.S.M. Williams read Theology at Jesus, and has been Fellow, Tutor, and Chaplain of Trinity since 1970. His publications include *Form and Vitality in the World and God* (1985).

PREFACE

The Religion of the Incarnation was the title first suggested by Gore for the collection of essays he was editing, which appeared in 1889 as *Lux Mundi*. Though the Latin phrase from St John's Gospel was preferred, Gore's suggestion survived in the sub-title and provided the running head for that 'founding document of liberal Catholicism in the Church of England'.[1] There is a better reason than the decline of Latin for reverting to the original title in this centenary celebration. That is the turn of the tide in Anglican theology against doctrinal reductionism.

This has little connection with the bigger swing to neo-conservatism elsewhere in the Christian world, or the more cheerful neglect of theology in large sections of church life. Far from the best insights of liberal theology being repudiated in English Christianity, they are widely taken for granted. But there is a growing recognition that they do not suffice to nourish a minority church in an aggressively secular society.

It is clear in retrospect that from *Honest to God* (1963) to *The Myth of God Incarnate* (1977) and beyond, two tendencies in modern theology have been confused in the public mind: the responsible clarification of the church's language, which now includes distinguishing between doctrine, myth, and history; and the embarrassed elimination of mythical language that had been misunderstood in a literalistic way, and with it large tracts of the doctrinal tradition. The first step (represented by Professor Wiles in *The Myth of God Incarnate*) is always necessary, the second a *faux pas* which most theologians nowadays are careful to avoid.

When the prevailing philosophical winds were positivist, and religious language scarcely taken seriously, it was fatally easy for theologians to slip from analysis into reductionist interpretations of the religious tradition. Their analyses rightly introduced distinctions unknown to the ancient authors, or at least not explicit in the material, and some of the categories used, especially myth and dogma, were defined by their contrast to the dominant paradigms of truth and rationality. It was then tempting to restate Christianity in ways that down-graded those problematic aspects of the tradition and to rely more heavily on the solid results of historical research and (so long as these remained persuasive) idealist metaphysics, or phenomenology.

In retrospect those worthy experiments of secular protestantism may be judged to have surrendered much that was essential to the Christian religion. The implication of our centenary retrieval of Gore's title is that 'the Incarnation' provides a label for what most Anglicans have never surrendered and would wish to claim is central to Christian faith and practice. The polemical edge of this proposal is directed primarily at liberal protestantism's hostility to the christological dogma. Bultmann's demythologizing of the New Testament also contained some residual positivistic elements, even though his hermeneutical theory was far more sophisticated than that of his predecessors. Some of the later English debate about the Incarnation also echoed the older doctrinal reductionism, obscuring its correct insistence that mythic and doctrinal language be distinguished from matters of historical fact. Some careless use of the word 'myth', with its pejorative connotations, added to the confusion. Earlier, Bishop Robinson's Sunday newspaper trailer, 'Our Image of God must go', like the occasional use of a striking phrase to mystify or demystify a discussion, have put pastorally-minded theologians into the guise of wolf's clothing.

Through all these media events some theological distinctions have presumably reached a wider audience. The word 'myth', already tainted in the New Testament, can hardly now be rescued by theologians and is best left to the anthropologists and phenomenologists of religion. But 'the Incarnation' remains essential Christian vocabulary, to be clarified rather than abandoned to the mythologists. Apart from those wider uses which are quite distinct from Christian theology, the word is used in Christian speech as a simple label for its founding revelation, as a statement of minimal Christian beliefs about that founding revelation, as a theological theory about these beliefs, and as a narrative description of part or all of that event. This fourth sense may properly be called 'mythical', in contrast to the second and third senses which are doctrinal, and the first which is merely conventional.

Students of religion who are unconcerned about the truth of Christianity may observe these distinctions without expressing a preference, but theologians committed to defending that truth will naturally stress the doctrinal meanings and may well be uneasy about mythical forms of expression. Thus Karl Rahner insists that the Incarnation is a mystery of faith and thinks 'we must to a greater degree than in earlier times avoid giving a mythological flavour to the expression of this mystery'.[2] Preaching today must allow 'the doctrine of the Incarnation to "make an impact" and not give the impression of being a merely mythological conception'.[3]

The essays which follow are no more 'essays on the Incarnation' or 'essays on the doctrine of the Incarnation' than were those of *Lux Mundi*. As our title and their sub-title imply, they are theological essays on

Christianity bound together with a claim that 'the Incarnation' is constitutive of the identity of the Christian religion. That implies less than the unified theological programme which *Lux Mundi* is usually taken to represent. But not even the more unified perspective of that volume provides the substance of an incarnational christology. It is the credal *form* of Christianity which is defended by these churchmen. With only slight exaggeration the Oxford Congregationalist A.M. Fairbairn could comment on *Lux Mundi* that 'Curiously, the Incarnation is the very thing the book does not, in any more than the most nominal sense, either discuss or construe.'[4]

None of the essays in either collection was originally written with this title in mind, nor with any suggestion that they should refer explicitly to the doctrine of the Incarnation, except where their title demanded that. In the present collection, the essayists were also given wide discretion about how much reference to make to the earlier essay taken as their starting-point. Predictably and appropriately, the better theologians in *Lux Mundi* have attracted the most attention from their junior partners. There is little attempt to rehabilitate the more justly forgotten Victorians. This is no disrespect. Theology always takes from the tradition what it can, but is directed at the present church and world. In our title, the word 'Incarnation' refers only to the identity mark of Christianity. How it is to be construed is a further question – the central question for Christian theology in every age. All that the Christian theological word itself insists on, as a rule of orthodox Christian speech, is that we claim to be confronted in Jesus Christ with the decisive revelation of God, and that it is the real historical person Jesus of Nazareth about whom we are speaking when we make this claim.

The contributors to *Lux Mundi* were agreed about much more than that. They shared a religious and theological outlook which led some of them to expound the doctrine elsewhere in terms of divine immanence. But it is equally possible to combine the doctrine of the Incarnation with a quite dualistic emphasis upon the transcendence of God, as the Fourth Evangelist arguably does. In celebrating Gore's original title this volume makes no claim to replicate the liberal Anglican catholicism of a century ago, securely rooted as that was in the Greek Fathers.

We do not claim the high degree of theological agreement found among the contributors to *Lux Mundi*, and would even make a virtue of our diversity and of our distance from our more famous predecessors. The world and our understanding of it have changed so dramatically over the past century that to be saying the same things as they did would be to be saying something very different. To live, a tradition has to change, as Gore insisted. He and his collaborators were convinced that, rightly understood, the Christian faith 'is as adequate as ever to interpret life and knowledge in its several departments, and to impart not less intellectual than moral freedom. But we are conscious also that if the true meaning of the faith is to be made sufficiently conspicuous it needs disencumbering, reinterpreting, explaining' (p.vii).[5]

That careful formulation sets limits to the change and development appropriate to the Christian tradition by implying that we have here something given, which we are not free to change or develop as we wish. On the one hand he insists that 'theology must take a new development', since 'the epoch in which we live is one of profound transformation, intellectual and social, abounding in new needs, new points of view, new questions; and certain therefore to involve great changes in the outlying departments of theology, where it is linked on to other sciences, and to necessitate some general restatement of its claim and meaning' (p.viii). On the other hand, he and his colleagues 'grudge the name development...to anything which fails to preserve the type of the Christian Creed and the Christian Church; for development is not innovation, it is not heresy', any more than it is 'merely an intensification of a current tendency', the contemporary Roman option of 'narrowing and hardening of theology by simply giving it greater definiteness or multiplying its dogmas' (pp.viiif.).

The Anglican liberal catholic claim to pursue a middle way between the Enlightenment's theological rationalism which dissolves the creed, and a papal system which renders it brittle and burdensome (Matt. 23:4), is bound to look different today from a century ago. But the diversity of theological approach in the essays which follow demands some account of our solidarity with each other and with our predecessors.

The present volume, like *Lux Mundi*, 'is primarily due to a set of circumstances which exists no longer. The writers found themselves at Oxford together between the years 1875-1885 engaged in the common work of university education; and compelled for their own sake, no less than that of others, to attempt to put the Catholic faith into its right relation to modern intellectual and moral problems' (p.vii).

Alter the century, and Gore's opening lines are still applicable. When in the late 1970s the idea of the present volume was floated, it was recognized that some of the then present Theological Faculty would by 1989 be past members. That point of similarity with *Lux Mundi* itself was not considered an obstacle, and it is the editor's special pleasure to 'welcome back' three contributors who still occasionally teach and examine for the Faculty, but who are now primarily engaged elsewhere: Mr Louth in the University of London, Dr Muddiman in the University of Nottingham, and Dr Nicholls at Littlemore.

Of these, the third echoes *Lux Mundi's* strong connections with the parochial ministry: Illingworth at Longworth, Moberly at Great Cudworth, and Talbot at Leeds. To some that connection between church and university will look now like another of the lost causes for which Oxford has a reputation. It is true that Oxford more than other places has clung to its history. The Tractarian associations of Littlemore and its more historic satellite Sandford make them appropriate symbols of what remains as programmatic for this centenary volume as for the original: the fruitful relationship between English Christianity (now including several denominations) and the university in which many of its clergy are still partly trained.

This connection is expressed not only by the authorial links of both volumes to actual parishes and cathedrals, but also by some strong if largely invisible links to the Anglican theological colleges. Two contributors are governors of Ripon College, Cuddesdon, and two others of St Stephen's House. Four have taught full-time, several part-time, and all occasionally in these or other theological colleges, and the connection is broadened by the inclusion of Wycliffe Hall among the present home bases of the contributors. That reflects a welcome decline in Anglican party spirit. In terms of Victorian church 'parties', high, low, and broad, we are all broad beyond obesity. More importantly, the Faculty provides a context in which all three colleges work together with other churches' institutions.

The historically explicable survival of an entrenched Anglican bias to the Oxford Faculty brings numerical strength. Some of the old established posts are still restricted to Anglican priests, but this anachronism results in more posts than would otherwise exist. Although all the contributors were appointed to their university or college posts on academic grounds, the majority were also required by statute to be male Anglican clergy. This makes the book less representative of the Theological Faculty than it would have been a century ago. The sub-title 'Anglican Essays', rather than 'Oxford Essays', is intended to acknowledge this institutional limit to our corporate liberalism and catholicity.

But as regards the present volume this limitation is by design, not accident. If 'dogmatic theology is the discipline which systematizes the doctrine prevalent in a Christian Church at a given time'[6] it is appropriate that a collection of essays which covers the main themes of systematic theology should stem from one particular church. If that argument creaks under the strain of the diversity which follows, that is itself instructive. Whatever the situation of Anglican theology today, this collaboration implies a programme, which may again be expressed in Gore's words. At the conclusion of his Preface he explains 'that we have written not as mere individuals, but as ministers, under common conditions, of a common faith. This unity of conviction has enabled us freely to offer and accept mutual criticism and suggestion; so that without each of us professing such responsibility for work other than his own, as would have involved undue interference with individual method, we do desire this volume to be the expression of a common mind and a common hope' (p.x).

That much at least can be said of what follows. Anglican churches give their ministers more freedom in interpreting their formularies than some would wish, but it remains true that we, like our predecessors, have written as servants of Christ (to borrow St Paul's words) and 'servants of the Catholic Creed and Church, aiming only at interpreting the faith we have received' (to borrow Gore's words, p.viii). Gore returned to this vexed question of authority in his longer Preface to the Tenth edition of 1890. He notes that 'the very grounds of (the theological authority of the Church) are for the moment too much in question to admit of the proper amount of deference being given to it' (p.xii in 15th ed.) but disclaims 'any desire to have "licence to say what we please" in our position as Church teachers. All meaning would be taken out of the effort and hope this book represents if we could not believe that we were speaking as the Church would have us speak' (ibid.). The formulation is ambiguous in a church where authority is dispersed, but given a true interpretation the contributors to this volume also would concur.

'Anglican essays' poses questions about Anglican theology today, and 'in commemoration of Lux Mundi' more precise questions about the aims of this volume, and its balance of historical and systematic interests.[7] None of these can be answered without a grateful recognition of the ecumenical context in which we all now do our theology. 'Essays in Anglican Theology', the originally preferred title (computer-coded EAT) would have claimed rather more than some Anglicans are happy about claiming. Is it not characteristic of Anglican theology to accept anything that is clearly Christian, and so to be forced to resist systematization?

In a fairly monolithic Christian culture, cut off by sea from neighbouring states, where Roman Catholic and other nonconformists could be penalized and marginalized, it was possible to maintain a church's boundaries largely by a common liturgy and polity. Theological controversy was necessary because opponents were far from silent, but this was not definitive of the faith of most English people. A knowledge of one's tradition, deepened by the study of history and supported by philosophical argument, could seem a satisfactory (even preferable) alternative to the systematic theology of Roman Catholic and Protestant schools.

Such a neglect of systematic theology is no longer defensible in a pluralist and secular society, and its recovery under ecumenical auspices can only be welcomed. Anglican theology should surely be more than theology (contingently) done by Anglicans. For the phrase to be meaningful it needs to say something about the character of such theology and its relationship to its antecedents.[8]

It would be impossible or else embarrassing to list specific items generally true of Anglican and not of other Christian theology, or even items more true of most Anglican than of most other theology. The necessary lists of exceptions would fortunately always undermine such an empirical approach. Judgements about the theological 'essence of Anglicanism' are partly an intuition based on the study of its history, partly a proposal about its future development, and partly a criticism of some of its manifestations.

It is tempting to claim that an emphasis upon the Incarnation is a peculiar emphasis of Anglican theology, in view of the development since *Lux Mundi*.[9] But this is neither desirable nor plausible. To be significant it would have to point to particular incarnational theologies and so use the phrase 'the doctrine of the Incarnation' more narrowly than is suggested here. Fairbairn found the origins of the modern emphasis on incarnational theology in Lutheran orthodoxy's self-definition against Calvinism, hardly a promising pedigree for a church that appeals to antiquity. He claimed that 'from the Lutherans the notion has filtered through various channels into the modern Anglican consciousness, which loves to describe Christianity as "the religion of the Incarnation", the Church as naturally of a piece with it, and as continuing its work.'[10]

It is true that Anglican theology refuses to play off the gospel against the catholic church, and that the church continues Christ's reconciling work (2 Cor. 5:19f.) by proclaiming his one oblation of himself once offered, and being the body of Christ in the world. But there is nothing particularly Lutheran about that, and the emphasis upon the event of 'God with us' (which includes the atonement) is shared by the Orthodox, Roman Catholics, and most Protestants. It is important for orthodox Anglicans that they share this definitional badge with other orthodox Christians.

A claim that the *Lux Mundi* writers' 'liberal catholicism' represents a typically Anglican stance is best based on their recovery, in a vastly changed intellectual environment, of the Caroline Divines' balance of tradition and reason. This balance was lost in the neglect of tradition by rationalists and evangelicals, and in the Tractarians' reassertion of tradition at the expense of reason. Its recovery by the *Lux Mundi* writers is an indication of their buoyant self-confidence and optimism. It is hard to be equally confident about the position of the churches in Western society today. Some of the available forms of Christianity are unattractive. But Western Christianity is surely in better intellectual shape than it has been for sixty years, though that may be partly a comment on the desperate lack of credible alternatives to the great religious traditions, and is in any case effective only insofar as it is expressed in genuine discipleship. Nevertheless, the Anglican balance of tradition and reason can be recommended with confidence, however acutely its advocates are aware of their own failures.

Whether the balance of liberal and catholic elements found in *Lux Mundi* is achieved in the essays which follow must be left to our readers to judge. A certain respect for tradition is implied in the authors' readiness to engage, however briefly, with the late nineteenth-century partners chosen for them by the editor. All the contributors represent something of the liberal and catholic traditions of Anglicanism, though not all would define them in quite the same way. Most of us would be more positive towards both the Reformation and the Enlightenment than most of our predecessors, as they in turn were more positive about German theology than their Tractarian predecessors had been.

But the greater degree of openness to Europe, both Roman Catholic and Protestant, and new appreciation of North American and Latin American theology, is no more than the natural consequence of greater mobility and ecumenical spirit. The latter may be underlined by some final comments on the changes in our Faculty since 1889. These will serve to reiterate the partial character of what follows in comparison with the wider spread of disciplines and perspectives represented within the Faculty. Both the Anglican Studies seminar and Week 0 Group of doctrine teachers, in which earlier drafts of these essays were presented, contain that broader denominational range. The contributions and criticisms of both students and colleagues, among them Dr Janet Soskice and Frs Fergus Kerr O.P. and Timothy Radcliffe O.P., now moved away, and Dr Paul Fiddes who is still with us, are here gratefully acknowledged. It is possible to envision a non-Anglican volume matched to the same topics and Faculty members not represented here. To name but some recent chairmen whose leadership of the Faculty should correct any misapprehensions of Anglican hegemony, Professor Barr of Christ Church and Oriel, Dr Yarnold of Campion Hall, Drs White and Mason of Regents Park, and the late Professor Caird of Mansfield and Queen's, would have graced any collection of theological essays on these topics. The wider perspectives of Greek Orthodox and Syriac Christianity which

Bishop Kallistos Ware and Dr Sebastian Brock provide within the Faculty would also have been an enrichment. The relationships of Christianity to other religions are touched on in 'The Incarnation and Development' but with such specialists as Professors E.P. Sanders and Dr Vermes for Judaism and the New Testament, Professor Gombrich for Buddhism, Matilal for Hinduism, and Gilsenan for Islam, the possibilities of expanding that side of the subject are considerable and highly desirable.

The Anglican representation in the Faculty is strongest in the posts which are partly state-funded because Oxford with its four canon professorships (the other four chairs are not tied) and surviving academic chaplaincies has retained far more of these historic links between church and university than other English universities, choosing to supplement them with new posts where necessary, rather than to abolish such patent anachronisms. But new theological posts in universities are not part of the contemporary political agenda and recent broadening of the Faculty has come from privately funded institutions, such as the Ian Ramsey Centre which specializes in medical ethics, and the St Theosevia Centre for Christian Spirituality.

That accords with the history of the University which has since the Middle Ages been a federation of independent institutions. It also corresponds to the way the Theological Faculty has broadened and expanded in the century since *Lux Mundi*. Though the Faculty was still Anglican in 1889, theology in Oxford had already begun its process of ecumenical enrichment. Mansfield College had been founded in 1886, with Fairbairn as its first principal and strong support from the Theological Faculty's greatest scholar, administrator, and poet, Edwin Hatch (1835-89), to provide 'a Free Church Faculty in Theology'. It opened on its present site in 1889.[11] Several of its later tutors, such as C.H. Dodd, T.W. Manson, and G.B. Caird were also University lecturers, and the college became a Permanent Private Hall of the University in 1955.

If this Congregationalist college has provided additional weight in New Testament studies, Baptists have been more prominent in the Old Testament field, Jesuits in Patristics, and Dominicans in spirituality and the philosophy of religion. Wheeler Robinson brought Regents Park (the Baptist college) to Oxford in 1940 and it became a Permanent Private Hall in 1957. Campion Hall was opened as Clarke's Hall in 1896, becoming a Permanent Private Hall in 1918, and makes a major contribution to the historical, liturgical, and ecumenical work of the Faculty. Blackfriars re-opened in 1921, 700 years after its foundation, and following its suppression in 1538.

Other associated institutions with long and distinguished pasts and (it is right to trust) futures, include St Benet's Hall, Greyfriars (restoring the brilliant Franciscan connection of 1224-1538), and Manchester College, which moved to Oxford in 1889, providing another superb library and succession of fine scholars. Mention should also be made of the Methodist College of Education, Westminster College, and the Roman Catholic Plater College, but enough history has been provided to correct any impression that the Faculty is all-Anglican, all-clerical, and all-male as this collection might otherwise have suggested.

That being said, the restriction of this volume to a group of liberal catholic Anglican clergy who know and more or less approve each other's views did simplify the editorial choices, much as the absence of several other Anglican colleagues is regretted. Like the absence of some important topics not included in this collection, that followed from the editorial decision to restrict the essays to the twelve titles in *Lux Mundi*, adding only an afterword from a Victorian church historian whose deep Tractarian loyalties remind some of us to value our roots. Gore as editor would no doubt have been happy had Liddon or Dean Church been able to perform a similar service.

This editor finally thanks both the contributors who accepted their assignments without murmuring and delivered their manuscripts punctually, and Mr Kim Richardson of the Bristol Classical Press, who herewith inaugurates the appropriately initialled BCP's expansion into fast and modestly priced theological publishing.

Theology Faculty Centre,   R.M.
Pusey Lane,
Michaelmas Term, 1988.

Notes

1. C. Welch, *Protestant Thought in the Nineteenth Century*, Vol.2 (New Haven 1985), p.168.
2. *Encyclopedia of Theology: A concise Sacramentum Mundi* (London 1975), p.695.
3. *Ibid.*, p.699.
4. *The Place of Christ in Modern Theology* (London 1893), p.451.
5. Quotations from *Lux Mundi* throughout this book are from the fifth (1890) edition, except where stated.
6. Schleiermacher, *The Christian Faith* (ET Edinburgh 1928), p.88.
7. In addition to Dr Rowell's 'Retrospect', much historical information will be found in the contribution of Dr Hinchliff.
8. See Paul Avis 'What is "Anglicanism"?', in Stephen Sykes and John Booty (eds.), *The Study of Anglicanism* (London and Philadelphia 1988).
9. L. Smedes, *The Incarnation: Trends in Modern Anglican Thought* (Amsterdam 1957).
10. n.4.
11. *Mansfield College Oxford: its Origin and Opening* (London 1890).

FAITH

Robert Morgan

Faith and theology

It was the broadly credal arrangement of *Lux Mundi* that gave Scott Holland's essay, 'Faith', its prominent position. The result was a sparkling beginning to a volume whose many virtues did not on the whole include lightness of touch. Gore, Moberly, and Illingworth deserve to be remembered as systematic theologians, and Gore's essay provoked the controversy which helped make *Lux Mundi* a landmark. But Holland's is the one most likely to inspire a centenary celebration. However elusive its theme, and vulnerable to changes in cultural mood, it can still be read with profit and even excitement. Without attempting to emulate his exuberance, this commemoration will find in Holland's discussions of (Christian) faith some suggestions for the shape of Christian theology a century later, and echo his insistence 'on the necessity for moving forward from a simple to a more theological Gospel'.[1]

Henry Scott Holland (1847-1918)[2] began his Oxford career at Balliol (1866-70), where he became a pupil and friend of the socially committed idealist philosopher, T.H. Green. During the *Lux Mundi* writers' period of teaching together, he had been a Senior Student of Christ Church (1871-84), but in 1886 had become a canon of St Paul's. He later (1910) returned to Oxford as Regius Professor of Divinity.

That was a surprising piece of prime ministerial patronage, because without disputing his fine philosophical and theological mind and historical sense, Holland was more the preacher and journalist than scholar. His genius found its most natural expression in several volumes of cathedral and university sermons, and in what he wrote as editor for the *Commonwealth*, the organ of the Christian Social Union, founded by Gore and himself in 1889. His speeches to its annual conferences were scintillating, whereas he never wrote the great book his friends expected on the Fourth Gospel, and his posthumously published introductions to this are disappointing.[3]

He has been called a prophet,[4] and that fits the occasional, oral, and non-specialist form of his deliverances, as well as their content. But prophets are in the deepest sense theologians, and Asquith's choice of a Regius was more appropriate than Scott Holland in his modesty would allow.[5] The ill-health that hindered his learning, so that like most clergy his thought was articulated mainly through sermons, was less destructive of the theologian's vocation than the ever-narrowing focus of modern historical scholarship. Academic research is necessarily a specialist task, and the main contribution of universities to theology lies in scholarship, not preaching. But theology's reflection on reality as a whole resists specialization, and it finds appropriate expression in the sermon's combination of faith and reason.

By 1910 the pulpit and books of sermons were an insufficiently public platform for theology, but the canonry at Christ Church, still associated with the chair, symbolizes the mutual dependence of primary religious discourse and the second-order discipline. Christian theology's aim to interpret human existence in the light of the Christian tradition, and that tradition in the light of Christian experience, requires a broad understanding of the world and human life, but also strong roots in the religion itself. How these are combined is now usually left to the individuals concerned, but social location influences thought, and the Victorian establishment's wisdom in attracting some of its best thinkers to explore the contemporary meaning of Christian faith and discipleship in comfortable and prestigious religious institutions is justified by Holland's works. His sermons and journalism are no substitute for a professional systematic theology, but they invite systematic elaboration, and the more probing account of human experience in the *Lux Mundi* essay on 'faith' offers an Anglican perspective on the shape of theology in the modern world.

The close relationship of theology to religious faith itself is as evident throughout that essay as in Holland's double career in church and university. The remark of Hollaz about theology being 'the most *practical* discipline' (*scientia eminens practica*), and Evagrius' view of the theologian as one whose prayer is true, indicate that the relationship is an old one. But an occasion to reflect on it is timely because over the past few years it has become both confused and also more urgent.

In a post-Christian culture the boundaries of faith are not so clear that it is possible to say who can truly do theology. Not even Evagrius claimed to know *whose* faith is true. The relationship to God which finds expression in verbal and non-verbal prayer is ultimately an individual and private matter, however dependent on the tradition and life of a community. But it seems that this connection with a religious tradition and community has to become more explicit now that talk of God is taken seriously only in religious circles. The institutional arrangements which Holland inherited were in need of reform, and he tried in vain to make them more ecumenical. But the close connection between theology and the religious life which he exemplified corresponds to the logic of a discipline committed to speaking of God.

This connection between theology and the religious life has usually been taken for granted. In a predominantly Christian culture, where everything stood in some relation to the church, the degree of control varied but no-one suggested that theology might be independent of its base in the believing and worshipping community. It was simply assumed that God is known by living the religious life, informed by scripture. Philosophy was merely the handmaid. In seventeenth- and eighteenth-century England, by contrast, religious ideas remained culturally important as the church's power declined. Belief in God was general and the Bible common property. Some Christian theology began to be done outside or on the periphery of religious institutions, for example by the Deists.

Their 'independent' study of the Bible and Christianity contributed significantly to modern biblical and historical scholarship. A degree of academic freedom from ecclesiastical controls (varying with time and place) made rapid advances possible in German universities, resulting in an academic theology somewhat detached from the worshipping community. Its rational methods do not directly yield knowledge of God, and only contribute even indirectly to this when set in a larger theological and philosophical framework. That was initially provided by the residually Christian culture, and by Christian universities like Oxford staging stubborn rear-guard actions and movements. But as these have shrunk to sectarian status under the tide of modern secularism and pluralism, the only chance of keeping academic theology truly theological (i.e. speaking of God) has been through revitalizing its links with its religious (i.e. worshipping) bases, the communities of faith.

Belief in God and immortality remained fairly general in the Enlightenment and have survived in an undefined way to the present. But this seems to be a residue of, or parasitic upon, more traditional forms of religion. Even the morally admirable 'natural religion', sympathetically discussed by the greatest Oriel theologian, Bishop Butler, existed more as a consequence than a foundation of Christianity. It proved sadly short-lived and ineffective except in combination with the more durable forms of the Christian religion, such as those which Butler shared with the later Oriel theologians, Keble, Newman, and Pusey. In the eighteenth century natural religion gave the real, i.e. revealed, religion of the Incarnation some rational support. But in itself it is an abstraction, and influenced by pietism and romanticism Schleiermacher rightly redirected his readers to religion as it actually exists. Scott Holland also was strongly influenced by romanticism. While defending the rights of reason in its proper sphere, like Coleridge he saw religion and life in broader terms.

This break with eighteenth-century theological rationalism, apparent in the title of his essay, is untypical of British philosophical theology. Discussions of 'faith and reason' still often run on evidentialist lines, and generally show more sympathy for Locke than for Kierkegaard. Scott Holland was not averse to propositional truth, and called the sermons published in 1888 *On Behalf of Belief*. But he knew that religion engaged the personality at a deeper level, and also that the older 'evidences' had collapsed. In the intellectual crisis of his time the most constructive apologetic was to consider religion itself, as this is known to the participant.

The essay on faith contains the rudiments of a theory of religion, a view of human existence, and a definition of Christianity. None of this is developed in much detail, but it is significant that the believer's account of faith unfolds in all these broader directions, rather than remaining in the sphere of psychological analysis. Faith is often spoken of as an experience. But it is closer to Holland's position to think of it as 'basal', prior to experience, and giving rise to the variety of religious experience.

The terms in which Scott Holland speaks of 'faith' include 'confidence in God, who can never fail' (p.5), 'the power by which the conscious life attaches itself to God' (p.17), 'the witness and the exercise of our sonship in God' (p.21), 'the act of willing adhesion to God the Father' (p.29), 'a spiritual intimacy, a living friendship with God' (p.46). In other words, faith is a relationship to God, and its definition presupposes and depends on a particular religious tradition's talk of God. No doubt the choice of the word 'faith' itself says something about the character of the relationship as one of confidence and trust, but the decisive factor is who is trusted. Religious faith is determined by its object.

As a believer writing for believers Holland can speak quite naturally about God. Recent theology has been more attentive to the experience of God's absence from contemporary Western culture, and this lies behind the common redefinition of 'faith' in purely anthropological terms. In opposition to that, what follows will restate and develop Scott Holland's more traditional approach. The danger of speaking so bluntly of God is that this can easily become an ostrich-like denial of contemporary experience, a flight back into the tradition rather than forward into a theology which fuses tradition and experience. It is tempting to bracket the word 'God' or substitute an evocative phrase such as 'the Holy One' which reminds us that the referent is the One who is worshipped, the mysterious ultimate, not the chiffre of some philosophy of religion or childhood images. But to avoid the word 'God' is to capitulate to secular pressures. The task of theology is rather to speak of God in appropriate ways. There is a time for silence, but where words are being used theology's first word remains *theos*.

It would not be hard to show that this Godward reference of 'faith' is characteristic of the Christian tradition. Where the New Testament speaks of faith or believing it generally refers to God, or the revelation of God in Jesus. The fact that in Christian experience and tradition the object of faith may be God or Jesus virtually interchangeably, is the challenge to intellectual elaboration set by the doctrine of the Incarnation. 'Faith' in the New Testament is not a general anthropological term, and 'believing' is not normally an epistemological stance. It involves 'ultimate concern', but that (as Tillich also insisted) is conditioned by its object, which may be appropriate (God) or inappropriate (idols). In Christian contexts 'faith' presupposes the revelation of God in Jesus, and refers to an alleged relationship based on that.

The clouds of epistemology which the word trails after it are not out of place. Christian faith makes truth-claims, and therefore faces questions about knowledge, including the relationship of our knowledge of God to the rest of our knowledge. But the relative lack of attention to these questions in the New Testament warns against giving them undue prominence in the conception of faith itself. Their importance for subsequent theological reflection should not obscure the less intellectual character of the primary religious response.

The English language has perhaps encouraged a distortion here. It distinguishes in the noun between 'faith', with its connotations of personal commitment, and 'belief', with its more cognitive overtones. But it does not make this distinction in the verb. The result is that unless a corrective is introduced by sometimes translating the New Testament *pisteuein* 'to have faith', the more usual choice of 'to believe' echoes 'belief' in contrast to 'faith' and causes the verb to be heard in a more cognitive way than the Greek usually intends. The German *glauben* avoids this cognitive bias, providing a better translation of passages which do not mean *für wahr halten*, 'to believe', with the emphasis on 'to consider true'.

Theologians have to be philosophers, however amateur. They are therefore especially prone to this intellectualistic distortion of 'faith'. Scott Holland avoided the snare which turns philosophical theologians into philosophers of religion, because his first responsibilities as a preacher taught him to keep his philosophical tools in the service of the gospel. His vocation and appointments cast him in the role of a 'confessional' theologian whose passion and commitment might even have methodological significance.

It would be anachronistic to depict him as a modern 'anti-foundationalist', but the fact that he was confident about the philosophical foundations of his belief in God makes it all the more striking that he did not build a natural theology on them, any more than he built a 'revealed theology' out of his in some ways quite traditional view of revelation. He broke the eighteenth-century rationalist mould of much English religious thought and substituted a more modern, 'confessional' approach, writing explicity from the standpoint of Christian faith.

Modern confessional theology is a large pool, but some of its biggest fish can help us to hear the lessons which Scott Holland has to teach us. Without claiming for him a place among the giants, it is possible to draw from his particular combination of tradition and modernity some guidance in absorbing their shared strengths while avoiding their different weaknesses. His account of faith is not unfolded in a formal systematic theology, but it can be drawn into contemporary discussions by being located between the two Church Fathers of modern Western theology, Schleiermacher and Barth.

Faith, theology and religion

Scott Holland was writing for Christians who knew who and what he meant when he defined faith in terms of a relationship with God. The apologetic thrust of his essay was aimed not 'at convincing a hostile disbelief, but at succouring a distressed faith' (p.4). It included some analysis of human consciousness, but presented faith as a 'basal' intuition prior to experience, and interpreted by believers as a relationship to God. It is not 'one among many faculties' with its own particular borders, limits and claims, over and against reason, feeling, and 'the other powers and capacities of our nature' (p.21):

> Faith is not to be ranked by the side of the other faculties in a federation of rival powers, but is behind them all. It goes back to a deeper root; it springs from a more primitive and radical act of the central self than they. It belongs to that original spot of our being, where it adheres in God, and draws on divine resources. Out of that spot our powers divide, radiating into separate gifts, – will, memory, feeling, reason, imagination, affection: but all of them are but varying expressions of that essential sonship, which is their base' (p.22).

Such an account is not based on empirical evidence, though it might be thought by some believers to correspond to their general experience and so confirm them in their religious stance. But it is itself an interpretation of experience based on a Christian presupposition, and therefore unlikely to persuade a non-believer.

It is thus possible to define faith primarily in terms of a particular religious system as 'relationship with God', rather than in general anthropological terms, which make no theological assumptions. But the price of choosing an explicitly theological definition is to lose one way of making talk of God intelligible by using the notion of faith to clarify in generally understandable language the human side of this supposed relationship. Since talk of God is problematic even for many Christians today, it is not surprising that some modern Christian apologetics has preferred to remove 'faith' from this 'insider' type of definition, and has described it in terms of a human experience which is expected to make sense to all.[6] The religious term is drawn from the analogy with inter-personal relationships, and it seems natural to return to that field of human experience in order to make sense of it. We know what 'faith' means in this sphere, and it is plausible to claim that it is an experience which bears some relation to religious experience, since other persons also are mysterious.

The attractions of using 'faith' as a bridge word, making talk of God intelligible where this is no longer self-evident, are considerable. The word is deeply embedded in the tradition of Christian talk of God and salvation, and it is tempting to see in the protestant emphasis on faith, and hostility to metaphysics and natural theology, a pointer to the day when rational arguments have to start at the human end, reflecting on common human experience. Faith would then emerge as an anthropological constant and reflection on this would clarify what Paul and Luther were talking about.

The human analogy characterizes the supposed relationship to God as one of confidence and trust. However, in Christian discourse this relationship term draws its essential content not in the first place from a human experience, but from its object, who is wholly other. God is not only prior in the order of being. Even in the order of knowing, the religious tradition that speaks of God is prior to, and shapes, Christian experience. The human love and trust characteristic of religious faith is understood as the appropriate response to the One who is revealed. Any attempt to elucidate the meaning of faith without at the same time speaking of Israel's God who is revealed in Jesus is likely to be speaking of something different from what Christian scripture and tradition mean by the word.

No term has had more theological weight placed upon it in the Western tradition than 'faith'. But the very factor that made it attractive to modern 'secular theology', namely, the difficulty of talking of God today, cautions against overuse of this word. In responding to the absence of God in a secular culture, talk of faith can easily become a substitute for talk of God. The more closely God and human existence are (rightly) thought of together, and especially where metaphysics is no longer expected to provide an ontological basis for religious belief, as in existentialist theology, there is a danger of talk of God and faith becoming talk of human existence only.

This suggestion that talk of 'faith' can become a black hole through which talk of God disappears without remainder into talk of human existence is perhaps surprising, in that the centrality of the theme in modern protestant theology owes much to the reaction of Barth and Gogarten against that anthropocentric tendency of liberal theology's talk of 'religion'. Commenting in 1924 on 'the latest theological movement's' charge that 'liberal theology has dealt not with God but with man', Bultmann concluded: 'The subject of theology is God. Theology speaks of God because it speaks of man as he stands before God. That is, theology speaks out of faith.'[7]

In Bultmann's kerygmatic theology, the notion of faith remains closely tied to the revelation 'event' that may occur when the Word of God is preached. But it is clear that this anthropological or existential orientation can lend itself to a talk of self-understanding that has little or nothing to do with the revelation of God in Christ, and so lead to a more radical secularization of Christianity than was envisaged by most nineteenth-century liberal protestantism, with its romantic attachment to 'religion'. Barth soon saw that his earlier Pauline-Lutheran emphasis on revelation and faith, developed by Bultmann, was not enough to turn the tide of anthropocentric liberal protestantism. He therefore moved towards a *Church Dogmatics* which restated and gave central place to an orthodox christology. Faith is here not merely obedient response to a punctiliar revelation event, but a faith in God revealed in the incarnate Son of God, Jesus of Nazareth.

That leaves unresolved most of the problems that troubled liberal theology. The older orthodoxy's talk of the 'object' of faith had receded because its ways of talking of God had lost credibility. It seemed necessary to abandon much of the tradition, and allow the Christian experience to draw fresh forms of expression from general human experience. It is odd for anyone who has learned not to identify revelation with a part of the Christian tradition to claim to start with revelation. We do not possess revelation, only traditions, including scriptural traditions.

On the other hand, Barth was clearly right to insist that the Christian church believes itself to be acknowledging a final and decisive revelation of God, uniquely revealed in its scriptures and preserved however unevenly throughout its sinful history. His conviction that it was the task of theology to communicate that knowledge of God would have been shared by most liberal theologians, even if a few biblical scholars and other historians insisted that this was not their responsibility. But Barth was also right in sensing that the liberals' attempt to speak of God by describing human religion historically was in deep trouble. It depended on an idealist metaphysics that was no longer plausible. He was also surely right to sense that in the process of accommodating Christian belief to a new intellectual and social situation the liberals had eliminated more than was necessary or expedient. The resultant 'neo-protestantism' of a Troeltsch was more neo than protestant.

A new way of thinking of revelation was necessary. The kerygmatic theology found in Paul and Luther was one possibility, soon modified and developed into a powerful new dogmatics. But this has not solved the epistemological problems of contemporary Christianity. Its account of the relationship of Christian belief to the rest of human knowledge has found few followers. The reason for the recent renewal of interest in Barth, especially in the later volumes of the *Church Dogmatics,* is a 'post-liberal' recognition that it is possible to learn from Barth's brilliant elaboration of the Christian doctrinal tradition without accepting his epistemology. We may not care to be taken over by Barth's system, but he has taught and encouraged many to use their Christian language and so sustain and live their faith, not whittle it apologetically away.

Barth's reassertion and restatement of the Christian tradition has revived Christian belief in God, not (as it initially appeared) by pitching 'revelation' against 'religion', but (ironically) by strengthening the Christian religion and enabling the system to work more effectively. That is compatible with his criticism of religion, even the Christian religion, in the light of the gospel, and would have been compatible with a more critical view of scripture. Theology always prunes the religious tradition in order better to communicate the gospel. The respect for scripture, which made Barth reluctant to criticize it theologically or historically, can be understood as a proper caution rather than a retreat to pre-critical views of revelation.

A reaction against modern anthropocentric interpretations of Christianity was necessary because (from the perspective of a more traditional standpoint) they were weakening and losing hold of the Christian sense of God. But it was not their turn to human existence that was at fault, and the cure could not be found in any easy appeal to divine 'revelation'. When pre-critical identifications of revelation with scripture are abandoned, theology can no longer be a matter of making deductions from revealed data. It has to start at the human end. But that means with some particular tradition and community, as well as with personal and corporate experience. Though it would have been misleading in 1799 to overwork the term, Schleiermacher believed in revelation just as much as Barth or Bultmann. The question (on which they too disagreed) was, and still is, how best to understand this.

The Bultmannian route of speaking of God by speaking of and from faith has proved precarious. Granted that theology in the modern world must start at the human end, with human experience, existentialist theology's talk of faith is too narrowly individualistic, and liberal theology generally underestimates the role of tradition in shaping experience, especially religious experience, in which convictions of divine revelation dawn.

Belief in revelation generally involves taking religion seriously – at least one's own religious tradition and practice, though it should not involve identifying revelation and religion. By criticizing religion in the light of the gospel Barth was following Jesus, Paul, and Luther. They all insisted on a critical distance between their religion, which was empirically given, and the revelation of God, with its human correlate 'faith', which may happen in and through a positive response to Jesus, and in the personal practice of religion. It may happen in other ways and places too, though it is unlikely to be understood as a revelation of God without the help of a pre-given religious tradition.

Theology depends on tradition and experience, but is concerned with a reality that lies beyond both. Like other believers, modern theologians typically speak of God from the standpoint of their own religious tradition, which they assume mediates a decisive revelation. They do not begin with God or with revelation, because these are not objectifiably available as a part of the tradition from which deductions can be made. We are ourselves involved when we speak of God on the basis of a tradition that we think bears witness to, and mediates a revelation. But to suppose that when the attempt to speak of God leads us to talk most intimately about ourselves, we are talking only of ourselves or human experience, is as fatal as talking only of the tradition (as some theology seems to do). If talking of God involves at the same time speaking of our human existence, a unity which the Reformers epitomized in the notion of 'faith', the reverse is also true. Any talk of faith which does not also talk with the tradition of God in Christ cannot appeal to the New Testament or the Reformers, and cannot be designated 'Christian'.

Trading on the ambiguity of the word 'faith', which can be used in religious and non-religious contexts, proved an unsatisfactory bridge between the Christian tradition and modernity because, whether one starts at the general anthropological end or with the theological meaning of 'relationship to God', it does not stretch to the other side of the great gulf between Christian faith and unbelief, or rejection of God in Christ. The Christian apologetic task of forging connections between a faith in God based on the revelation in Christ, and contemporary knowledge and experience, must find a better framework.

Rejecting the particular apologetics that seeks to make Christian faith intelligible by appealing to the general anthropological meaning of 'faith' does not have to involve a wholesale rejection of apologetics. Barth was right to distinguish dogmatics from apologetics and to recover the word 'faith' for the 'insider' contexts and meanings, referring to a relationship to God, that it has in the New Testament. But rejecting apologetics wholesale, itself a subtle apologetic move, was not a good idea. In the pulpit of Safenwil and elsewhere, preaching is appropriate, and theology is among other things a 'ministry of the divine word'. But in a secular society it is also necessary to place religious belief on other maps of reality. It may ultimately prove strong enough to absorb all other knowledge into its own overarching framework, but to pretend that other (apparently cognitively stronger) frameworks do not exist is to cherish illusions. The 'insider' tasks of dogmatic theology, developing the system from within, are important. But the system itself must also be located in reality, and in the absence of a generally accepted metaphysics that requires a theory of religion. Christian claims to truth cannot be divorced from questions about the nature of human life, including the nature and validity of religion.

The importance of 'religious studies' for Christian faith and theology in a secular and pluralist society has been obscured from both sides. Much 'scientific' study of religion from Marx and Freud down to some less impressive religiously alienated academics has been hostile to Christianity, and so distasteful to theologians. Despite the common translation of *thrêskeia* (worship) as 'religion' at James 1:27, the word's main roots are in the secularism and pluralism of the Enlightenment. It now generally implies (unlike 'true religion and virtue') an 'outsider' perspective. As such it cannot suffice for theologians, who need also to speak of faith in God. It also retains something of the Enlightenment's critical stance. But theologians have learned to live and even do business with opponents. The discussion of 'religion' offers them common ground with the humanities and social sciences which cannot be ignored by a discipline committed to forging links with other areas of human knowledge and feeling.

The notion of 'religion' is itself a contested concept, and the Christian apologist will have to argue for a theory of religion which (unlike Marxist and Freudian definitions) is compatible with belief in God. Understanding religions as cultural systems of symbols[8] gives due weight to the doctrinal tradition, and to moral and ritual practice, while also leaving open the question of *how* the system refers, and to what (if any) transcendent reality it refers, and in what (if any) transcendent reality it makes participation possible. Theories of religion can be argued about, corrected, and rejected, on the basis of empirical, historical, sociological, and psychological data. But the phenomenon of religion cannot be dismissed as an unfortunately influential illusion. It may be based on an illusion, namely faith in God. But there is clearly something here that needs discussion and study, even if its invitation to participate is resisted.

The descriptive study of religion can thus fulfil an apologetic role and is arguably the most promising modern equivalent of a natural theology. It is in principle quite distinct from the 'insider', participant's language of faith in God. But the wires have been crossed by modern theologians using the word 'religion' with heavy theological overtones to refer to their own religion or faith in God. That is justified by usage, but it makes for confusion, and Barth's sharp contrast between them is helpful even though his hostility to the very notion of 'religion' was unfortunate. A theology which does not take its empirical religion seriously loses contact with reality. But Barth was surely right to insist that theology is essentially insider talk, concerned with God, revelation, and faith in God. It uses, but is distinct from, the historical and social-scientific study of religion.

Bultmann recognized that what Barth called 'faith' was more or less what Schleiermacher and Herrmann had called 'religion'. He accepted Barth's turning theology back to the New Testament and Reformation word 'faith', which implied God, and left 'religion' to the social scientists. Others have returned to Schleiermacher's larger map of theological activities which accepts the primacy of the 'insider' tasks performed by Barth and Bultmann, but also attempts at the outset to relate Christian faith to the rest of the human search for truth and meaning. Religion is too important for theologians to leave it to the social scientists.

The study of this important human phenomenon as it actually exists involves studying particular religions, and observing that when Christians talk of their faith in God they have in mind the God of Israel revealed in Jesus. This observation that the object of faith is definitive for religious faith both supports the proposed line of demarcation between insider and outsider perspectives, and suggests that the tangential relationship is useful to theology. The study of religion cannot demonstrate the truth of a particular religion, but it can help to make it intelligible before handing over, as Evans-Pritchard does at the end of *Nuer Religion*, to the theologian who talks of God and faith.

Faith, theology, and the religious tradition

Clarifying the truth of faith in God is the main responsibility of theologians. As believers or participants in a religious tradition and community their task is to clarify what is in some sense given, not demonstrate it to the satisfaction of outsiders, or 'convicting a hostile disbelief' (p.4). They presuppose the reality of God and the foundation revelation of their own community, and the faith relationship to God that has followed from that supposed revelation. But none of these supposed realities is available for public inspection, or even to private introspection. Even believers can only assume the reality of their faith, supported by the community and whatever experience is vouchsafed to them in their moral and spiritual life. Holland speaks of 'not being able to bring it under direct observation' (p.8), and insists that this is of the essence.

But while faith itself is as non-objectifiable as God and revelation, it exists only in conjunction with the tradition through which the revelation finds expression and is communicated, and this is open to public inspection and can be challenged. Believers seek to relate their faith to all their knowledge and experience, and in doing so sometimes make mistakes. However intangible faith in God is, its moral consequences and theological statements are open to moral and rational criticism. The work of theology includes testing the tradition and developing it, to ensure that it corresponds to whatever truth is available.

This is partly an appeal to scientific knowledge and moral experience, but it is also an appeal to the tradition itself, including scripture, in which past experience is embedded, and the religious community's knowledge of God has found classic expression. Some correction and revision will be required by new growth in knowledge and experience, but there is also an assumption that (within the limits of a particular historical epoch) past formulations have as a whole mediated a genuine knowledge of God.

If membership of a religious community involves standing in a tradition and accepting it as a whole, coupled with a readiness to criticize and discard some formulations, entrusting them 'to history for safekeeping'[9], then the question of the criteria for this sifting is crucial. Both the tradition itself and the experience of believers are essential here. In the last resort 'conscience is always to be followed', and we will be guided by our own always provisional understanding of the gospel, informed as this constantly is in worship and by study of the tradition. But every religious community defines itself, and has some idea of what is essential to its identity. It is impossible to avoid some form of the older protestant orthodoxy's question of what in the tradition is fundamental for a Christian knowledge of God, or faith. This may take the modern form of defining the essence of Christianity.[10] Such definitions need to be fixed enough to guarantee continuity with past forms of the religion and flexible enough to permit openness to new knowledge and experience. They also need to refer to the founding revelation event on which the religion is based. Authentic Christian faith must include reference to this much traditional content, however lightly it sits to the rest of the tradition.

The theological or gospel criterion by which believers judge material in the Christian tradition itself is the tradition's own witness to the reality of God, decisively revealed in Jesus, as the resolution of the human predicament. That tight-knit unity of God, Jesus, and salvation has generally been taken as essential to the Christian message,[11] and christologies (which always include a soteriology) can be judged by reference to this criterion. The adequacy of their attempts to articulate the gospel can be tested in several ways for coherence, intelligibility, and fruitfulness, but their continuity with what orthodoxy has 'always, everywhere and by all' affirmed is best tested by reference to this.

What Christian orthodoxy says about God, and about Jesus, and about salvation (which includes its anthropology), is dependent on what it says about each of the other two. The case for an incarnational type of christology (which still allows for some theological diversity) and the Trinitarian doctrine of God which follows from this, is that no other type can adequately express the Christian conviction of the saving presence of God in Jesus. Enlightenment 'historical Jesus' types of christology loosely associated with a deist doctrine of God say less about Jesus, God, and salvation, because they fail to include the other two in what they say about each. They can only strictly speak of the faith *of* Jesus, not faith *in* him.

Believers must claim a kind of absoluteness for their revelation event if they are to say that in it they have to do with God, not some intermediary. Since Christians (unlike Jews and Muslims) locate the decisive revelation event in a human person, 'manifested in flesh, vindicated in Spirit', Christian theology thinks of God in a Trinitarian way. The basis of this doctrine (secondary in the order of knowing, but central in Christian doctrinal construction) is the doctrine of the Incarnation, God's self-identification with a first-century Jew. Consistent Hegelian interpretations of the Christian doctrines of Trinity and Incarnation fail to speak of this man from Nazareth as the object of Christian faith in God. They are at least as unorthodox as the Enlightenment proposals whose doctrine of God they aimed to improve on. Neither of these classical heresies articulates the Christian conviction of God's total self-identification with humanity in the full depth of its need.

Our reason for rejecting the modern attempt to make talk of God intelligible by means of 'faith' as a general anthropological constant, and returning instead with Scott Holland to the classical Christian tradition epitomized in the creeds and christological dogma, was that despite its soteriological dimension, the 'faith apologetic' has tended to obscure the very reality of God that Barth and Bultmann wished to affirm. Scott Holland avoided that reductionist precipice by reserving the word 'faith' for contexts in which the reference to God is implied, namely to believers' talk. That restriction is in step with the early Barth and Bultmann's reaction to the anthropocentricism of liberal theology's apologetic based on 'religion', an apologetic revived in twentieth-century 'secular theology' under the banner of 'faith'.

However, Barth's hostility to 'religion' and history, his rejection of apologetics and natural theology, and some elements of an uncritical attitude to scripture, are all foreign to Anglican tradition and sensibility, which in these respects is closer to Schleiermacher than to Barth. The distinction between 'insider' and 'outsider' perspectives was therefore introduced in order to retain the 'religion apologetic' of the liberals and to welcome their study of real history – not merely the existentialists' 'historicity (or historicality) of human existence'. Faith is then reserved for the 'insider' perspective that the word presupposes in the New Testament, Fathers, Reformers, and dialectical theology.

Barth's first step led him to a second, which brought him and his 'post-liberal' followers much closer to Scott Holland's critical orthodoxy than his earlier kerygmatic theology had been. But before returning to Barth's retrieval of the tradition in an incarnational christology his first step invites further consideration. It contained elements which Barth shared with Scott Holland, as well as those which jarred on Anglican sensibility. The shared heritage included the acceptance of Schleiermacher's double critique of eighteenth-century rationalism and pre-critical orthodoxy. Holland and Barth converge, because without losing their strong roots in the tradition the *Lux Mundi* group was open to the new knowledge which liberal theology had long since assimilated, including a cautious biblical criticism, and because Barth did not go back behind these insights as he recovered a stronger continuity with the doctrinal tradition.

The argument for following their restriction of the word 'faith' to the narrower religious meaning which includes the reference to God is that there is no through train from a phenomenology of faith to belief in the reality of God. This must therefore be written into the definition of religious faith itself. Most discussions of the 'psychology of faith' and the 'experience of faith' are in fact describing not faith but religion and psychological states. The confessional word 'faith' finds its way into these descriptive scientific discussions because many of them are conducted by believers, who accept already the reality of the referent, or by phenomenologists who for methodological reasons make a pretence of doing so. When now that scientific standpoint is adopted by theologians for apologetic purposes, they may be better advised to adopt the vocabulary of religious studies and call their descriptions 'dimensions of religious experience',[12] thus avoiding the word which in religious contexts traditionally implies its object.

The great theologians of faith, from Augustine through Luther to Kierkegaard, were admittedly men of considerable psychological insight. But they were, like Scott Holland, religious writers who presupposed the reality of God, not dispassionate analysts of religion. The reference to God could be taken for granted by Augustine and Luther when they spoke of faith. In a secular culture it needs to be made explicit lest the basic polarity of humanity and God is obscured, and the hiddenness of God becomes the disappearance of God. That reference to God is best guaranteed by building it into the definition of the religious word faith.

This reservation of 'faith' for 'insider' participant contexts, rejecting the 'faith apologetic' strategy, implies no hostility to Christian apologetics as such. These must appeal to a human reality that none can gainsay, and that is not 'faith', whose reality non-believers can readily deny.[13] They cannot deny its moral and religious fruits, but effects can follow from an illusion. The real, visible, undeniable human side of this supposed relationship is not 'faith', but 'religion'. This cannot be called an illusion, though it may be said to be based on illusion, the alleged illusion shared by millions, of being in a relationship to God.

Faith is an 'insider' term, ill-suited to provide a bridge to a secular culture that does not seriously speak of God, because, despite the analogy, religious faith in God is essentially different from the general anthropological term. It is different because it is defined by its object, not by the feelings it may evoke.

The still widespread religious use of the word 'faith' outside contexts presupposing the practice of religion reflects a residual religiosity. The boundaries between Christian and non-Christian cannot easily be drawn in a culture retaining many Judaeo-Christian roots. But to blur the boundaries or deny their existence is a fatal policy for Christianity to adopt in a pluralist situation. When historical and parochial realities are blurred, theology needs to keep its conceptual distinctions sharp. The distinction between insiders and outsiders has in principle (and in the New Testament) a sectarian sharpness. To distinguish on these lines between religion and faith opens the door to an alternative apologetic strategy based on 'religion', to replace the general anthropological use of the word 'faith'. It also preserves the notion of faith for the more difficult role of maintaining the integrity of Christian talk of God. That cannot be justified by appeal to human nature as such, or to anthropological constants such as faith. Its validity cannot be demonstrated by reference to religious experience. It is in the first place simply given in a religious tradition and accepted by participants. Rational argument comes later, as the tradition is defended and related to the rest of our knowledge, and if necessary modified.

This feature of religious talk of God as pre-given in a tradition and generally accepted before any attempt at justification is made, both supports the religious definition of faith as relationship to God and opens up the question of the tradition's doctrinal language, through which it is communicated and expressed. Where this strong reference to the theological tradition is not emphasized, talk of faith is in danger of turning inwards and losing its reference to the transcendent God. Feuerbach was able to make a *prima facie* case from some of Luther's novel statements for saying that he was speaking merely of human existence.[14] That is surely grotesque, but the shadow of Feuerbach hangs over modern theology from Schleiermacher to the present, not least where Luther is venerated, and faith made theology's central theme.

If the threat of anthropological reductionism is never far from modern discussions of faith, but Luther himself not guilty of this, one indication of the direction by which to outflank it may be found in what Luther shared with St Paul, John Wesley, Karl Barth, and Scott Holland: an overwhelming sense of God, expressed in the practice of religion, including saturation in a tradition and an energetic use of a deeply venerated scripture. Their understanding of faith was firmly rooted in religious practice, which involves a general acceptance of the community's tradition and use of its central doctrinal symbols before ever the question of how they are true, or of their possible cognitive content is even raised. This lived tradition supports an already presupposed conviction of the reality of God. That sense of God cannot be produced to order, but the fact that all these five theologians were already exceedingly zealous for the religious traditions of their fathers (Gal. 1:14) when their new understandings of God in Christ dawned indicates how it may be nurtured. Their use of the word 'faith' from the perspective of a powerful sense of God is opposed to the apologetic strategy of cutting 'faith' from its religious contexts, and also refers us to their religious traditions.

When pre-critical theology identified part of the tradition with revelation it was natural to misunderstand faith as merely believing certain propositions to be true. That is no longer defensible, but the truth contained in the tradition is still presupposed, and accepting the tradition is a prerequisite for participating in a religion. This tradition is indispensable and ancient (some of it is always older than the decisive revelation), but its role in making revelation understandable and faith possible is always subsidiary. It is subordinate to the revelation event itself. Believers attend to and engage with their tradition; they are not enslaved by it. It mediates the revelation of God in Jesus, but is not itself revelation. Parts of it, notably scripture, but also the creeds, have great authority for Christians. That means they are used frequently and respectfully. But they do not have absolute or unconditional authority — only God has that.

Christians submit to what in conscience they believe God's will for them to be. But they cannot finally objectify the event of revelation in a series of propositional truths. Timothy is urged to 'guard the deposit' (1 Tim. 6:20), to preserve the tradition; pastoral theologians (and there are no others in the English church) take care not to mutilate it unnecessarily as they sift it, and where necessary criticize it. They are professionally concerned to develop it in ways that express the truth of the gospel in their own day, and that requires both loyalty and daring, both continuity and innovation. But it does not involve identifying it with revelation or being committed to the truth of all its statements in an uncritical way.

From the perspective of Scott Holland's critical orthodoxy the problem with modern theology (in his later years he had liberal protestantism in his sights) is not overvaluing but undervaluing the classical Christian tradition. He defended the christological dogmas (and he thought all dogmas were concerned with christology) because he thought they were true. But he thought they were true, not because they had been dropped out of heaven in an infallible book, or (even more absurdly) had been dictated to an infallible general council or synod, but because they 'are statements of what He must be, if He is what our hearts assure us; if He can do that for which our wills tender Him their life-long self-surrender. Unless these rational considerations stand, then no act of faith is justifiable; unless His personality corresponds to these assertions, we can never be authorized in worshipping Him' (p.50).

The language of 'personality' goes beyond the early church's dogmatic formulae and into some modern theologians' attempts to make sense of these today, or rather a century ago. Even if neither the fourth- and fifth- nor the nineteenth-century theologians distinguished clearly between the dogma, which is fixed, and their theological elucidations, which must vary from one culture to another, the logic of Holland's position seems clear. The doctrine of the Incarnation, based on the 'fact' (another word overused a century ago) or divine event of the resurrection, is the lynch-pin of the Christian system. God's self-identification with the man Jesus is the 'given' in Christianity. No-one has even seen God; the only-begotten Son who is in the bosom of the Father revealed him, declared him, made him known. That is why, for Christians, faith in God and faith in Christ are inter-changeable. In having to do with Jesus we have to do with God. That is Christianity, and its elaborate tradition of belief and practice, rejected by secular protestantism, holds believers in living relationship to God by holding them fast to Christ in his church. Christian faith in God is attachment to Christ, in the fellowship of the Spirit, which means in his body the church. It is not a personal subjective experience, though it gives rise to several.

In the absence of secure philosophical foundations, it is the religious community's common life and worship that sustains the sense of God and provides the soil out of which any rational talk of God must emerge. Such theology is important because without rational self-criticism religions are prone to illusion and can become demonic. But the community also needs a strong tradition to support its religious life. Christian theology prunes the tradition to strengthen it, cutting out error and consigning much to the lumber room of history, for safe keeping. But parts of this tradition remain definitive for a Christian faith that is faith based on the saving event of Jesus Messiah, our crucified, risen, and expected Lord. That indispensable and central reference to the decisive saving revelation of God in Jesus of Nazareth is what is meant by calling Christianity 'the religion of the Incarnation'. Which of the many incarnational theologies is preferred is a further question. But to count as 'incarnational' it must (against gnostic docetism and some modern German idealism) refer to the historical figure of Jesus, and (against ebionism and some modern liberalism) find the decisive saving revelation of God, the God of Israel and all the world, in his life and death and vindication.

Faith, truth, and credal orthodoxy

Most English discussions of faith and reason, or reason and revelation, have focussed on the truth of Christian doctrinal statements. Truth is Christian theology's central concern, and that has since the second century drawn it into a close relationship with philosophy. It now brings the discipline into contact with the various areas of human knowledge and experience, especially the human sciences and literature, but also the natural sciences and the visual arts.

But the 'truth of Christianity', or truth of faith, the reality of the saving relationship with God based on the revelation in Jesus, the reality of the 'life hid with Christ in God' (Col. 3:3), is a different kind of question from the truth of particular statements in the tradition. Many of these can be modified without fundamentally altering the shape of the tradition. This is constantly being developed in order to bear witness to the same Lord, the same faith, in the same community of the baptized, who worship God in the same way as Father of all, and (to give an example of such development we may now add) Mother of all. New knowledge and sensibility stimulates new ways of speaking of God, Jesus, and salvation, but if this unstitches their tight-knit unity, which the doctrine of the Incarnation preserves, the whole shape of the tradition is changed and what has normally been considered Christian faith is weakened by the slow disintegration of its symbols.

A reassertion of the classical doctrinal tradition as essential to an orthodox Christian account of 'faith' need not imply the pre-critical view of the relationship between revelation and the tradition residually present in some discussions of faith and reason. That view identified revelation with a part of the tradition, whether scripture alone or scripture plus some later tradition, and twisted 'faith', whose object is the revelation of God in Christ, into the intellectual assent to certain propositions in the tradition. Many still think of the creeds in these terms, and the distortion is hard to correct because it contains an important grain of truth. Faith in God requires a religious tradition, and it is important that credal statements are true. But their truth is relative to the religious system in which they occur, and to start with assent to individual propositions is not the way to understand or justify religious practice and belief.

Ever since modern philosophy, science, and history rendered untenable the simple identification of divine revelation and human traditions, the task of Christian theology has been to restate Christianity in ways that would not be vulnerable to these criticisms, but would nevertheless preserve its claim to a saving knowledge of God in Christ. The old protestant orthodoxy had preserved and developed the patristic doctrinal tradition in the earthen vessel of a now untenable doctrine of revelation. When in the eighteenth century this was smashed, the doctrinal content was liable to be lost. Schleiermacher's turn to the human subject's religion, and his partial retrieval of the classical tradition as a 'doctrine of faith', rescued theology by responding appropriately to the new intellectual situation. The weaker theologies of later liberal protestantism, the strong protest of the early Barth, and the post-liberal theology that draws on the later Barth, are all variations on the same apologetic theme. Like Scott Holland they all express their faith in God as 'insiders', members of a tradition-shaped community which identifies its founding revelation in the specific event of God in Jesus. They all totally depend on more or less of this tradition, but avoid identifying it either with the revelation itself or with general truths of reason, thus turning faith into an insufficiently warranted pretender to knowledge.

Barth himself is admittedly equivocal. In a climate hostile to tradition dogmaticians often come close to pre-critical views of revelation in order to preserve from erosion the tradition that they rightly see is indispensable. But now that the Enlightenment prejudice against tradition has been challenged[15] theologians are less defensive and can affirm the truth and value of their tradition and the social world structured by it without confusing it with the revelation event on which it is based and to which it points. Their attempts to develop their tradition in order to incorporate new knowledge and moral insight can also be frankly acknowledged. Such adjustments show that respect for truth and the conscience by which in the moral and religious realm this is perceived take theological precedence over respect for tradition.

Religious faith is totally dependent on tradition for its knowledge of God, but it is not faith in the tradition (Holland, pp. 42-6). It is faith in God:

> the personal intimacy with God in Christ which alone is our concern. We do not, in the strict sense, believe *in* the Bible, or *in* the Creeds: we believe solely and absolutely in Christ Jesus. Faith is our living act of adherence in Him, of cohesion with God. But still, once more, we must recognise that this act of adhesion has a history: it has gradually been trained and perfected: and this has been accomplished through the long and perilous experiences recorded in the Old Testament; and it has been consummated in the final sealing of the perfected intimacy attained in Him, in Whose person it was realised and made possible for us: and it has been guarded and secured to us in the face of the overwhelming pressure of eighteen strong, stormy, and distracted centuries. And therefore it is that we now must attain our cohesion with God, subject to all the necessities laid upon us by the fact that we enter on the world's stage at a late hour, when the drama has already developed its plot and complicated its situations. This is why we cannot now, in full view of the facts, believe in Christ, without finding that our belief includes the Bible and the Creeds (pp.45-6).

Scott Holland's loyalty to his tradition, coupled with a complete openness to truth from any quarter, is not uncommon among theologians. What makes his essay an advance on his predecessors and suggestive for his successors is the way he combines the modern theological turn to the human subject with a strongly tradition-based sense of God. Schleiermacher and Barth have been drawn into the discussion in order to sharpen the contours of a view of Christianity which shares their strengths, avoids their different weaknesses, and can claim continuity with Scott Holland's account.

'Faith' for him is faith in God and Christ. But this emphasis upon the object of faith, and the refusal to obliterate the distinction between subject and object, is different from pre-critical talk of the *fides quae creditur*, or content of what is believed. The object of faith, to whom the believer is attached, is Christ the revelation of God. He cannot be identified with the tradition that defines him, necessary as that is for faith's relationship to him. Acceptance of this tradition sustains and expresses the faith in Christ which is Christian faith in God.

The tradition also serves as ballast which prevents this faith in God from shrinking into existential self-understanding. The christological dogma in particular preserves the otherness of the object of faith and worship. That function of dogma has taken on a new importance since the demise of classical metaphysics, which once helped theology to preserve a sense of the transcendent reality of God. A Christian philosophy may still fulfil this role for believers, without commanding general assent. But if it does not, the deficit will have to be made good by the doctrinal tradition itself. This need not provide philosophical foundations for belief in the object of religious faith, but must so point to it that believers are drawn into the system and attend to God. The christological dogma points to Jesus as the decisive saving revelation of God, and so gives shape to the particular religious symbol-system of worship (which includes religious ethics) and belief, through which Christians claim to draw near to God in the relationship they call 'faith'.

Calling religions 'systems of symbols' introduces into the discussion a theory of religion. It is impossible to adopt an 'outsider' perspective on Christianity or any other religion without implying some such theory, whether or not it is made explicit. Since the development of Scott Holland's theology attempted in this commemoration turns on the distinction between the insider perspective which speaks confessionally of God, revelation, and faith, and the outsider perspective which describes religion, preferably without prejudice to the question of the reality of its transcendent referent, it has presupposed a theory or definition of religion. The notion of 'symbol system' is usable by theology, as Marxist and Freudian theories are not, because it leaves open the question of the religion's truth, i.e. the reality of its transcendent referent. Students of religion stand (methodologically speaking) outside the religious system they are describing and analysing and do not presuppose the reality of God or faith's relationship to God. Historians, sociologists, and philosophers of religion can raise the question of God, and comment on the coherence and intelligibility of the answers given in religious traditions as these struggle to express and communicate what they claim to reflect. But the reality of God and faith is affirmed only from within a religious tradition, based as that is on a claim to revelation.

What Schleiermacher, Barth, and Scott Holland share is a strong sense of God nurtured in traditional Christian worship and structured by a christocentric dogmatics which relates all Christian belief and practice to the saving revelation of God in Jesus. Scott Holland is closer to Schleiermacher in his philosophical idealism based on close study of Plato and Kant (two philosophers in Barth's background also), and in their assumption, based on a relatively uncritical reading of the Fourth Gospel, that the roots of incarnational belief are clearer than a later generation would confirm. More important than these contingenciesa rising from the history of philosophy and biblical criticism (England being fifty years behind Germany, and several degrees less adventurous – though none the worse for that) both their theologies (unlike Barth's) relate faith and reason, Christ and culture, religion and history, as positively as possible. In contrast to these similarities, Holland did not follow Schleiermacher's radical reorientating and daring criticisms of the tradition. He made the believing subject a theme of reflection without forcing the whole fabric of Christian doctrine into the procrustean bed of religious self-consciousness or dissolving the *fides quae creditur* (doctrinal content) into the *fides qua creditur* (act of faith). His English conservatism provided a kind of bulwark against the anthropocentric tendency of Schleiermacher's rethinking the doctrinal tradition.

But this defence against anthropocentricism was no mere conservatism. Scott Holland assumed that the dogmatic definition of Christ was true, and one way to attempt to develop his position is to support that assumption by explaining how it is true, recognising with Holland that it is more than a transcript of religious self-consciousness but less than itself revelation. The old apologetic arguments for the divinity of Christ, based on the appeal to miracle and prophecy, were destroyed early in the eighteenth century, and those based on the historicity of the Johannine discourses in the nineteenth. Today there are no generally acceptable arguments, yet most believers accept this doctrine, as they accept the reality of God and salvation. How can these be justified?

The apologetic strategy implicit in this essay has been to say that the essential truth of a religion's reference to God through God's saving revelation in history is convincing only to 'insiders' and that it has an essentially pragmatic character. Believers accept the system or tradition they have 'received' because it is clearly valuable and seems to make sense of their lives and the world. It works, and is not at variance with the rest of their knowledge. They do not need to demand philosophical foundations before accepting it.

Without implying that Scott Holland would have been happy with a pragmatist account of religious truth it may be suggested that this is at least compatible with the non-foundationalist, confessional style of doing theology, which starts from Christianity (or any other religion) as it is. Whereas Gore's later trilogy *The Reconstruction of Belief* (1921-4) starts with the philosophical basis for belief in an immanent God who might be expected to reveal himself, Holland is more modern in starting with Christianity as it is.

Such an approach must seek to modify the tradition where it is at variance with the rest of contemporary knowledge, as Scott Holland does in accepting the death of the older evidential apologetic. Beyond that it must ensure that the Christian religious system is in good working order, and that requires a clear perception of what that system is. Calling Christianity 'the religion of the Incarnation' implies that the dogmatic definition of Christ is central to and constitutive of this system, and that the Enlightenment and liberal alternative of reducing christology to what most non-believers will accept – Jesus as a great moral and religious teacher – is a disastrously false step. Such christologies 'from below' have failed to climb up to the level of assertion which the New Testament and classical Christian orthodoxy have, like Holland (above p.18), felt constrained to confess.

Scott Holland, like Schleiermacher and Barth, recognised that it would be inappropriate to deny these rationalist and liberal theological experimenters, with their 'historical Jesus' versions of Christianity, a place in the community. Anglicanism's unwillingness to call heresy by its name has the merit of encouraging the exploration which belongs to the venture of faith. It also recognizes that the limits of the theological diversity which is both desirable and inescapable today are not always immediately obvious. But after 200 years there are good reasons for thinking that an experiment which abandoned what the New Testament authors, Fathers, and Reformers, thought constitutive of Christianity, has failed. A recovery of the true humanity of Jesus was salutary, but a denial of his divinity gradually destroys the Christian religious system, because this hinges on the claim that in having to do with Jesus, our crucified and risen Lord, we have to do with God, that faith in God and faith in Christ are identical, that the worship of Christ is worship of God.

What we mean by the divinity of Christ requires clarification, and theological exposition of the dogma will vary from culture to culture. But parameters are necessary, and the history of liberal theology, insofar as it abandoned the doctrine of the Incarnation (as opposed to abandoning particular patristic incarnational theologies which are plainly superannuated) suggests that this doctrine, which holds faith in God, faith in Christ, and salvation inseparably together, is still the best criterion of authentic Christianity.

Unlike Hegel's incarnationalism, which at least in the 'left wing' form given it by Strauss denies the doctrine of the Incarnation, Schleiermacher struggled to combine an incarnational christology with a historical perception of Jesus. As the last great theologian to die before the radical gospel criticism of Strauss and Baur undercut their appeal to history, he has more in common with liberal Anglican incarnational christologies which rejected this criticism than with his liberal and radical German successors who accepted it. His attempt to replace the rationalists' moral teacher with an incarnational christology, i.e. one that finds the reality of God in Jesus of Nazareth, (not in some 'idea', or even in the 'kerygmatic Christ') has more in common with the later Barth and subsequent narrative theology than with the early Barth and other dialectical theologians. Despite its partial failure Schleiermacher's compromise between tradition and modernity in a revisionary incarnational christology remains more true to orthodox Christian faith than much of what followed. In Germany especially, the doctrine of the Incarnation was fractured by christologies built on the historians' separation of the so-called 'historical Jesus' and Christian faith perspectives.[16]

In contrast to some theological idealists' embarrassment about the historical particularity of the Christian revelation, Schleiermacher and Holland were clear that the subject of christological predication is the man from Nazareth. That necessitated historical criticism: 'concrete historical facts...must be subject to the thumb of critical discussion, and to all the external handling of evidence and argument' (p.44). But in contrast to Enlightenment and later liberal protestant theologies they were also clear that what is said about Jesus in christology must bear the weight of subsequent Christian experience. When historical criticism of the Fourth Gospel robbed Schleiermacher's proposal of its visible means of support, that was the first part of his theological system to be jettisoned. Some of what followed justified Barth's theological reaction, as the great achievements of the liberals' historical scholarship were no substitute for a theological interpretation of scripture, i.e. one which spoke with scripture of God, and elicited and clarified the response of faith. With the decline of the idealist metaphysics which had made Baur's historical scholarship at the same time talk of God, historical research and theology went their separate ways. The re-unification provided by kerygmatic theology omitted too much doctrinal substance to sustain the Christian religious system, and Barth found himself impelled to retrieve the classical tradition in his *Church Dogmatics*.

By ceaseless exploration Barth thus arrived close to the traditional Christianity with which he had started, and knowing the place for the first time he came close to the credal orthodoxy maintained by Scott Holland, who travelled and wrote less. Barth unfolds the tradition with a genius that no-one claims for the theological preacher and teacher of St Paul's and Christ Church. But the extent of Holland's literary output does not affect the claim that he offers valuable pointers to the shape of a theology that is traditional without being tradition-bound, and open to new knowledge without being blown off-course by it. Neither Barth nor Holland interpreted the tradition they explored as a system of symbols, but both can be read today in the light of some such theory of religion. If 'post-liberal' Americans can set Barth's interpretation of the tradition in a new framework, post-liberal Anglicans can similarly understand Scott Holland's advocacy of the religion of the Incarnation.

Holland did not elaborate the tradition very much. His writings are more like Schleiermacher's sermons than *The Christian Faith*. His point of reference is usually the creeds,[17] which epitomize the tradition, giving central place to the christological dogma, its narrative basis in the gospels, and the trinitarian pattern of belief which follows from it. A typically Anglican account of the relationship between the three-fold authority of scripture, tradition, and reason would be to say (as Holland implies) that *the creed guides our understanding of scripture*.

That Anglican guideline gives scripture a primacy which unreformed catholicism and uncontrolled enthusiasm would seem to deny. But it also recognizes that scripture is interpreted by thinking people, whose 'understanding' embraces the rest of their knowledge and moral insight. Further, this understanding takes place in the context of the church where the tradition's fundamental beliefs about God as creator, redeemer, and sanctifier, made known through the saving revelation of Jesus Christ, are assumed and expressed.

The credal point of reference highlights the worshipping context that is essential to Christian belief.[18] It is here that the creed is recited, and its recitation is essentially doxological, despite the new secondary uses found for it in some fourth-century controversies. This rehearsal of the Christian story, summary of the Christian tradition, acknowledgement of a common participation, and affirmation of personal commitment, is in principle far removed from tests of orthodoxy. Christian truth and orthodoxy are taken for granted in Anglican worship, not made into an issue.

Such a relaxed attitude would soon sink into complacency if it were not accompanied by theological scrutiny of the tradition, including scripture, in the light of the gospel and its engagement with contemporary knowledge and social realities. But the scrutiny has to be sensitive to the symbol system of beliefs and rituals through which faith in God is sustained. Credal items are not isolated propositions whose validity can be rationally tested, but parts of a working system through which millions believe they are in a worshipping relationship to God that makes sense of their lives, and motivates their behaviour.

Only a handful of theological statements are prominent in most Christians' symbol system. Scott Holland's credal point of reference also relegates to secondary status those matters not included in the creeds. They are scarcely matters of faith, even if some other Christians seem inordinately attached to them. One example whose absence from the creed was noted by Gore is the inspiration of scripture. It would be wrong to deny it, but also wrong to make a fetish of it. Others are mariological and sacramental doctrine, the ministry, predestination – and justification by faith. No Anglican theologian would deny the necessity of sacramental doctrine or church order. For understandable historical reasons, 'apostolic succession' has received a degree of emphasis not warranted by the creeds. It is a matter for Anglican self-criticism that theological positions have sometimes been adopted on appeal to tradition alone (including scripture) rather than shown by theological argument based on tradition and experience to be required by the gospel of God in Christ.

Even 'scriptural doctrines' such as justification by faith alone and predestination are essential only insofar as they can be shown to be required by the gospel of the Incarnation. They are non-credal, and not obviously integral to the Christian symbol system.

It was therefore not unAnglican of Holland, as it would surely have been unLutheran, to write a long essay on faith without even mentioning justification. Medieval and Reformation controversies, echoed in such historical landmarks as the 39 Articles, should not dominate the contemporary agenda.

This does not mean that Scott Holland's Anglican understanding of faith is unPauline. The apostle is the most incisive if not the most direct scriptural witness to the Lord, and the epistles secondary only to the gospels in Anglican faith and worship. But 'justifying faith' belongs more to the history of doctrine (including the 39 Articles) and biblical interpretation than to Paul himself. If it were Luther who 'guides our understanding of scripture' justification would be central; since it is the credal summary of the Christian symbol system that provides that guidance, it is not.

St Paul himself will presumably have spent most of his time preaching Christ and evoking faith in Christ without any mention of justification. The Old Testament language concerning God's righteousness and ours, especially Hab. 2:4 and Gen. 15:6 which alone connect it with faith, have generated some profound theological reflection in Western Christianity. But whenever it has caused anthropology to usurp the central position of christology in the Christian system, the gospel has been misunderstood.

Luther's use of this Pauline antithesis to criticize medieval catholicism is valid only on account of its underlying appeal to christology (*solus Christus*) as the sole criterion of Christianity, not on account of what he says about faith. That is psychologically far more interesting than Paul's understanding of the word, but it has no normative significance for Anglicans.

Without mentioning justification by faith Scott Holland shares with Paul and Luther the fundamental conviction of the creeds that Christian faith is a saving relationship to God in Christ. It calls for a belief in God, and a christology which asserts that in having to do with the crucified and exalted Jesus, we have to do with God – i.e. it calls for an incarnational christology. This conviction also presupposes the Christian community which proclaims this gospel and lives from this relationship to God in Christ. Beyond that it can sit lightly to the details of doctrinal discussion. Holland writes powerfully of the necessity of belief in the resurrection of Jesus, leading to an incarnational christology that finds God in Jesus, without himself offering a new christological construction. St Paul apparently accepted the early church's tradition of the atoning death of Jesus as a sacrifice for sins (1 Cor. 15:3), without developing his scriptural argument for the sole sufficiency of faith in Christ into a forensic theory of how God wrought this salvation. Scott Holland also was content to insist on the fundamental shape of a Christianity based on scripture as understood in the light of the church's tradition – a tradition epitomized in its creeds.

This high value set upon the creeds does not rest on some special Anglican interest in the fourth century. That has left its mark on all subsequent orthodoxy only because here the christological heart of the gospel – Emmanuel, God with us – received its decisive dogmatic definition. Holland defends the dogma, but he is at his most persuasive when preaching on the resurrection. Without that there is no doctrine of the Incarnation and no Christianity. Again this shows Holland starting with Christianity as it actually exists, a religion (or functioning symbol system) whose shape is determined by the event in which the decisive saving revelation of God is acknowledged: that is, by reference to the person who is acknowledged, 'My Lord and my God'.

That 'supreme act of personal surrender, for which Christ unhesitatingly asks, cannot conceivably pass beyond its child-stage without forming a direct and urgent challenge to the intellect to say how, and why, such an act can be justified or such a claim interpreted' (p.44). The event of revelation and faith, in which Jesus is disclosed and recognized as more than a teacher or prophet, gave rise to doctrinal definition and led also to the attempt to encompass all knowledge and experience. Scott Holland wrote in a church still adjusting to the break-down of its favoured apologetics. He wisely aimed 'to sift the questions which beset us, and to distinguish those to which Faith is bound to give an answer from those which it can afford to let alone' (opening paragraph, p.3). The evidentialist apologetics were dead, but that was no reason to abandon the dogma by which Christianity is identified.

Maintaining this incarnational structure of the tradition provides a framework within which the saving revelation may be actualized afresh for subsequent believers. That is what motivated the Fourth Evangelist's recasting his tradition in an incarnational mould in the first place (John 17:20; 20:31 etc.). The rationalists' combination of deism and the historical Jesus has not been able to claim much continuity with traditional Christianity, and has not been widely accepted as true to Christian experience. The credal alternative still beckons: 'For us and our salvation, He came down from heaven', however the religion of the Incarnation is articulated theologically today.

Distinguishing 'insider' talk of God, revelation, and faith, from the outsider perspective adopted by apologetics, helps preserve Christian talk of God and faith from distortion. Apologetics rightly cultivates the ground common to believers and outsiders. It can plead the human value of religion without reducing God to a function of human needs, whereas to defend faith in that way is to trivialise it. Believers in God claim to be responding to something greater than themselves, and will not sell God as a commodity. They 'let God be God', and recognize Christian religious faith as faith in God who is worshipped in joyful and obedient response to the saving revelation in Jesus.

Apologetics, natural theology, philosophy of religion, and other good works can follow in another context. Christians use their reason, and they engage in theology as soon as they begin to think. Faith seeks connections with the rest of knowledge and the older natural theology performed tasks which ought not be neglected. If philosophy no longer sums up human knowledge it is no longer the special partner of theology, but forging connections remains vital if its claims to truth are to be credible. On the other hand a premature combination of faith and unbelieving reason, when the dominant rationality is hostile to religion, is likely to prove as damaging to faith in God as their too severe disjunction. 'Faith and reason' arguments need quite drastic revision in a pluralist and secular culture, whether or not the approach advocated in this essay is accepted.

Re-reading Scott Holland has provided an opportunity to retread some familiar territory in the new 'post-liberal' shoes he can be said to have anticipated. The modest contribution of theological prolegomena to the life of faith is to focus the material theological task of pruning the tradition and engaging with the rest of human knowledge and experience. It may therefore serve as an introduction to the essays that follow. An essay on 'faith', like the first word of the creed, is more concerned with the form than the content of Christian believing. But our argument has been that the word is rightly used in Christian discourse only where a conviction of divine disclosure is implied, and where the tradition in which this is apprehended and expressed is used to refer to that ineffable content. Talk of faith is not Christian unless it refers to the revelation of God in Christ, any more than talk of God is Christian unless it speaks of that revelation and that faith. None of this is possible without the community life in which the tradition is preserved and actualized in word and sacrament.

Support has been found in Scott Holland for starting theology with the tradition- and community-dependent life of faith itself, whether or not respectable philosophical foundations are available. It is no doubt necessary to clarify what we mean by God, and metaphysical reflection seems indispensable here, however far that may be from the mainstream of school philosophy. But since the 'we' who speak meaningfully of God in a secular culture are religious believers, clarification of our God-talk leads to an investigation of our religion, not in the first place to philosophical analysis of the concept of God, much less to arguments about God's existence. Discussion of divine attributes belongs later in the doctrinal system, not in the 'preamble' to faith.

Specifically, investigation of Christianity (as of some other religions) directs attention in the first place not to its rational foundations,[19] but to its claim to a foundational revelation which is narrated, proclaimed, responded to, and elucidated in scripture. It also directs attention to the life of faith in the community that arose from women and men acknowledging this event of divine disclosure. Both these foci require theological interpretation of scripture to be placed higher on the Anglican agenda.

Christians speak of God in Christ, and understanding our confessional statements involves analysis of the Christian system, not merely historical study, indispensable and important as that dimension also is. Such analysis requires some definition or theory of religion which is tested by the empirical data and so confirmed or discarded. Theological prolegomena today need to clarify the nature of religion as well as the various apologetic and dogmatic tasks of Christian theology. All that is even further removed from the actual life of faith that the substantive doctrinal tasks of pruning the tradition which might otherwise choke it, and of harnessing to it the scientific and historical knowledge which might otherwise extinguish it. Our introductory mapwork relating faith to theology, religion, and the tradition is equally far removed from the inspirational quality of Scott Holland's sermons. Those who seek the reality of faith will turn not to such prolegomena, but to theologically informed preachers such as Schleiermacher and Barth in Berlin and Switzerland, or between them in England, Henry Scott Holland, whose essay on faith can still communicate something of the joy in Christian believing.

Notes

1. *Old and New* (London 1903), p.viii.

2. See S. Paget (ed.), *Henry Scott Holland: Memoir and Letters* (London 1921); E. Lyttleton, *The Mind and Character of Henry Scott Holland* (London 1926). W. Lock, *Oxford Memories* (Oxford 1932), pp.70-8 is disappointingly slight. See also J.H. Heidt, *The Social Theology of Henry Scott Holland*, Diss. (Oxford 1975), with extensive bibliography.

3. *The Fourth Gospel* was edited by W.J. Richmond and published with his own reconstruction of Holland's thought, *The Philosophy of Faith*, in 1920, then on its own in 1923. Its focus is on historicity and apostolic authorship, but the editor has added in Note 2 a fragment from lecture notes, on the epistemology of faith.

4. E.g. Lyttleton *op. cit.* ch. 3; A.M. Ramsey, *From Gore to Temple* (London 1960), p.12; Heidt *op. cit.* ch. 1.

5. Paget *op. cit.* p.236 records his self-deprecating reaction to Asquith's offer of either the Regius chair or the Deanery of Christ Church: 'We must have a scientific theologian honourably representing learning ... I have absolutely no scholarship whatever about me'.

6. E.g. S. Ogden, *On Theology* (New York 1986), p.69: 'To exist as a self at all is possible solely on the basis of faith, so that the statement "Unless you believe, you shall not understand", is true in a sense not only of the Christian or of the religious believer but of every human being simply as such.' W.C. Smith, *Faith and Belief* (Princeton 1979), writes of faith as 'generally human' (p.129). The more common English approach to the topic from the philosophy of religion is well represented by John Hick, *Faith and Knowledge* (London 1957), and his teacher H.H. Price, *Belief* (London 1969). Both are also contributors to the symposium edited by Hick, *Faith and the Philosophers* (London 1964). Peter Carnley, *The Structure of Resurrection Belief* (Oxford 1986), echoes English concerns in looking for an epistemology of faith.

7. *Faith and Understanding* (ET London 1969), p.52.

8. Clifford Geertz's essay, 'Religion as a Cultural System', in M. Banton (ed.), *Anthropological Approaches to the Study of Religion* (London 1966), reprinted in his collection *The Interpretation of Cultures* (New York 1973), has been influential. Cf. G. Lindbeck, *The Nature of Doctrine* (London 1984).

9. Cf. Schleiermacher, *The Christian Faith* (ET Edinburgh 1928), p.475.

10. Cf. Schleiermacher, *Brief Outline on the Study of Theology* (ET Richmond 1966); Ernst Troeltsch, *Writings on Theology and Religion* (ET London 1977), and S.W. Sykes, *The Identity of Christianity* (London 1984).

11. E.g. E. Schillebeeckx, *Christ* (ET London 1980), esp. pp.62, 803, 838.

12. W.W. Meissner, *Life and Faith: Psychological Perspectives on Religious Experience* (Washington D.C. 1987), uses this phrase as a section heading, but then includes faith and hope as its contents.

13. E.g. R. Needham, *Belief, Language, and Experience* (Oxford 1972). Although Needham avoids the word 'faith' much of his argument refers to this.

14. L. Feuerbach, *The Essence of Faith according to Luther* (1844, ET 1967).

15. H.-G. Gadamer, *Truth and Method* (ET London 1975). Equally important for theology is A. MacIntyre, *After Virtue* (London 1981).

16. I have elaborated on this in 'Historical Criticism and Christology' in S.W. Sykes (ed.), *England and Germany: Studies in Theological Diplomacy* (Frankfurt 1981).

17. This is apparent in some of the titles of his collected sermons and papers: *Creed and Character* (1887), *On Behalf of Belief* (1888), *Creeds and Critics* (1918). The centrality of 'faith' in his writings is also clear; e.g. *Fibres of Faith* (1910), *Facts of the Faith* (1919).

18. See D.W. Hardy and D. Ford, *Jubilate* (London 1984).

19. This approach can now find philosophical support from A. Plantinga and N. Wolterstorff (eds.), *Faith and Rationality* (Indiana 1983) and D.Z. Phillips, *Faith and Foundationalism* (London 1988) - but in no way depends on that. Theology pursues its own path without waiting for a licence from philosophy.

THE CHRISTIAN DOCTRINE OF GOD

Andrew Louth

Et hoc omnes intelligunt Deum:
quam omnes Deum nominant;
quod omnes dicunt Deum;
et hoc dicimus Deum;
et hoc dicimus Deum.

Not a Latin poem with a strangely modern ring, but the words with which Aquinas closes each of the Five Ways: 'and this everyone calls God', or some variant. Fitfully philosophers criticizing Aquinas' five ways of proving the existence of God have drawn attention to the daring or implausibility of such a conclusion – it could be argued that all Kant's criticism of such arguments focus on that phrase – but for the most part attention has been directed to the substance of the arguments. Certainly Aquinas hardly gives the impression that these concluding words bear very much weight. But it seems to me that it is the implausibility of meaning anything much by such a phrase in our modern culture that is the biggest problem in trying to say anything on the doctrine of God (to begin with, anyway). *Omnes* – all men and women – do not normally mean anything by God nowadays: our religious talk about God is really the only kind of talk about God there is. That was not the case for Aquinas, it was not the case in the last century: in particular, it was not the case for Aubrey Moore when he composed his contribution to *Lux Mundi*. People talked about God in various contexts: nature, society, morality, politics, economics even – in all these areas of discourse God could be evoked (in some cases one might have to add 'still' or 'with difficulty'), and poets evoked God in their verse. That seems to me to be no longer the case. The job of the theologian is not to clarify or purify a use of the notion of God that already has currency: for the notion of God has scarcely any currency at all, except when people want to be religious. This is all very obvious, and I must seem to some to be labouring the obvious: but if it is true, then it means that to discuss the doctrine of God now is to do something very different from what we would have been doing in the nineteenth or the thirteenth century. One cannot just launch into the subject assuming that others will know what one is talking about: unless one is to be content with talking to a few (or even many) like-minded souls, which is only different in degree from talking to oneself.

In a way this was recognized in what seems to me (perhaps through ignorance) one of the more interesting utterances on theology by an Anglican this century. In *Theology* in 1939, just before the outbreak of the Second World War, William Temple reflected in an article called 'Theology Today' in a way that was critical of much of his own theological work. He spoke of the spirit in which he had written his *Christus Veritas*, a spirit in which he felt that 'what is needed is the exposition of the Christian idea of God, life and the world, or, in other words, a Christocentric metaphysics' , as a spirit that seemed 'very remote' to him in 1939. He spoke of theologians such as himself as having outlined 'a Christian map of the world' and said that men and women in the late 1930s 'rightly refuse to listen' to such: 'the world of today is one of which no Christian map can be made.' He summarized what he saw as the changed task of the theologian thus:

Temple

> Our task with this world is not to explain it, but to convert it [here Temple echoes, presumably consciously, the well-known remark of Marx's]. Its need can be met, not by the discovery of its own immanent principle in signal manifestation through Jesus Christ, but only by the shattering impact upon its self-sufficiency and arrogance of the Son of God crucified, risen and ascended, pouring forth the explosive and disruptive energy which is the Holy Ghost.[1]

Temple referred back to his remarks in the introduction he wrote as chairman to the report, *Doctrine in the Church of England*: there he made much the same contrast, this time giving giving it a more specific historical reference by contrasting the needed theology of redemption with the older theology of Incarnation which he associated especially with the 'influence of Westcott reinforced by that of the *Lux Mundi* school'.[2] It seems to me that Temple's analysis here was right, especially significant perhaps in that it took the form of a self-criticism that consigned much of his own work to the dustbin. How much Temple's analysis has been heeded is another question. Not, perhaps, very much, even though no-one reads Temple nowadays: it is perhaps quite difficult for Anglicans, especially, to realize that they are not part of the map of modern England – they seem all too obviously part of any such map. If they are on the map, surely it can be read in some way as a Christian map? But on an Ordnance Survey map, some things are marked in Gothic script, as being of historical interest – later than the Romans.

It might be thought that I am overdoing this sense of the contrast between the theologian's task nowadays, and what it was in the past. Certainly, Temple's contrast between theologies of Incarnation and redemption suggests a difference merely of emphasis: and Temple understood it so himself, though he spoke of a 'vast difference...in direction of attention and estimate of relative values'.[3] But it does seem to me that a situation, in which discourse about God and the divine has no real currency, is a new situation for Christian theologians – a new situation which is disguised when modern Christians talk of living in a pagan culture. Pagan cultures, in any proper sense of the word, have an often very elaborate sense of the divine and its impingement on human life: our society has very little sense of anything impinging on it at all – human cares and concerns are self-contained, though they do, of course, conflict a good deal. Certainly paganism is part of the society we live in in a way that it was not in the time of *Lux Mundi*. Moore spoke of polytheism as being 'not merely untrue, but impossible and inconceivable':[4] but nowadays Indian religions are part of our society, both by immigration and by their appeal to some people's need for religion. But it remains that society *as a whole* embraces religions, including Christianity, by ignoring them: maybe in its folly.

Perhaps, though, I am only talking about the deadened consciousness of modern society: not that other societies have not succumbed to such a deadened consciousness themselves, but custom and convention wore religious garb and disguised the essentially irreligious nature of societies that seemed religious (think of Pascal on *divertissement*). Poets, it might be claimed, have not lost a sense of the sacred, of the divine, of God. But it seems to me that the case of R.S. Thomas, for example, bears out, rather than undermines, my case: that lack of public currency for the notion of God renders use of the term 'God' very problematic. Though R.S. Thomas is thought of as a religious poet (especially by religious people), most of his early poems have little about God. But in those early poems, 'God' can be used without much difficulty: e.g., in 'Priest and Peasant' from *Song at the Year's Turning*:

> While I watch you, and pray for you,
> And so increase my small store
> Of credit in the bank of God,
> Who sees you suffer and me pray...[5]

In his later poems, however, there is more and more about God, but this mention of God is associated with images of waiting, silence, absence...In *Not that He brought Flowers,* a priest (or preacher) kneeling before the altar prays

> Prompt me, God;
> But not yet. When I speak,
> Though it be you who speak

> Through me, something is lost.
> The meaning is in the waiting.[6]

Other poems speak of 'the silence/that is his chosen medium/of communication...';[7] 'Never known as anything/but an absence, I dare not name him/as God';[8] 'the eternal/silence that is the repose of God';[9] or, at the end of a poem 'Correspondence' about his own silence in failing to reply to letters, he says, 'I wish there were as simple/an explanation for the silence of God.'[10] Or in a poem called 'Via Negativa':

> Why no! I never thought other than
> That God is that great absence
> In our lives, the empty silence
> Within, the place where we go
> Seeking, not in hope to
> Arrive or find.[11]

That title – 'Via Negativa' – suggests something traditional: negative language of silence, darkness, absence, waiting, is all part of the familiar repertory of traditional theology. But one has only to compare R.S. Thomas with another Welsh poet, Henry Vaughan, in his poem 'The Night' to sense a difference:

> There is in God (some say)
> A deep, but dazling darkness; As men here
> Say it is late and dusky, because they
> See not all clear;
> O for that night! where I in him
> Might live invisible and dim.

Vaughan's darkness is the blinding light of God, an unbearable presence; Thomas' silence is something rather different, a sense of absence, always teetering on the brink of nothing, of agnosticism, often treated very evasively.[12] But it is not easy, either, to treat his poems as the record of a gradual relinquishment of faith. The poem 'Alive' uses negative imagery very positively, ending:

> The darkness
> is the deepening shadow
> of your presence; the silence a
> process in the metabolism
> of the being of love.[13]

The linking there of silence and darkness with the quiet creativity of nature is a theme that appears elsewhere, often in the form of a contrast between that and the efficiency of the machine, of technology, an efficiency which is devoid of meaning.

The point of that digression was immediately to underline my contention that discourse about God has no natural currency nowadays: R.S. Thomas normally speaks of God in his poems in the same breath as he evokes doubt and agnosticism. But the way he does this is by his use of imagery of silence, absence and waiting: imagery that can as easily be regarded as *anticipatory*, than as simply negative.

One traditional way of securing discourse about God a place within human discourse as a whole has been the traditional proofs for the existence of God. Moore starts his paper in *Lux Mundi* by saying that he is *not* going to discuss these proofs, though at the end he recaps the proofs, treating them not as establishing anything, but precisely as relating his notion of God to related areas of human discourse: morality, existence, etc. Philosophers will probably always be interested in such proofs (certainly they still regularly write about them), but such an interest need not be theological: it is interesting, anyway, to see what lies at the remoter reaches of human speculation. But if such proofs are generally regarded as problematical – as I should have thought they are – they are not much use to theologians in a context where discourse about God is not current: for then an enormous *onus* is being put of them which they could only bear if irrefragable.

It has however sometimes been thought by Christians, or apologists for Christianity, that God's existence cannot be established and that this tells us something significant about the nature of God. Notable thinkers who have held this have included Pascal, Kierkegaard and Dostoevsky. In none of these cases is the point simply that deprived of reason one is driven to resort to faith, and it is only faith that counts: still less the modern version of this which reduces religion almost to a matter of personal taste. The point – or part of it, at least – is rather that were the existence of God to be proved, what would be established by such a proof would be a certain kind of coherence between God and the world that would force us to see God in a particular (false) light and would also oblige us to turn a blind eye to some aspects of the world. For Pascal the world of nature is ambiguous: there are signs that God made it, there is evidence too that no God of love such as Christians believe in could ever have made it. God, if he exists, is a hidden God, *deus absconditus, dieu caché*.[14] Any proof would amount to reading this ambiguity as something more straightforward. But if one could prove the existence of God one would end up with a notion of God that followed the tendency of such a proof – a *limited* notion of God:

> The Christian's God does not consist merely of a God who is the author of mathematical truths and the order of the elements. That is the portion of the heathen and Epicureans. He does not consist

> merely of a God who extends his providence over the life and property of men so as to grant a happy span of years to those who worship him. That is the portion of the Jews. But the God of Abraham, the God of Isaac, the God of Jacob, the God of the Christians is a God of love and consolation: he is a God who fills the soul and heart of those whom he possesses: he is a God who makes them inwardly aware of their wretchedness and his infinite mercy: who unites himself with them in the depths of their soul: who fills it with humility, joy, confidence and love: who makes them incapable of any other end but him.[15]

For Pascal the means by which we grasp the notion of God must be commensurate with God as he reveals himself: it is not therefore a matter of comparative indifference what traces of the divine or the sacred we take to be the traces of God. In a society where (however untruly) the alternative to belief in God seems to be no belief at all, any sign of God, any trace of the sacred is likely to seem valuable to the apologist: to someone like Augustine there would have been no such indifference – it was important not to fall into the hands of the demons! In Pascal's approach, with its insistence on ambiguity (an ambiguity which is present in everything belonging to this world, even the scriptures – hence allegory, even the miracles of Christ which were ambiguous in their import), there is a corresponding stress on the importance of discernment. But we shall come back to that: here I want to introduce Dostoevsky into our considerations.

Dostoevsky's *The Brothers Karamazov* famously contains many of his theological and religious ideas. Here I want to look at one thing only: the kind of Christianity Dostoevsky seeks to commend in the persons of Fr Zossima and Alyosha. I do not want to raise the question as to whether Dostoevsky accurately represents Orthodox theology in his account of Fr Zossima: it seems to me that Fr Sergei Hackel has made a strong case for seeking Dostoevsky's inspiration in this elsewhere, but that is irrelevant here.[16] Books 5 and 6 bring the question of Christianity to a head with the long conversation between Ivan and Alyosha Karamazov, culminating in the poem or legend of the Grand Inquisitor, followed by the lengthy summary of Fr Zossima's teaching by Alyosha in Book 6.

Ivan's attack on Christianity has two salvoes: the first is focussed on the idea of the cosmos as an eternal harmony established by God, the second (the legend of the Grand Inquisitor) focusses on the Church as an authoritative sacramental system establishing harmony among mankind (the fact that Dostoevsky gives Ivan a story about the Roman Catholic Church in fifteenth-century Spain is clearly intended to present this as a distortion of Christianity: but it is a distortion not limited to fifteenth-century Seville.) What is attacked in both cases is presented in analogous terms: in terms of a harmony in which the greater good of the whole outweighs suffering or distortion in little things. The first time Ivan outlines what he believes,[17] he underlines his idea of God creating the world as a mathematical system, and this remains Ivan's premise. The second and longer presentation, in the chapter called 'Rebellion', with its examples of pointless cruelty to children that cannot be excused and could never form part of the 'eternal harmony' culminates in Ivan's 'respectfully returning his ticket': 'rebellion', as Alyosha says. To which Ivan replies,

> 'Imagine that it is you yourself who are erecting the edifice of human destiny with the aim of making men happy in the end, of giving them peace and contentment at last, but that to do that it is absolutely necessary, and indeed quite inevitable, to torture to death only one tiny creature, the little girl who beat her breast with her little fist, and to found the edifice on her unavenged tears – would you consent to be the architect on those conditions? Tell me and do not lie!'
>
> 'No, I wouldn't.' Alyosha said softly. [18]

Alyosha then raises something he maintains Ivan has missed: Christ, the innocent victim who died for all, who can 'forgive everything, everyone and everything and *for everything*'. Which leads into the legend of the Grand Inquisitor.

The legend of the Grand Inquisitor is too well-known to need recounting. The focus of the story is the Grand Inquisitor's visit to Christ, held in a dungeon, after his having been arrested when he appears in the flesh in fifteenth-century Spain. The Grand Inquisitor sees Christ's appearance as a threat, a threat to the religion that has been built up in Christ's name in the fourteen centuries since his life and death. This religion, he tells Christ (who says nothing), though called Christianity, systematically undermines the religion Christ preached. Whereas Christ, in his temptation in the desert, refused to do anything that would encroach on human freedom since he had come to teach men to love, and love implies freedom, the religion that the Grand Inquisitor serves systematically takes away from men and women their freedom and rules them by means of the 'miracle, mystery and authority' that Christ renounced at his temptation. The 'fearful burden' of 'freedom of conscience' is taken from men and women and they are thus able to be happy. The Grand Inquisitor presents this as a work of *compassion*: freedom is too much for the frailty of men; they would rather be led like sheep. At the end of the long explanation by the Grand Inquisitor Christ says nothing, but then suddenly goes up to the old man and kisses him on his lips. He is let out of the dungeon and vanishes.

The whole of Ivan's argument with Alyosha is an indictment of religion and a religious view of the universe as a system of control at the expense of conscience. But it is not the whole story: Ivan's speeches form a kind of diptych with the teaching of Fr Zossima preserved by Alyosha. The heart of Fr Zossima's teaching is contained in his first address, much earlier on in the novel: 'For you must know, beloved, that each one of us is beyond all question responsible for all men and all things on earth, not only because of the general transgressions of the world, but each one individually for all men and every single man on this earth.'[19] The inspiration behind this teaching in Fr Zossima's own life, we find in his account of his elder brother, Markel. He had become a young atheist to his mother's horror. Later he falls ill of consumption and upsets his mother still further by refusing to fast and go to communion. But then, for his mother's sake – 'to please her and set her mind at rest' – he agrees to fast and go to church. A sudden change comes over him, he becomes 'calm and gentle, cheerful and joyous', even though by now his consumption is far advanced. He explains the source of his joy by saying that he realizes that he deserves no-one's love, that the love shown him is a gift to be appreciated, and goes on to say, 'every one of us is responsible for everyone else in every way, and I most of all';[20] and that with that realization he is in paradise: for we are all in paradise, only none of us knows it. And very soon he dies. The heart of Fr Zossima's teaching can be seen to be the very opposite of the kind of Christianity Ivan rejected: it is not at all a matter of a system, a contrived harmony upheld at the expense of suffering and the conscience of the individual. Rather it starts at quite the opposite end: no-one *else* is responsible, we are each of us responsible. Whereas Christianity as a system relieves the individual of responsibility, this understanding of Christianity starts from the acceptance by the individual – by me – of responsibility. But neither does Zossima's teaching reduce to a mere individualism: for we are each responsible for *everyone*. If we are each responsible for everyone, then we can never hold anything against anyone else; nor can we disclaim responsibility by living in accordance with mere appearances, and so on. The barriers we set up between one another, barriers that constitute claims against one another, are taken down. Fr Zossima is quite confident that there will be an ultimate harmony, the kingdom of heaven, but 'it's a spiritual, a psychological process. To transform the world, it is necessary that men themselves should suffer a change of heart. Until you have actually become everyone's brother, the brotherhood of man will not come to pass.'[21]

Put together, the two parts of the diptych – Ivan's argument and Fr Zossima'a teaching – amount to the rejection of the notion of God as the ultimate underwriter of a system of control, whether cosmic or ecclesial, and the affirmation of freedom as the central term in any understanding of God and man and their relationship. Berdyaev, who owed much to Dostoevsky, put it well when he said:

> In opposition to Schleiermacher and many others it must be stated that religion is not a 'sense of dependence' (*Abhängigkeitsgefühl*) but, on the contrary, a sense of independence. If God does not exist, man is a being wholly dependent on nature or society, on the world or on the state. If God exists, man is a spiritually independent being; and his relation to God is to be defined as freedom.[22]

Freedom – as that which makes love possible and which in turn is enhanced or made possible by love. And by their very nature both freedom and love are non-coercive: force and coercion have no place here.

This leads to several lines of reflection. First, one way of expressing what I have been considering is to make a distinction between *explanation* and *meaning*. It is meaning that men and women are in search of, not, or not necessarily, explanation. Explanation can only provide meaning at a comparatively humble level, and in many cases explanation ousts meaning: we talk of 'explaining away'. The contrast between explanation and meaning is the contrast between Ivan Karamazov and Fr Zossima's brother, Markel; it is the contrast between Pascal's *esprit* and *coeur*, his *esprit de géométrie* and *esprit de finesse*. And the doctrine of God belongs to the realm of meaning. Now much natural theology sees things differently: it tries to present God as the supreme explanation. And such an attitude to God can spill over into other aspects of theology, even spirituality. God is seen as an ultimate solution to problems: in that context prayer becomes a last resort to the ultimate answer. The Garden of Gethsemane and the Cross show us, beyond a shadow of doubt, that God the Father is not such a being: he is the source of costly meaning, not easy explanations. And to speak of God the Father is to speak of God the Trinity. To speak of God in this way may seem to envisage a style of theology rather different from what has often been customary in Christian theology, at least in the West. Western ideas of predestination strike the wrong note; Eastern language of *synergy*, a working together of God and man, seems much more appropriate. There seems to be, also, a fairly close correlation between God as meaning, and God as perceived in the categories of freedom and love, which are essentially non-coercive.

I mentioned earlier that the temptation to pursue any trace of the sacred that seems to lead to the divine is one to be resisted: the 'divine' with a small 'd' includes what others would have called the demonic. The sacred, the divine, in its primitive manifestations, is usually understood as powerful, terrifying, not to say violent, something to be propitiated. René Girard, in his *La Violence et le sacré*,[23] has suggested, as an anthropological theory, that sacrifice is a way of diverting the violence provoked by human conflicting desires: that, if you like, the idea that humans form a society by means of some sort of social contract is too tame an idea and fails to take account of the power and disruptive capacity of human desire. Sacrifice, licensed violence, lies at the heart of human society, and thus at the heart of religion. In his more recent *Des choses cachées depuis la fondation du monde*,[24] he suggests that Christianity offers another possibility – though not, by any means, a possibility that has been often understood or adopted – the possibility of seeing in Christ one who offered no violence to anyone but who became the object of the violence of others. Although Christ's death is often understood as a sacrifice, he argues that in the New Testament such an understanding is rare: none of the gospels, he argues, seriously suggests it. (It is an argument that at times sets the theologian's teeth on edge, but the broad lines of his case seem to me compelling, if not absolutely convincing.) Rather, Christ's life and teaching are about non-violence, about love as the way to such non-violence, about the Christian community as a new kind of society based not on violence institutionalized in the sacred, but on non-violence understood as following the way of Christ who reflects the nature of God. (Girard professes a very orthodox christology, including a vigorous defence of the Virgin Birth.)[25]

All we have said so far seems to suggest an important correlation between various contrasts: explanation and meaning, coercion and freedom, violence and non-violence, reason and the heart. Let us exolore this correlation a little further. Pascal's distinction between *raison* and *coeur*, between *esprit de géométrie* and *esprit de finesse* (which echoes, of course, an older distinction between *scientia* and *sapientia*) is a distinction which sees the heart as an organ of discernment. It is *principles* that the heart grasps,[26] and it grasps them by feeling them (*sentir*: 'Dieu sensible au coeur'[27] etc.). Such a distinction could easily be read as a licence for a Romantic understanding of religion as essentially a matter of feeling, emotion, where reason has no place (cf. Schleiermacher in his *Reden*). That is not Pascal's point ('le coeur a ses raisons...'),[28] nor is it mine. The point is rather that reason must have somewhere to start from and cannot provide its own starting-point. That is always the case: the everyday world impinges on us; even though reason (and language) shapes our perception of the world, it shapes *something*. It is at least analogous with our understanding of God, and no starting-point will be found unless reason recognizes that there is a limit to its competence ('Reason's last step is the recognition that there are an infinite number of things which

limits of reason

are beyond it. It is merely feeble if it does not go so far as to realize that'):[29] that it cannot control everything it brings within its grasp, but must be sensitive to what can impinge on its procedures. The distinction being groped for here is something like the distinction Wittgenstein draws at the end of his *Tractatus*. 'It is not *how* things are in the world that is mystical, but *that* it exists'; 'Feeling the world as a limited whole – it is this that is mystical'; 'Es gibt allerdings Unaussprechliches. Die *zeigt* sich, es ist das Mystisches'.[30] How do we feel (or perhaps better, sense) principles? How do we feel or sense that which shows itself? For Pascal (and, I think, for Wittgenstein) this is not something we can turn into a procedure or a method: we can prepare ourselves, indeed unless we do the glimmering of what shows itself will scarcely be noticed. But the glimmering is outside our control, we cannot produce it. Recall, too, what we suggested earlier: that R.S. Thomas' *negative* language in relation to God could be regarded as *anticipatory*. We endure, in patience and often bewilderment and doubt, the silence: we wait for what we cannot coerce. If faith is in one sense a starting-point, providing the premises of what we believe, it is, in another sense, the end of a life-time's striving. Remember Kierkegaard's ironic words in the preface to *Fear and Trembling*:

> In those old days it was different, then faith was a task for a whole lifetime, because it was assumed that dexterity in faith is not acquired in a few days or weeks. When the experienced old campaigner drew near to his last hour, having fought the good fight and kept the faith, his heart was still young enough not to have forgotten that fear and trembling which chastened the youth...Where those revered figures arrived, that is the point where everybody in our day begins to go further.[31]

If freedom and love are non-coercive and characterize most deeply the nature of God, then God's manifestation of himself must be similarly non-coercive. And so, too, we might suppose, will be his being, if we dare venture that far. For to think of the being of God in terms of freedom and non-coercive love, is at least to glimpse something of what the doctrine of the Trinity means. There, at the heart of reality, beyond any kind of constraint or condition, traditional Christianity suggests we see God as three persons bound together in mutual love, neither overriding the other or coercing the other, but each letting each other be, and forming the space in which the being of persons can make sense. If that is the nature of God's being, a non-coercive, free and loving existence, then his manifestation will be similarly without coercion. Hence, perhaps, the problem at the beginning of this paper: there is no way in which we can be *forced* to talk about God. Hence, perhaps, a kind of solution to this problem, in that the contrast I emphasized to begin with is maybe more apparent than real. For God is only part of general discourse if the notion of God includes much that should rather be relegated to the category of the divine...or the demonic. If God is only who God is, that is much more difficult to cope with than if God is a kind of being or a quality of transcendence. And to speak of God as essentially one *who* is, is, as we have learnt from Karl Barth, to speak of the Trinity. To know the kind of ambiguity Pascal knew, the kind of ambiguity R.S. Thomas explores, is perhaps a sign that we are on the right track, rather than a cause for despair: but even such a sign is ambiguous. And so nothing could be more appropriate than that the ultimate sign of the God of the Christians is the death of a man, so little ambiguous as to seem clearly negative – how could something so purely and ordinarily human be a sign of God? – and yet, if a sign of God's love, perhaps reaching beyond ambiguity with the only obviousness that does not coerce.

> Our religion is wise and foolish: wise, because it is the most learned and most strongly based on miracles, prophecies, etc.; foolish, because it is not all this which makes people belong to it. There is good enough reason for condemning those who do not belong, but not for making those who do belong believe. What makes them believe is the Cross.[32]

> There is no other sound
> In the darkness but the sound of a man
> Breathing, testing his faith
> On emptiness, nailing his questions
> One by one to an untenanted cross.[33]

Bel état de l'Église quand elle n'est plus soutenue que de Dieu.[34]

Notes

1. See *Theology* 39 (1939), pp.328-30.
2. *Doctrine in the Church of England* (1938), p.16.
3. *Ibid.*
4. *Lux Mundi* (15th (cheap) edition., 1904), p.48.
5. *Song at the Year's Turning* (1955), p.109.
6. *Not that He brought Flowers* (1968), p.29.
7. 'The New Mariner', in *Between Here and Now* (1981), p.99.
8. 'Adjustments', in *Frequencies* (1978), p.29.
9. 'The Gap', *ibid.*, p.8.
10. *Between Here and Now*, p.85.
11. *H'm* (1972), p.16.
12. Cf., e.g., 'Llananno', in *Laboratories of the Spirit* (1975), p.62.
13. *Ibid.*, p.51.

14. See Pascal, *Pensées*, Nouvelle edition établie pour la première fois d'après la copie de référence de Gilberte Pascal par Philippe Sellier (Mercure de France, 1976), nos. 681f. (numbered in Lafuma's edition (=L) as translated by A.J. Krailsheimer in Penguin Classics (1966), 427, 429).

15. *Pensées*, no. 690, pp.377f. (L449).

16. See S. Hackel, 'The religious dimension: vision or evasion? Zosima's discourse in *The Brothers Karamazov*' in *New Essays in Dostoevsky*, ed. M.V. Jones and G.M. Terry (Cambridge 1983).

17. *The Brothers Karamazov*, tr. David Magarshack (Penguin Classics 1958), pp.274f.

18. *Ibid.*, pp.287f.

19. *Ibid.*, p.190.

20. *Ibid.*, p.339: a statement that the philosopher, Emmanuel Lévinas, is fond of quoting ('que je cite toujours'), see *De Dieu qui vient à l'idée* (1982), pp.134f.

21. *The Brothers Karamazov*, p.356.

22. *Dream and Reality* (Engl. trans., 1950), pp.179f.

23. Grasset 1972.

24. Grasset 1978 (page references to the paperback edn. in *Le Livre de Poche*, 1986).

25. *Ibid.*, pp.313-23.

26. *Pensées*, no. 142 (L110).

27. *Ibid.*, no. 680, p.359 (L424).

28. *Ibid.* (L423).

29. *Ibid.*, no. 220 (L188).

30. *Tractatus Logico-Philosophicus* (new edition, 1972), 6:44, 45 and 522 ('There are, indeed, things that cannot be put into words. They *make themselves manifest*. They are what is mystical.')

31. *Fear and Trembling*, tr. W. Lowrie (slightly modified) (Princeton 1941), pp.5f.

32. Pascal, *Pensées*. no. 427 (L842).

33. R.S. Thomas, 'In Church', in *Pietà* (1966), p.44.

34. Pascal, *Pensées*, no. 427 (L845: 'A fine state for the Church to be in when it has no support left but God!').

THE PROBLEM OF PAIN

David Brown

The original *Lux Mundi* article of this title was written by J.R. Illingworth, the person in whose vicarage the meetings of the group were held and whose influence on the group as a whole was in fact considerable, despite his withdrawal from Oxford to the country living of Longworth on grounds of ill-health.[1] Indeed, though Gore's essay was to become the most famous, with its developmental view of inspiration it too can be seen as breathing something of the strongly progressive, Hegelian outlook of Illingworth, despite the predominance of Platonic ideas elsewhere in Gore's writings. Intriguingly, the author of the entry in the *Oxford Dictionary of the Christian Church* describes Illingworth as 'a philosopher rather than a theologian'.[2] That his background was predominantly in philosophy, with a strong influence from the Hegelian T.H. Green, is of course true,[3] but the comment is unfair if it is intended to imply that he did not take theological issues seriously. His already noted ill-health meant that the problem of pain was more than just an academic issue to him, and his essay is in fact an impressive attempt to combine the insights of natural and revealed theology. Perhaps therefore the best tribute that I can offer him a century later is to continue that typical Anglican tradition and attempt to explore the relation between philosophical and theological approaches to the problem of evil.

While in general there continues to be no sharp distinction drawn in Anglican writing, as is well illustrated by the two best known popular writings on the subject of the last half-century, C.S. Lewis' *The Problem of Pain* and Austin Farrer's *Love Almighty and Ills Unlimited*,[4] increasingly one is aware of hostility to philosophical approaches in German theology and of the way in which this is in turn influencing the attitudes of English-speaking theologians, most notably of late perhaps in Kenneth Surin's *Theology and the Problem of Evil*.[5] Likewise analytic philosophers, when they read someone like Moltmann, express surprise at how any of this could be thought of relevance in offering a 'solution' to the problem of evil. The result is that philosopher and theologian view one another across a divide of mutual incomprehension, and that is a pity since both have useful things to say and the approach of each is impoverished by their failure to take the other's questions seriously.

Indeed, what I want to argue in this paper is that the problem arises precisely because each fails to appreciate adequately the true nature and limits of the question that is their own proper domain. That is, I shall argue that the philosophers err, when they think that they have anything of importance to say to a specific case of human suffering, the theologians when they deny that there is any general problem of pain to be answered, or, putting the matter more positively, it is the philosopher's task to deal with the general problem, the theologian's with the specific case. To show how this is so, I shall look first at the philosophical issue, and then at the theological.

The first thing to note is that the philosophical problem in its classical form is essentially a logical problem, that is of showing that there is no contradiction involved in holding together the following three propositions, (1) that God is all-good, (2) that God is omnipotent and (3) that evil exists in the world. Thus this is the way in which the problem was seen as early as Epicurus[6] and the way in which it continues to be seen by America's most distinguished philosopher of religion, Alvin Plantinga.[7] I stress this point for two reasons, first because, as we shall see, the problem is being viewed rather differently in England in the writings of Richard Swinburne and secondly, and perhaps more importantly, it explains why despite the protests of many theologians it is none the less entirely appropriate to speak of a 'solution' to the problem. Far from representing any lack of sensitivity to the issues, all such talk represents is the claim that the purely logical problem of the apparent contradiction in the Christian simultaneously holding these three beliefs is in fact resoluble.

To show that this is so is Plantinga's strictly limited aim and it is important that this should not be lost sight of, amid all the complexities of the argument in terms of 'possible worlds' and 'transworld depravity' that have resulted from his debate over the issue with the atheist J.L. Mackie.[8] The structure of any possible solution is in fact quite simple. Since omnipotence is bound by nothing save the laws of logic, the only way out of the dilemma must be to argue that the existence of evil is a logically necessary concomitant of the existence of some good that is willed by the Creator, whether the concomitant be as a consequence of or as a means to, that good.[9] Plantinga's version is of the former kind, and his argument is that, if God wished to give his creatures the good of freewill, then as a logically necessary consequence of this must come the possibility of them doing moral evil. Where possible worlds then becomes relevant is in Plantinga's further claim that it is possible that in every conceivable world which God might have created with creatures enjoying such freedom, its misuse would have occurred. For if that is so, then God in surveying the possible worlds that might have been created would have seen that, whatever choice were made, human beings would do wrong. In other words, 'transworld depravity' exists, and, so even God could not avoid a world with evil in it. Mackie responds[10] by arguing that a world with free, perfectly good human beings is easily conceivable, but significantly he has to change the definition of freedom in the process, to one in which it is compatible with determinism. So it is perhaps worth stressing that this so-called 'free will defence' is only intelligible in terms of a contra-causal view of freedom, one in which, though many factors may incline us in particular ways, nothing ultimately causes our actions except our own free decisions.

The extent to which Plantinga views the problem as a purely logical one is particularly highlighted by his willingness to use precisely the same sort of strategy to deal with natural evils (disease, earthquakes and so forth) which do not appear to have their origin in any moral evil. For here he resorts to an explanation in terms of fallen angels, who like men have misused their freedom. Significantly, however, he adds the comment: 'The Free Will Defender, of course, does not assert that this is *true*; he says only that it is *possible*' (his emphasis).[11] His point is that, to show that there is no contradiction involved in holding the three propositions, all one need do is establish their compatibility, not make the means of that compatibility plausible.

It is perhaps not very surprising that philosophers in general have not been content to have their role so narrowly circumscribed. One of many such examples is his fellow American, Stephen Davis, who after discussing 'the logical problem of evil' goes on to tackle what he calls 'the emotive problem of evil' (EPE),[12] which he introduces thus: 'But even if it is true that theism is logically consistent, there is another difficulty that remains, namely, what I call the EPE...To show that "God is omnipotent and God is good and evil exists" is possibly true does not show that it is true or even probably true, i.e. it does nothing to show that people should believe in God's omnipotence and goodness.'[13] Davis then goes on to make just such an attempt, and, though he has no doubts about the existence of Satan, he is honest enough to admit that 'Plantinga's luciferous defence may be both true and theologically satisfactory, but at least it is not clear that it is.'[14] Certainly it is an explanation which the Anglican philosopher, Richard Swinburne, is careful to eschew, his own suggestion being that the existence of natural evil is logically necessary if we are to be free agents in a world where the consequences of our actions matter.[15] He describes this as 'the argument from the need for knowledge' and points out that, since we learn inductively, there could be no acquiring of knowledge unless consequences of good and bad kinds regularly followed specific sorts of actions in accordance with natural laws. He develops this argument at considerable length, compared to another, better known argument that also makes a logical point, that evil is a logically necessary condition for the occurrence of certain virtues.[16] Thus, for example, the notion of courage makes no sense unless there is something bad to be feared, compassion no sense unless there is suffering to be alleviated, and so on.

Personally I find this latter argument a powerful one. Admittedly sometimes it is objected that compassion, courage and so forth only have value because the world is the way it is, and that in the absence of suffering they would never have been accorded such independent value. But such an objection seems to me a mistake. For there are surely other obvious reasons for valuing, for example, compassion, than simply the relief of pain which is involved. To give an illustration from the original essay, compassion helps build up a strong sense of human solidarity or, if this is thought to reflect too strongly Illingworth's Hegelianism, one might mention the more general point that such virtues are thought to produce the type of character that fits us for heaven, and yet, though that character will no doubt be exercised there in numerous ways, none of them will have anything to do with the relief of pain.

However that may be, as already noted Swinburne devotes more attention to another argument, his so-called 'argument from the need for knowledge'. This is to be explained by the way he conceives of the problem of evil. For him the issue is not merely a logical one; it is also a question of probabilities. Can the fact of evil be accommodated within his cumulative, probabilistic case for theism? This is why he is concerned both with the quantities of evil in the world and with specific cases, and not just with the purely logical point with which he begins. It is thus this that leads him to say in respect of the amount of evil in the world: 'There must be naturally occurring evils...if men are to know how to cause evils themselves or are to prevent evil occurring. And there have to be *many* such evils (his emphasis), if men are to have sure knowledge, for as we saw, sure knowledge of what will happen in future comes only by induction from many past instances.'[17] Again, as an illustration of his willingness to consider specific instances we might take the following: 'Actually seeing a friend have to have his arm amputated as a result of standing too close to a dangerous machine in a factory and getting his arm trapped in it is rightly going to deter me from standing too close to the machine much better than is a notice which says "Dangerous".'[18]

It is comments like these which have led to some of the harshest criticisms one is ever likely to read in the contemporary philosophy of religion. Thus D.Z. Phillips remarks of another of his examples that it is 'a sign of a corrupt mlnd...to ask of what use are the screams of the innocent',[19] while Surin comments on Swinburne's reply as follows: 'This incapacity to acknowledge that a particular reality is mind-stopping betoken an irremissable moral blindness, in less serious cases it testifies to a real lack of moral imagination, to an unshakeable moral coarseness. But in all cases the failure to lend a voice to the cries of the innocent (and there can be few more glaring instances than the willingness to construct a divine teleology out of innocent suffering) is to have lost the capacity to tell the truth.'[20] In a volume stemming from the Oxford Theology Faculty, all the contributors will readily perceive the gross unfairness of such accusations. Nevertheless it does seem to me that Swinburne, admittedly in common with many others, has made a serious error of judgement in going beyond the purely logical problem into considerations of quantity and specific cases.

Taking quantity first, consider one of Newman's more controversial utterances: 'The Church holds that it were better for sun and moon to drop from heaven, for the earth to fail, and for all the millions who are upon it to die of starvation in extremest agony...than that one soul... should commit one single venial sin, should tell one wilful untruth though it harmed no one, or steal one poor farthing without excuse.'[21] My point in quoting this particular utterance is not to endorse it, but simply to draw attention to how far removed traditional Christian morality is from any utilitarian calculus, any attempt to weigh good and evil in the same balance. Yet very often responses to the problem are phrased in ways which, whatever the intention, can easily admit of a utilitarian reading. For example, Davis in discussing the amount of evil in the world sees the issue in terms of whether 'this freedom has turned out to be cost-effective', whether we have 'the best possible balance of good over evil'. [22] Likewise Swinburne responds to the objection that 'the game...is not worth the candle' by an admission that seems to concede that such weighing is the heart of the problem: 'This is, I believe, the crux of the problem of evil. It is not the fact of evil or the kinds of evil which are the real threat to theism; it is the quantity of evil.'[23] It is little wonder therefore that, when theists themselves speak like this, their opponents also inevitably express the issue in terms of whether the good outweighs the evil it involves.[24]

But, if we take this hint from Newman, what we shall see at stake is not at all the quantity of evils in the world but a different system of values. That is, the existence of evil in the world should simply be seen as a tragic consequence of certain goods being valued by God, not something that has to be weighed in the same balance as them. As Christians we attach supreme worth not to the creation of happiness, nor any attempt to balance out good and evil, but find it instead in the radical freedom that

God has given us to shape our own destinies, including a type of character and virtues that simply would have no intelligibility, no meaning in the absence of pain. Thus it is just not the case that the argument with the non-believer takes place within a shared system of moral values. Rather, the heart of the debate lies in the fact that the Christian has opted for a different moral universe, one in which freedom, compassion, sympathy, courage and so forth exist. This is not to say that non-Christians never attach a similar high worth to these values; only to draw attention to the extent to which Christian as well as non-Christian can be infected in the modern world by utilitarian assumptions in making the issue of quantity primary.

But to this it may be objected that I have ignored one vital fact, that God can foresee the future and so must have had the choice between various possible worlds, some of which had more evil than the present one, some less, and so, even if he was not concerned with weighing evil against good, he still had the option of creating a world with less evil in it than at present and so quantity of evil remains a relevant issue, even if we are only comparing it with other possible levels of evil rather than with the good *per se*. Some contemporary philosophers[25] would argue that, since God can only know what it is logically possible to know, he cannot know future, free human action since this remains undetermined until the individual makes his decision. That would be one way of responding, but even if we take the traditional account of omniscience it still remains unclear to me how we can make any objective assessment of the quantities of evil in the world. It is a commonplace in modern theology to speak of the need for a post-Auschwitz theology and indeed it is also a theme in contemporary philosophy, but I quite fail to see the point. God infinitely values each one of us and the tragic dimension of suffering would seem to me just as acute, whether we were to envisage just one individual suffering or millions. Here C.S. Lewis is more astute than many a modern writer: 'We must never make the problem of pain worse than it is by vague talk about the "unimaginable sum of human misery"...Search all time and space and you will not find that composite pain in anyone's consciousness. There is no such thing as a sum of suffering, for no one suffers it. When you have reached the maximum that a single person can suffer, we have, no doubt, reached something very horrible, but we have reached all the suffering there ever can be in the universe. The addition of a million fellow-sufferers adds no more pain.'[26]

Since questions of quantity can enter consideration of the problem of evil in a number of different ways, it is perhaps worth pausing at this point to clarify what it is that is being affirmed and denied within the Christian tradition, as reflected in the writings of Newman and Lewis.

As I understand it, the relevance of quantity is being denied in two specific ways. First, in contrast to those who think the argument is just about arithmetic, about what the total balance of pleasure and pain is, the claim is that the disagreement is in fact much more fundamental, there being no shared calculus in which to measure quantities, no sufficiently shared system of values. Secondly, given the traditional Christian stress on the unique, irreplaceable worth of each individual, the claim is that total quantity of pain in the world cannot be the issue, since that would be to suggest that persons were somehow dispensable in relation to a larger whole. Rather, the key issue must be the maximum amount of pain suffered by any particular individual. Of course, in a sense there is more tragedy in more suffering simply because more are suffering but the tragedy lies in what each suffers, not in some mysterious total summation of suffering. That being so, the only proper question of quantity must be whether God was justified in allowing the maximum quantity of suffering that can happen to the human condition to befall some particular individuals among us. There is thus no global question of quantity, only the tragic conflict between the moral value of freedom and the virtues and the maximum pain that any of these particular persons of infinite value could suffer.

Should someone still object that I have ignored one issue which remains crucial for them, namely that too many suffer this individual maximum of pain, my response would be that, once one has conceded that it is legitimate for God to let that happen to one individual, no further moral question can arise about the legitimacy of letting it happen to more than one. That one was already of infinite value in God's eyes, and so the tragic dimension in the divine decision is already present and in no way significantly increased by many others also suffering in this way. This is not to say that God would not try to keep the number who suffer to a minimum. But it is to claim that with free will there is no way of effectively controlling this and that the really important moral issue must be expressed in terms of the legitimacy of allowing just one individual to suffer, not by means of an irrelevant introduction of numbers.

The reference to Auschwitz may also be used to illustrate the other main failing in contemporary philosophical approaches, the appeal to specific cases. Part of the problem is that discussion of whether pain could serve some point in a particular case can easily lend credence to the idea that what is at stake is whether or not that particular pain was engineered by God to serve that point. In other words, by discussing particular cases it is very easy for a major shift of perspective to occur without its full implications being realised. For from the fact that God allows pain to occur as part of the general divine purposes, it by no means follows that such pain befalls this particular individual also as part of God's plan. The system is such that it is inevitable that some individual will suffer, but this does not mean that God has deliberately chosen a world in which it is this specifiable individual. Rather, it is entirely arbitrary whether the pain befalls A or B. That is to say, if the goods that God wants are to be realised, then tragically pain has to be part of the world, but who bears that pain is irrelevant. For the same results can be achieved, whoever it is. It is thus a logical mistake to discuss specific instances, because the philosophical 'solution' requires only that some individuals suffer, not that any actually uniquely identifiable individual should do so. [27]

The main reason why this conclusion is resisted is, I think, because of the desire of philosopher as much as theologian for a total explanation. He thinks that there must be a reason why one individual suffers rather than another, and so wants to give that reason. Again, equally he may feel that it is incompatible with omnipotence to admit that any evil could finally frustrate the divine purpose and so all evil must ultimately be caught up to serve the good. Thus, for example, Nelson Pike tells that omnipotence can only be safeguarded if God succeeds in shaping all the evil that exists to ultimate divine purposes, [28] while, to give a theological example, Barth expresses himself in very similar terms with his emphatic declaration that God 'would not be God if he were...restricted in his actions' and so he has no hesitation in concluding: 'The effect of the creature is in the hands of God...It is wholly subordinated to the contexts of his wider purposes.'[29]

That I just cannot believe. If God has given free will to man, this must have introduced a radical indeterminacy to the world, which even God cannot fully control. So if one accepts the free will defence there just is no avoiding the admission that there is an incurably tragic dimension to the creation, both in the sense that not everyone *may* be redeemed, since that is ultimately in our hands, not God's, and in the sense that not every event in our lives can now be used for the good, since the opportunity for that to be so has passed, and here again God has no power to alter the nature of time.[30]

But, if philosophers err by attempting too much, so too do theologians. If the philosopher's mistake is to search for reasons everywhere, even where none are to be found, as on the questions of quantity and the pain of specific individuals, the theologian's characteristic error is to suppose that everything can and must be given a christological reference. Traditionally Anglicanism has avoided this mistake by accepting the Catholic distinction between natural and revealed theology, but that it is under threat is evident from the increasing influence of Lutheranism noticeable even among some of the contributors to this volume. Certainly it is from Germany in the writings of people like Dorothee Soelle, Jürgen Moltmann and Eberhard Jüngel that the strongest attack on the sort of position that I have so far outlined has come. For them only the cross can offer an answer to the problem of evil and indeed Jüngel in particular wants to go further in not only seeing philosophical approaches as an irrelevance but as positively responsible for the rise of atheism in the modern world. What is wrong with his argument I have tried to point out elsewhere.[31] So here perhaps it will suffice to draw attention to the need to take seriously the fact of the cross as a 'scandal of particularity'. For that very particularity must surely mean that it can only provide answers to questions set by man already situated in his particularity, not to questions that are prior to any particularity, the very sorts of questions with which we have been dealing in the first section of this paper. One cannot help in fact wondering whether much modern theology is not based on a pious conceptual confusion between a logically necessary and a logically sufficient condition. For, while of course since Christ is the source of our salvation, and the final end of the creation finds its point in him, his role must be an indispensible one, it by no means follows from this indispensable role that in many areas of thought his role will not still be very remote and not as it were centre stage, as in the purely logical issue of the consistency of our beliefs with which this paper began.

But where then does the contribution of revealed theology lie? The answer must surely be in the very particularity which Christ came to share. But, that said, one finds the writings of contemporary theologians on the subject sadly disappointing. Perhaps because of the christological assumption to which reference has already been made, they seem to assume that it suffices to say that God himself entered into human suffering in Christ and leave the matter at that, without trying to make the precise nature of the connection explicit. Yet surely we must make it so, since the fact of another's suffering of itself does nothing to reduce the tragedy of an individual's suffering, even if that other be God himself. Two wrongs never of themselves make a right. Let me therefore draw attention to the two ways in which it seems that the cross can deal with the scandal of particularity that it shares, the arbitrariness of the particular case.

The first thing to note is the arbitrariness of the form of Jesus' death. Had he lived a few centuries earlier and lived in a different land it might have taken the relatively painless form of drinking hemlock, as with Socrates. Again, were it to have taken place this century in some of the countries of Latin America, it could well have been much more gruesome still – years of torture producing a wasted body that is finally just dumped in an anonymous grave. Indeed, depending on one's theory of atonement, one might even be prepared to go further, and question whether the story had to end brutally. For it is not so much the fact of the suffering itself that produces its impact on us, as the way in which Jesus responded to the diverse actors in the story as the drama unfolded.

Now of course such reflections are appropriate only to a limited degree, since there comes a point at which it becomes problematic whether we are still talking about Christianity, so much is our religion bound up with a particular story set in the framework of a particular prior religious tradition. But what they surely can be allowed to do is to emphasise the way in which God's involvement with suffering in Christ is an involvement with that most frightening aspect of suffering, its essential arbitrariness. There is no providential reason why one of us will die in his forties of cancer, while another will enjoy a ripe old age; no reason why a Mother Teresa of Calcutta lives universally honoured by almost all, while a fellow-believer languishes in a Soviet psychiatric hospital, forgotten even by his fellow Christians. It is this which makes Christ's cry of dereliction from the cross the cry of all sufferers – Why me? Why has God abandoned me to this fate? Of course, the cry had been heard before, most poignantly of all perhaps in Psalm 88 with its unrelieved gloom. But here in Jesus we have God himself endorsing that cry, the tragic element in his creation that each new sufferer must discover for himself, that there is no reason why it has befallen him rather than another. Many a hospital chaplain has commented on the need for patients to let their anger loose against God. In the Incarnation we have God taking part in the tragic element in his creation by railing against himself.

But that in itself would serve little point unless the Incarnation had also brought with it a way beyond and out of the suffering into its creative transformation and redemption, I find myself fully persuaded by Moltmann's view in *The Crucified God* that the Incarnation implies God's involvement in suffering to a degree that cannot be adequately described, if the patristic doctrine of the divine impassibility is maintained.[32] All analogies for God are inadequate, but the following may be of some help. Some children have the misfortune to be born without the ability to experience pain and so unless they are educated in time about the consequences of their actions they end up by doing themselves permanent damage, even accidentally killing themselves. However, if they survive to adulthood, then they will have acquired a good knowledge of the consequences of pain, but even so they will remain without any experiential knowledge of what it feels like to be in pain. Similarly it seems to me with God. Of course, without the Incarnation he already had perfect knowledge of the consequences of pain, but only the Incarnation could have brought him knowledge of what it feels like to be one of us.

But more important for our argument here is not the difference the Incarnation makes to God, but the difference it makes to us, and here Moltmann is disappointing. The connection he makes is largely through a modified penal theory of the atonement,[33] whereas the more interesting question seems to me to be how this suffering God can help us in all our suffering, not just where it bears some connection with our sins. Dorothee Soelle's stress on God's solidarity with us in our suffering[34] initially sounds more promising, but on examination it turns out to be a case of God in Christ as one of the oppressed identifying with the oppressed rather than effecting its creative transformation. So let me offer an alternative account.

The key problem in pain seems not to be its physiological level, but what is happening psychologically. Thus it is a fact well known to doctors that the same level of physiological pain can lead one individual to take early retirement, another to have frequent absences off work and yet others to show no apparent traces in their conduct at all. Again, a large part of the rationale for the hospice movement has been that patients' attitude to the pain is very heavily a function of the background environment against which it is set, that is whether it is a caring and loving one or not. Requests for euthanasia in hospices are in fact almost unknown. In other words, it is the question of meaning that is primary in pain, not its degree.

But when we address that question to Christ's suffering, what we discover is that God in Christ experienced pain at its most apparently meaningless and yet brought good out of it. The Epistle to the Hebrews tells us that Jesus experienced temptation from the inside.[35] But to that we can also add guilt. For, simply in being born a Jew feelings of social guilt must have been inevitable, given the numerous occasions on which the nation had failed God, and so, though objectively Jesus had no guilt, to baptism he went to purge that guilt. Now dying, he finds himself abandoned by all and so enters that most painful human experience of them all, the assigning to one's life by others of a label one cannot accept – to the Jewish authorities a blasphemer, to the Romans a common criminal and, worst of all, to his own disciples a failure. Here we have the story of Job relived, because, of course, Job's tragedy was not that he was innocent but that his friends believed him to be other than he was. The answer that book gives is not entirely satisfactory,[36] whereas in the case of Jesus we do clearly see meaning emerging out of the meaninglessness. This is most conspicuously so in the case of Luke and John. But even Mark twice implies the acquiring of a meaning. Most obviously is this so in the judgement of the centurion in that it suggests that there must have been something in the manner of Jesus' dying to evoke this comment, while it does not seem too fanciful to suggest of the cry of dereliction that Mark intends us to recall the confident note with which the Psalm ends, from which the quotation is taken.[37]

So it is a God who has entered into the most awful pain of all, the pain of meaninglessness, who offers us his aid in giving our pain a meaning. It is surely here that special providence enters the picture. It is no part of the divine plan that any specific individual suffer pain. But because pain is a tragic consequence of the values the creation embodies, God has chosen to enter into our pain at its most acute and now is always available to help creatively transform whatever befalls us as one who knew pain at its worst and potentially most destructive.

Perhaps I should add that in speaking of such creative possibilities both for the sufferer and for others in his environment I should not be taken as referring to anything that can be measured. It is not for us to judge how people use their opportunities. A smile may require heroic effort; the gift of a large cheque the vapid movement of a langourous hand. God alone knows how easy or how difficult is the exercise of our free will in terms of our antecedently formed character.

Thus my conclusion is that current approaches in both philosophy and theology err in claiming too much and in despising the other. Anglicanism's *via media* of accepting both natural and revealed theology is surely right. For it is only from the former that we can learn why pain in general exists in the world (because pain is the tragic price that has to be paid for the realisation of certain values), while it is only from the latter that we can obtain a response to the specific suffering individual (that it is a God who has fully entered into pain at its most arbitrary and threatening who now comes to our aid to help give that pain a meaning, if we will allow this). Goodness and tragedy are thus inextricably linked not just in the crucifixion but in the nature of creation and thus in the nature of God, and it is to that one and the same reality that both natural and revealed theology point.[38]

Notes

1. The nature of his illness seems to have been more psychological than physiological. Thus his wife speaks of a 'delicacy of body and nerves' inherited from his mother (*The Life of John Richardson Illingworth*, ed. by his wife (London 1917)), while Henry Scott Holland too refers to 'nerves' and 'incessant physical trouble under any mental strain', though his death seems to have been caused by a combination of eczema and blood-poisoning (*ibid.*, pp.318 & 322). However, the *Church Times*' obituary movingly asserted that 'pain was the secret of his power' (*ibid.*, p.315) and we know that it gave him

particular pleasure that his essay was reproduced as a pamphlet for use during the First World War in the year of his death (1915).

2. *The Oxford Dictionary of the Christian Church*, Second Edition, F.L. Cross & E.A. Livingstone (Oxford 1974) p.691.

3. Such was the influence of Green on Illingworth and others associated with *Lux Mundi* that Mark Pattison was led to remark: 'Green's honey goes to the ritualistic hive' (*The Life of John Richardson Illingworth*, p.84).

4. C.S. Lewis, *The Problem of Pain* (London 1940); A. Farrer, *Love Almighty and Ills Unlimited* (London 1962).

5. K. Surin, *Theology and the Problem of Evil* (Oxford, 1986).

6. Epicurus is quoted by Lactantius (*Patrologia Latina* VII, 121). Latin and English are conveniently both available in M.B. Ahern, *The Problem of Evil* (London 1971), pp.11 & 2. Cf. also Augustine, *Confessions*, VII, 5.

7. A. Plantinga, *God and Other Minds* (Ithaca 1967) chs. 5 & 6; *The Nature of Necessity* (Oxford 1974) ch. 9; and more popularly, *God, Freedom and Evil* (London 1975), Part 1.

8. J.L. Mackie, 'Evil and Omnipotence' in *The Philosophy of Religion*, ed. B. Mitchell (Oxford 1971); *The Miracle of Theism* (Oxford 1982) ch. 9.

9. Moral evil will be an unwanted consequence of the good of free will, while natural evil will be a necessary means to the two sorts of goods mentioned later in the paper, namely the creation of the virtues and the growth of knowledge. If an analogy with the human situation is desired, one might in the latter case think of the way in which the surgeon's infliction of pain was necessary to the restoration of health, and in the former of the sorts of cases covered by the doctrine of double effect, where a good intention is approved despite the consequence of evil that will also follow, for example the death of innocent civilians in what is none the less a just war. Of course in our case the limitation is physical necessity, whereas in God's it is only logical, but logic, as the text shows, can also impose considerable constraints. If, following the analogy with the doctrine of double effect, the objection is raised that despite what I say later proportionality between good and evil is still relevant, my response would be twofold: First, in so far as the introduction of proportionality to double effect is relevant, this seems to me to have more to do with finding an easy way of testing the sincerity of the good intention than with the moral situation as such. Thus if the alleged unwanted effect is radically out of proportion to the intended good effect, this can give good grounds for suspecting the motives of the agents concerned. But secondly, in any case God is faced with a vastly different moral dilemma, not with the preservation of a particular good that will, whatever happens, continue to exist elsewhere but with whether a supreme good can be brought into existence at all.

10. *The Miracle of Theism*, pp.162-76, esp. pp.166-72.

11. *God, Freedom and Evil*, p.58.

12. S.T. Davis, *Logic and the Nature of God* (London 1983) ch. 7.

13. *Ibid.*, p.106.

14. *Ibid.*, p.113.

15. R. Swinburne, *The Existence of God* (Oxford 1979), pp.202-14.

16. *Ibid.*, pp.214-15.

17. *Ibid.*, p.207.

18. *Ibid.*, p.206.

19. D.Z. Phillips, 'The Problem of Evil' in *Reason and Religion*, ed. S.C. Brown (Ithaca 1977), p.115.

20. *Op. cit.*, p.184.

21. J.H. Newman, *Difficulties felt by Anglicans* (London 1850), Lecture VIII, p.199. The point of the lecture is to contrast the utilitarian standards of the world with those of the Church. Significantly a few pages earlier (p.196) he had already made a comment that could be used to reinforce my point that what matters morally is the individual and not the numbers involved: 'The Church looks and moves in simply an opposite direction. It contemplates not the whole, but the parts; not a nation, but the men who form it; not society in the first place, but in the second place, and in the first place individuals.'

22. *Op. cit.*, pp.110 & 108.

23. *Op. cit.*, p.219.

24. E.g. Mackie, *The Miracle of Theism*, p.154.

25. E.g. J.R. Lucas, *The Freedom of the Will* (Oxford 1970), ch. 14; R. Swinburne, *The Coherence of Theism* (Oxford 1977), ch. 10.

26. *Op. cit.*, p.104. The central role given to Auschwitz in the theologies of Soelle, Moltmann and Metz is usefully summarised and discussed in Surin, *op. cit.*, pp.112-32 & 146-9. Davis mentions the Holocaust (p.100), and Swinburne, Belsen (*The Existence of God*, p.219).

27. Of course with some virtues it is logically necessary that the pain be present in the individual himself. For example, it is only courage present if it is exhibited by someone who himself has reason to be afraid. But with most virtues this is not so and there seems to be no essential link between degree of virtue and the amount of pain experienced by the individual himself in his own life. Swinburne does at one point speak of 'victims of the system' (*ibid.*, p.210), but he seems to think this of only limited applicability.

28. Nelson Pike, 'Plantinga on Free Will and Evil' in *Religious Studies*, 1972, pp.472-3. Here he is following Augustine in *Enchiridion*, ch. 100: 'How would a Good Being permit evil to be done except that in his omnipotence he can turn evil into good?' It should of course be noted that many a philosopher has been content with a weaker thesis, namely that all evil must have the potential for good, not that it actually achieves this.

29. K. Barth, *Church Dogmatics* (Edinburgh 1960), pp.133 & 153-4.

30. In stressing the fact of unredeemed evil, we should not of course lose sight of the other side of the equation, of the considerable degree to which we are what we now are and want to be is only so in virtue of a past history of evils both in our own case and that of our ancestors (for further development of this argument, cf. R.M. Adams, *The Virtue of Faith* (Oxford & New York 1987), pp.65-93.

31. D. Brown, *Continental Philosophy and Modern Theology* (Oxford 1987), pp.202-3.

32. J. Moltmann, *The Crucified God* (London 1976), ch. 6.

33. *Ibid.*, chs. 4 & 5. For a brief critique, D. Brown, *op. cit.*, pp.117-19.

34. D. Soelle, *Suffering* (Philadelphia 1975). Soelle is certainly also concerned to argue that Christians must do all they can to eliminate the suffering. But what one misses is any recognition of the transformative power of the pain itself, so violent is her reaction against what she labels 'Christian masochism' and 'theological sadism' (cf. esp. pp.9-32), admittedly often inadequate and insensitive ways of expressing that point. Indeed, the force of her case seems decisively blunted, if my argument is accepted that one cannot describe as part of the divine plan what happens in the particular case.

35. Heb. 4:15.

36. Though more satisfactory if one stresses 42:5 with its assurance of God's presence through the suffering rather than 42:3 with its appeal to divine inscrutability. For an indication of the range of possible interpretations, cf. N.N. Glatzer (ed.), *The Dimensions of Job* (New York 1969).

37. This is the view of D.E. Nineham, *Saint Mark* (Harmondsworth 1963), p.428. But even if this is not so, Mark's narrative still moves from the meaninglessness of Psalm 22:1 at 15:34 to the centurion's assertion of meaning at v.39. In this he is followed by Matthew. But Luke and John can also be seen as having a similar progression, the former in his move from his initial stress on Jesus' death between two common criminals (23:32) to his confident handing of his spirit to his Father (v.46), the latter in the transition from the poignant 'I thirst' to the triumphant 'It is finished' (19:28-30).

38. I am grateful for helpful criticisms from a number of individuals, especially David Redhouse, Rod Sykes and Rowan Williams.

PREPARATION IN HISTORY FOR CHRIST

John Barton

> Beloved in Christ, be it this Christmastide our care and delight to prepare ourselves to hear again the message of the angels, and in heart and mind to go even unto Bethlehem and see this thing which is come to pass, and the Babe lying in a manger. Therefore let us read and mark in Holy Scripture the tale of the loving purposes of God from the first days of our disobedience unto the glorious redemption brought us by this Holy Child.[1]

The King's College, Cambridge, Carol Service is the perfect expression of what Christians have meant by 'preparation in history for Christ'. Behind the selection of the traditional Nine Lessons lies the conviction that the sacred history of Old and New Testaments is not an aimless assemblage of old tales, nor a collection of timeless examples, but a story with a plot. Its dénouement is to be found in the 'things concerning Jesus' – the Christ-event, to translate Greek into German. For Anglicans, it is in general probably the liturgy – and not only in the form of carol services – that helps to define the shape of this plot. Indeed, recent lectionary revisions and adjustments to the liturgical year have tended to heighten the emphasis on salvation history. The Elizabethan Church chose lessons for the major festivals from the wisdom books of the Old Testament wherever it could, aiming at moral edification.[2] But the Church of England to-day prefers readings that speak of the 'mighty acts of God' in history. It has reorganized Advent and the preceding weeks to make sure that its people know the 'tale of the loving purposes of God' in the Old Testament, and has made Epiphanytide and Lent into a chronological presentation of the life of Jesus according to a kind of harmony of the gospels.[3] At the same time the Eucharistic Prayer in most Christian traditions has recovered its (presumed) original connection with Jewish *berakoth*, with the effect that the Preface, for so long a rather perfunctory seasonal variation, has expanded into a full account of the works of God in creation and redemption. Eucharistic Prayer D of the 1977 American Book of Common Prayer, modelled on the Anaphora of the Liturgy of St John Chrysostom, is a particularly clear example:

We acclaim you, holy Lord, glorious in power. Your mighty works reveal your wisdom and love. You formed us in your own image, giving the whole world into our care, so that, in obedience to you, our Creator, we might rule and serve all your creatures. When our disobedience took us far from you, you did not abandon us to the power of death. In your mercy you came to our help, so that in seeking you we might find you. Again and again you called us into covenant with you, and through the prophets you taught us to hope for salvation. Father, you loved the world so much that in the fullness of time you sent your only Son to be our Savior. Incarnate by the Holy Spirit, born of the Virgin Mary, he lived as one of us, yet without sin. To the poor he proclaimed the good news of salvation; to prisoners, freedom; to the sorrowful, joy. To fulfill your purpose he gave himself up to death; and, rising from the grave, destroyed death, and made the whole creation new.[4]

Why is this turn to salvation history, to the preparation in history for Christ, a problem for a modern biblical scholar or theologian? There is one extremely general objection which I shall say little about, though if valid it is utterly devastating to the whole history-centred approach of modern liturgy. This is the objection that God is not revealed in the particular events of history at all: that providence is always general, never particular; that there cannot in any sense be divine actions in the world. If I do not spend time on this objection, it is not because I think it unimportant, but because I do not have the philosophical expertise to handle it. It is clearly one of the great questions in modern Anglican theology, as witness the very different recent contributions of Maurice Wiles[5] and of the Bishop of Durham.[6] There are, however, three more small-scale objections to the current liturgical preoccupation with what is now sometimes called the 'story' understanding of the eucharistic offering.[7]

First, is there something a bit too optimistic, even triumphalistic, in Christian insistence that human history was providentially guided in such a way as to run up into the Christian dispensation? Jewish commentators on Christianity are forever asking where, in the world after the Holocaust, is the evidence that God has 'loving purposes' which he is working out in the history of mankind; and how, in particular, it can be affirmed that he accomplished some decisive act, fit to be seen as the climax of all his purposes, in the events surrounding Jesus, when the sad tale of human wickedness and persecution continues unabated. If we must speak teleolgically, they protest, let us at least say that the messianic age is still to come, for if this is it, then God must have a black sense of humour. For some, of course, post-Holocaust theology can only be agnosticism or despair or wry gallows humour. A Jewish tailor told his customer it would be a month before his suit was ready, and he complained, 'A month you should need? In six days God made heaven and earth.' 'So have you looked at them?' asked the tailor.[8]

But even without astringent Jewish criticisms of Christian raptures about the loving purposes of God, there is an uncomfortable gap between the liturgical celebration of the sacred story, in which 'the hand of God has guided his flock from age to age', and the understanding of world history to be found even in those few historians who are prepared to risk themselves on such a wide sea. As soon as we ask some 'cash-value' questions about the fourth American Eucharistic Prayer, instead of being content to glory in its sublimity, it starts to sound like the Whig interpretation of history; and the one matter on which modern historians agree with Dr Johnson is that the first Whig was the devil. Indeed, the new-style nine-week Advent of the Church of England, tracing God's providence from creation through fall to prophetic predictions of the Saviour and the fulfilment of God's faithful promises in Christ seems (from this point of view) an astonishing thing for liturgists in the 1970s to have invented: a monument to a nineteenth-century liberal belief in progressive revelation, foisted on the Church just at the moment when no-one can possibly believe in it any longer. Perhaps it confirms the suspicion that the Church of England is the Whig faction at prayer. Nothing in Edward Talbot's essay 'Preparation in History for Christ' seems quite so dated as his title. Once given the brief, he handled it with great skill and was far from accepting a simple, optimistic, and progressivist interpretation of human history; but the brief itself belongs to a world of thought that seems to have passed away except in the liturgical sphere, where the antiquarianism of modern liturgists has given it an artificial new lease of life.

But if 'preparation in history for Christ' seems to some not to do justice to history, others may ask whether it does justice to Christ. Anglicans have generally felt comfortable with the picture of human history under God as a seamless garment, the old dispensation and the new complementing each other perfectly, the new concealed in the old, the old revealed in the new. Like the Fathers to whom they have always returned as an inspiration, they have believed that the word of God was known in the world before his incarnation in Jesus, both in Israel and in the wider world of human culture. In Austin Farrer's words, the rays of light that stream from the eternal Word are concentrated like the sun's rays through a burning-glass in order to enter in unique fashion into our world through Mary, the Lord's mother;[9] but this incarnation does not mark a break or disjunction in human history, rather its culmination and goal.

Matters look different from a Lutheran perspective, of course. English readers react with a kind of mildly baffled amusement when German writers speak of Christ as the end of history, as the abolition of religion, as an eschatological event that breaks the matrix into which it irrupts. They do not necessarily think such language exactly false, but they find it exaggerated and perhaps a little tasteless. German Lutherans have no doubt their own reasons, often the opposite side of the coin from the Jewish reasons of which we have been speaking, for distrusting Whiggery in matters of religious faith. If Christ is to save us, it cannot be by accentuating or concentrating aspects of human culture or religion that had existed before him. The sanctification of existing human culture, human history, human institutions, a German may well feel, is the road to Auschwitz, and no-one goes down that road any longer. Yet the Lutheran stress on the disjunction introduced by Christ actually long antedates the post-war suspicion of history in German life, and is *echt lutherisch*. Genuinely Pauline, too, surely: 'Christ is the end of the Law' (Rom. 10:4); 'if anyone is in Christ, there is a new creation; the old has passed away, behold, the new has come' (2 Cor. 5:17). Anglican talk of Jesus as the promised Messiah, seen in the extreme reluctance in Britain to this day to accept any understanding of Old Testament prophecy incompatible with the King's Carol Service, strikes Lutherans as a failure to see that in Jesus something genuinely new and unprecedented has arrived. It is part of that same English unawakened innocence which also fails to see that the Reformation actually made a difference to Christian faith and life, which regards the French Revolution as a little local unpleasantness, absolutely typical of the French, and the student revolts of the '60s as a campaign for the abolition of academic dress. Can you not see, they ask us, that the skies have fallen? that the only 'preparation' for Christ took the form of hopeless and irremediable unpreparedness? that all who came before him were thieves and robbers? We may (I think we should) resist this rhetoric; but we should not go on talking as if it were all just a storm in a teacup.

Even from an English perspective, we must be on our guard against making the Christian faith merely a kind of intensification of existing culture, one more step in 'the education of the world', to move from *Lux Mundi* back to *Essays and Reviews*.[10] Talbot was wisely anxious not to overplay his hand by presenting the preparation for Christ as so perfect that he might appear as no more than someone whose time had come, the man of the moment, the one than whom nothing more inevitable can be imagined. Yet to Lutheran eyes even this caution does not save the project from looking like an apologetic attempt to make Christianity plausible, by showing that it is the infinity at which the various parallel lines of human thought, in Israel, in Greece, in mankind in general, finally converge. And the Chair of Christian Apologetics has been gathering dust now for many decades in most German theology faculties.

A third and less obvious problem for a modern Christian in accepting the idea of salvation history lies in the direction indicated by Hans W. Frei in his *The Eclipse of Biblical Narrative*.[11] Modern readers, Frei points out, are in a radically different position from their Christian forbears because they know, as earlier generations did not, that the narrative account which forms more than half of the Bible is not an accurate report of the course of world history, but a *story*. This story is anchored in history at various points but, taken in sum, it is not 'history' in our sense. Frei coined the expression 'history-like' for the character of biblical narrative. For pre-critical readers, a commitment to the sacred history as told by the Bible was not a decision *either for or against* a secular reading of world history, since no such option existed. For the modern reader, on the other hand, the biblical text stands against what a literary theorist might call a counter-text – the secular historian's reconstruction of human history. The problem is not merely that this secular reconstruction is often non-religious: even a highly theological account of world history – indeed, even a fundamentalist version of it which insists on the accuracy of the biblical account at all points – is still different from an uncritical and unquestioning acceptance of the Bible's version as the sole horizon of thought. In a critical age, to trace 'the tale of the loving purposes of God' cannot be a matter of entering naively into the world of the biblical text. It entails making a decision between two options. Either modern Christians who wish to go on affirming that God directs human history and brings it to fulfilment in Christ must break out of the world of the biblical text, and try to show that the hand of providence can be detected in history, not as narrated in the Bible, but *wie es eigentlich gewesen*; or they must adopt the kind of attitude sometimes called 'second naivete' (much adopted by Paul Ricoeur, but anticipated in Barth[12]), and declare that so long as they are thinking in the Christian mode they will allow the biblical narrative to function as their horizon of thought. Either course may be defended, but it is important not to confuse the two.

The modern liturgical recovery of the virtue of 'narration' as the means by which Christians declare their allegiance to God often looks, from this perspective, like an uneasy compromise. This is in fact the case in the Eucharistic Prayer already quoted, but perhaps it is even clearer in the (notorious) Eucharistic Prayer C of the American Prayer Book:

> God of all power, Ruler of the Universe, you are worthy of glory and praise. At your command all things came to be: the vast expanse of interstellar space, galaxies, suns, the planets in their courses, and this

fragile earth, our island home. From the primal elements you brought forth the human race, and blessed us with memory, reason, and skill. You made us the rulers of creation. But we turned against you, and betrayed your trust; and we turned against one another. Again and again you called us to return. Through prophets and sages you revealed your righteous law. And in the fullness of time you sent your only Son, born of a woman, to fulfill your law, to open for us the way of freedom and peace.[13]

The problem about this from the point of view of Frei's analysis is not, as British readers will tend to feel, a lapse of literary taste. It is an impossible mingling of two idioms of thought: critical reconstruction of the history of the world (indeed of the universe) and the retelling of the biblical story. An account in which the human race was made the rulers of creation, in which there is something called 'the fullness of time', and in which prophets and sages revealed God's righteous law, is not part of the same world of thought as the one in which the universe contains the vast expanses of interstellar space and the earth as a fragile island within them. That is not necessarily to say that the two stories *conflict*, in a 'science versus religion' opposition; it is to say that they are incommensurable.

Frei's book did not present a clear programme, but others have developed from his careful distinctions the project of a narrative theology, in which there is a conscious decision for the second option, the acceptance of the biblical story not as a basis for the reconstruction of 'real' history but as the irreducible frame of reference for Christian thought.[14] In this there are of course heavy influences from Barth, from the entire tradition in German Protestant theology which declares (in Lessing's famous words) that the 'ugly, broad ditch' between truths of historical research and truths of faith is for ever unbridgeable, and – in the last few years – from Wittgenstein's ideas about encapsulated language-games. 'Canonical criticism' of the Bible marches to much the same tune.[15] For people of this persuasion, Eucharistic Prayer C would represent a failure of nerve: a radically unsatisfactory attempt to connect the language of faith with the language of secular history and science. And talk of 'preparation in history for Christ', at least as interpreted in Talbot's essay, would presumably evince a similar confusion of thought. For the phrase makes sense only in the context of the biblical story of prophets and kings and messiahs, and the attempt to make it apply to 'real' history is faintly ludicrous – and also theologically undesirable, for would not any divine plan or providence that could be caught in the nets of human historical study be by definition less than fully divine?

But to this question, expecting the answer 'yes', the tradition of English theology answers 'no'. The religion of the Incarnation is faith in a God who presents himself for historical inspection; the light of the world is not confined to the Holy of the Holies, not encapsulated in the Bible or in formulations of doctrine, but let loose upon the world to bring illumination to all spheres of knowledge and action. And the notion that historical study can contribute to our understanding of that light should not be given up without a struggle, however quaint such phrases as 'preparation in history for Christ' sound in twentieth-century theology.

In this context, the similarity between Christian 'narration', especially in liturgy, and Jewish liturgical custom is really less close than it looks. *Once given* a canon of scripture containing Old and New Testaments, understood as a single seamless work, the Christian listing of the great events of salvation looks formally just like the Jewish one, the sole difference being that the things concerning Jesus are of course added to the catalogue. Jewish thanksgivings list the creation, the exodus, the giving of the promised land; Christian thanksgivings go on to include the death and resurrection of Jesus and the coming of the Spirit. A 'narrative theology' therefore seems, superficially, adequate to account for either; both communities of faith have a story to tell, which runs parallel to begin with; though it then diverges.

But the resemblance is far more apparent than real. Jewish thanksgivings, like the Hebrew canon of scripture on which they depend, do not just happen to stop short of the events of the New Testament period; they never go beyond the end of the exile, and more often than not stop far earlier, at the entry to the promised land or even at the death of Moses. The sacred history which they narrate is the sacred history contained in holy scripture, for which most of the Persian and the whole of the Graeco-Roman age form an empty blank. Salvation history, in the kind of Judaism that produced the extant *berakoth*, does not mean an account of the purposes of God from creation *to the present*, but the narrative of Israel's history during the sacred period covered by the law, the prophets, and the writings – or even by the Pentateuch alone. Now when a past age, seen as closed and completed, forms the entire content of historical narration, especially in a liturgical context, the effect is quite the opposite of historical in any normal sense of the word. What happens is rather that the sacred events become paradigms for understanding present experience. This process is already at work in Deuteronomy, which most think had a liturgical origin, in the reiterated 'today' motif: 'not with our forefathers did the LORD make his covenant, but with us, who are all alive here today' (Deut. 5:3). The effect, in fact, is exactly the same as in the Christian context when (for example) the account of the crossing of the Red Sea is read at a baptism. As James Barr puts it, 'The more one hears of the exodus of Israel from Egypt as part of the liturgy for the baptism of infants in water, the less one is concerned to ask whether any Israelites ever came out of Egypt and, if they did, how they got out.'[16]

People sometimes describe the process by which Jewish festivals ceased to be primarily harvest festivals, and became instead celebrations of the mighty acts of God, as a 'historicisation' of the Israelite cult; but it might be truer to say that it represents the 'mythicisation' of the history of Israel. And for most varieties of Judaism in the New Testament period, and for the mainstream from the Tannaitic period onwards, there is little sense of historical events as part of a *continuing* divine story. Contemporary events never belong to the sacred history; liturgical narration does not make the historical reality of the narrated events important, but on the contrary empties them of historicity, making them into timeless symbols. The Christian observation that there are no debates in Judaism about the historicity of Moses analogous to those about the empty tomb or the Virgin Birth accurately reflects the far smaller importance that questions of historicity have in mainstream Judaism.

Now of course for us, at a remove of two thousand years from the events concerning Jesus, the narration of the stories in the gospels tends to function in much the same way as the narration of the exodus does in Judaism: as a potent symbol of the character of God and as a paradigm of his action in the world. But from the beginning it was not so. In adding references to the life, death, and resurrection of Jesus to the list of the *magnalia Dei* in their *berakah*, early Christians were taking a radical step, and breaking the mould they were using. Very recent events, which fell entirely outside the sacred period to which the holy scriptures belonged, were set alongside, indeed, said to be greater than, the traditional sacred history. Furthermore, the Christian eucharistic narration was not content to leave matters even there, but spoke also of the activity of God through the Holy Spirit in the present: sacred history continued to this day. The creation of a New Testament, and its eventual inclusion in a single codex as part of an undifferentiated Bible, had the fateful effect of concealing this highly innovative move. But for early Christianity, the narratives about Jesus and the present experience of the Spirit lay firmly outside holy scripture, and *yet* were held to tell of the activity of God in human history even more 'classically' than the stories that *were* scriptural.

This claim that the events of contemporary history are not merely some kind of re-enactment of the holy events of old, which have passed into myth, but the locus of a fresh and unprecedented encounter with the living God, at once (so I believe) cuts the ground from under the 'narrative theology' approach and both legitimates and requires an engagement with real, as opposed to sacredly-narrated, history. The contrast between Christianity and what was to become mainline Judaism on this point has been made well by Krister Stendahl, who has championed the cause of getting *behind* the biblical text against narrative theology in his article, 'The Bible as a Classic and the Bible as Holy Scripture'. After noting that modern Christian theology has moved away from a concern with history towards a concern for 'story', he continues:

> There is a striking analogy to such a move from history to story and wisdom. I think of the major move of rabbinic Judaism after the fall of Jerusalem and the Bar Kokhba catastrophe. Rabbinic Judaism – a child of the very tradition which is often credited with having given 'the idea of history' to the world – cut loose from the frantic attempts at finding meaning in and through history. At Jamnia and through the Mishnah the center of religious existence was placed in Halakah, i.e., in the lifestyle and wisdom of Torah. To be sure, the historical consciousness remained strong in Judaism, but not any more as the center of attention. It becomes exactly 'story', Haggadah, with far less binding authority. To be sure, the Mishnah and the Talmud are not the sum total of Judaism. There are the prayers and the memories, but the center, the equivalent to what Christians came to call theology, is in Torah as Halakah. Those Jewish writings that struggled with meaning in and through history, writings like 4 Ezra and 2 Baruch, have survived through Christian transmission. They were not part of the living tradition of Judaism. It was the Christians, new on the block, who inherited and renewed the historical mode. To them history was not mute, for now 'in these last days God has spoken to us by a Son' (Heb. 1:2).[17]

All this implies, to my mind, that we should adopt not Frei's second option, but his first, and go down the road that is said to be blocked and in any case to lead nowhere: the road called 'preparation in history for Christ'. The question is not: How does the Christian story fit into the sacred story of Israel? – or, as it is sometimes put, What is the relation of the New Testament to the Old? These are questions about inner-textual relations, and they make sense only if Christianity is the religion of a book. The question we should be asking is: What can be said about Jesus in the context of human history and human religious thought? If it is in Jesus that we encounter God, what is new in either his message or his mission? What is old? Where is he continuous with the culture into which he came, where discontinuous? These are directly historical questions; they are also theological or religious questions, because on them hang decisions about whether he is worth believing in and being committed to.

To put the matter somewhat sharply: it is customary to say that the English obsession with asking purely historical questions about Jesus shows a philistine insensitivity to real theology, of a piece with our notorious failure to produce systematics. Those who hold that nothing of religious importance can hang on the contingencies of history are supposed to be the people who are really serious about theology. Precisely the opposite is the case; for theology is not a game played among those already in a charmed circle, but a set of assertions about the way things really are; and if it fails to connect with what may be discerned through other modes of study, history, the natural sciences, and so on, then it is saying nothing worth saying. It is therefore precisely those students of Christian origins who are most scrupulous about religious neutrality, most purely descriptive, who seem to me to have most to contribute theologically, because they are contributing some real knowledge rather than a self-contained system of religious thought that might as well exist on Mars.

Preparation in history for Christ is a question, therefore, about the world into which Jesus came; and Edward Talbot's decision to treat it by asking about the confluence of religious and moral ideas form ancient Israel and from the Graeco-Roman world to form the matrix within which Jesus taught, lived, and died, seems to me still entirely the right approach. But this does not, of course, acquit it of the other two charges with which we began: that it is inclined to a triumphalistic or over-optimistic interpretation of the hand of God in human religious progress, or, on the other hand, that it allows too small a place for the radical discontinuity of Jesus with what preceded him.

Here, it seems to me, the question is one of balance and proportion. The radical discontinuity of Christ with existing culture is indeed a very important truth. One can understand why German theologians in particular are so touchy about it; but one may also wonder if it is not being used to solve a problem which is a Lutheran creation in the first place. Of course National Socialism deified the (supposed) orders of nature and society, and thought in terms of religion as subservient to the historical process that would vindicate all things German; and of course the Confessing Church was right to say 'no!' to that, and to insist that the call of Christ cuts across all human cultural allegiances. But an Anglican may wonder whether a less extreme separation of the orders of nature and of grace in Lutheran thought, a less rigid insistence on the idea that the gospel does not speak in the political sphere, less of a political *via negativa* in Lutheran theology, might have produced a context less congenial to Nazi ideology in the first place. If a stress on the discontinuity of Christ from all that preceded him is part of the cure, it looks surprisingly like a homeopathic cure. This does not mean that we have to rush to the opposite extreme, and talk as though Jesus and his gospel are a mere epiphenomenon of the onward march of human culture. The relation of Christ to those aspects of human religion and philosophy that may be seen (from a Christian point of view) as a preparation for him is surely best seen as dialectical: a reaffirmation that transforms what it reaffirms, a transformation that respects what is transformed. Classic formulations of the doctrine of the Incarnation provide just the kind of paradoxical terminology we need: Christ is *totus in suis, totus in nostris*; he fulfils all human hopes, yet redefines them in the very moment of fulfilment.

From an Anglican perspective the need to stress the unexpectedness or distinctiveness of Christ springs rather from the desire to insist that it is God with whom we have to do in him – that he is not explicable in merely human terms. But I do not find that the distinctiveness of Christ is understated in Talbot's essay in any case. Much more serious, in my judgement, is the suggestion that the whole idea of a preparation in history can make sense only within the biblical way of telling the story of the world, and that when we abandon the narrative framework of the Bible for secular historiography the notion that human history has any direction at all, let alone a progressive one, is so nonsensical that Christian faith must on no account be risked on an association with it. The idea that history is going somewhere is as much of a bad dream for modern German theology as the idea that human culture is sacred; and world history is deeply unpopular with most professional historians anyway, while any teleological form of it is quite beyond the pale. Is it still possible to speak other than mythologically of the 'loving purposes of God' in human history?

The possibility of answering 'yes' to this question has recently come from a surprising (because essentially Lutheran) source: Gerd Theissen's *Biblical Faith: An Evolutionary Perspective*.[18] On Theissen's model, something really new happened in ancient Israel, which is the precondition for mankind coming to terms with the physical and cultural world within which human life is set, and reacting to it creatively rather than destructively. This new thing is the recognition of the single God confessed by the monotheistic faiths, a God who offers mankind the opportunity of adapting to the pressures of life in nature and culture by moral change, and especially by concern for the rights of the disadvantaged, rather than by being simply swept away by the historical process. And this new thing was repeated and intensified in the life of Jesus of Nazareth, in the commitment which led him to his death. To give thanks that this is so is, implicitly, to say that God was himself behind these two ventures of human faith, the prophetic movement in Israel and the ministry of Jesus. The history of human religion as presented by Theissen is not itself a theologically neutral history, because within it these two stages can be recognized as genuine breakthroughs, points at which the human religious quest showed itself to be adapted to ultimate reality.

All that went to make these breakthroughs possible, the whole long and winding history of ancient Near Eastern religion and the entire intellectual and spiritual background to Jesus and his disciples, is therefore properly seen as a preparation in history for Christ: the remote preparation that made it possible for a decisive mutation – which is none the less a random mutation – to occur. Jesus, as Theissen puts it,[19] is the black moth which embodies properties apparently, and at an earlier stage of evolution really, dysfunctional, but in the advanced stage of human culture at which he appeared offering a model which alone can ensure the survival of the species.

Now in this Theissen is not concerned, like the narrative theologians, with the Jesus of the New Testament as a literary character, and with the canon of the Old Testament as the literary matrix within which he is to be understood, but with Jesus of Nazareth, the person studied by historians (not necessarily the same as the 'Jesus of history' theologians abstain from studying out of theological asceticism). Similarly, he is concerned with the beliefs that were actually held by the prophets of Israel, people we can reconstruct only by digging *beneath the surface* of the Old Testament and other ancient Near Eastern literature. He is concerned, that is to say, with Jesus in the context of Israelite, Jewish, and world history. Furthermore, he is concerned with the development of human religious consciousness, especially in its Jewish and Christian forms, in the context of intellectual history in general and of the account of the emergence of man from nature provided by the natural sciences through the theory of evolution. Theissen believes that Jewish belief in the one God, and Christian faith in Jesus Christ, can be seen as two giant leaps forward in human evolution, through which the possibility arises that mankind may at last break out of the iron laws of competition for survival which, left unchecked, will eventually destroy the earth. Discontinuity is stressed – they are leaps; and Whiggery is avoided – they are random mutations, not part of an inevitable 'ascent of man'. Nevertheless, like all evolutionary changes, they presuppose the context from which they come, and are not examples of direct divine intervention in the world. If God is at work here, it is through the most natural of means, letting the world and mankind make themselves, not by suspending the laws of nature.

Working in terms of Hans Frei's models of biblical narrative, there is no doubt that Theissen belongs (with the Anglo-Saxon tradition) in the reconstructive camp. He does not claim to be restating the biblical idea of prophecy and fulfilment, or of goal-directed narrative; still less to be telling us that this was what the old idea of prophecy and fulfilment 'really meant'. The theory that the faith of Israel and the gospel of Christ represent two leaps in evolution is not in any sense a restatement of what the Bible says, but a completely new theological theory appealing to biblical material as evidence for the developments it traces. In that sense, it must be called a 'liberal' theory: it lies to the left even of Eucharistic Prayer C (the one about interstellar space), because it is not in any sense merely a retelling of the biblical story. But it can claim, I believe, to be a cogent modern statement of a theory about 'preparation in history for Christ'; and in essentials it strikes me as perhaps the new version of Talbot's essay which the Church of England needs today. It would be good to think that some of his ideas might rub off on English theology, for which he has evidently more time than many German theologians.

For I am convinced that it is correct to speak of 'preparation in history for Christ', and to mean by it some tendency that can be detected in human history as it has in fact unfolded, not merely in history as the Bible narrates it. Human culture is not empty of traces of God or of rumours of angels: and God was seen at work in a human life, not merely in narratives about a human life. Theissen's thesis seems to me to offer the most hopeful possibilities for rehabilitating the idea of a preparation; indeed, for asserting not only that the ground in which the seed was to be nurtured was providentially prepared, but also that God is not absent from its subsequent growth, and by his Spirit is still active today. What is needed is a development of Theissen's theme that will avoid the shoals of triumphalism and over-optimism that are always a lurking danger for those who try to give a theistic account of human cultural history, so that it may not go the way of Teilhard de Chardin. If it can be combined with the recent upswing in the cause of natural theology, we may be about to witness new possibilities for seeing the hand of God in history and culture; perhaps European theology is at last ready to return to this theme. The older liberalism failed us; a chastened, more tentative, and more humble liberalism might still succeed, and might still achieve what to me is the great prize for theology: to connect at every point with secular study, humanistic and scientific alike, and to work towards a unification of knowledge, not as an imperialist queen of the sciences but as a humble learner who accepts all sources of knowledge as the gift of God.

Notes

1. From the Bidding Prayer of the Service of Nine Lessons and Carols, King's College, Cambridge.

2. In the Elizabethan Book of Common Prayer the first lessons for Morning and Evening Prayer on saints' days are not chosen with regard to the particular saint being celebrated, but are a selection from Proverbs, Ecclesiastes, the Wisdom of Solomon, and Ecclesiasticus read in continuous series.

3. Cf. the lectionary in *The Alternative Service Book* 1980.

4. *The Book of Common Prayer according to the use of the Episcopal Church* (Seabury Press 1977), pp.373-4.

5. M.F. Wiles, *God's Action in the World* (London 1986).

6. D.E. Jenkins, *God, Miracles, and the Church of England* (London 1987).

7. Cf. K.W. Stevenson, *Eucharist and Offering* (New York 1987).

8. I am grateful to my colleague Dr. Glenda Abramson for this story.

9. Cf. A.M. Farrer, *Lord I Believe* (London 1962), p.88.

10. Cf. Frederick Temple, 'The Education of the World', *Essays and Reviews* (London 1860).

11. H.W. Frei, *The Eclipse of Biblical Narrative: A Study in Eighteenth and Nineteenth Century Hermeneutics* (New Haven 1974).

12. Cf. P. Ricoeur, *Essays on Biblical Interpretation*, ed. L.S. Mudge (Philadelphia 1980, London 1981); K. Barth, *Church Dogmatics* I/2 (Edinburgh 1956), pp.493-4 and IV/2 (Edinburgh 1958), pp.478-9.

13. *The Book of Common Prayer according to the use of the Episcopal Church*, p.370.

14. Cf. R.E. Thiemann, *Revelation and Theology: The Gospel as Narrated Promise* (Notre Dame 1985); G.W. Stroup, *The Promise of Narrative Theology* (London 1981); and the *Festschrift* for Hans Frei, *Scriptural Authority and Narrative Interpretation*, ed. G. Green (Philadelphia 1987), which contains a critical evaluation of narrative theology by Maurice Wiles, 'Scriptural Authority and Theological Construction: The Limitations of Narrative Interpretation' (pp.42-58). See also my comments in *People of the Book? The Authority of the Bible in Christianity* (London 1988), ch.4.

15. Cf. B.S. Childs, *Introduction to the Old Testament as Scripture* (Philadelphia and London 1979), and *The New Testament as Canon: an Introduction* (Philadelphia and London 1984); J.A. Sanders, *From Sacred Story to Sacred Text* (Philadelphia 1987). See also the critical comments of J. Barr, *Holy Scripture: Canon, Authority, Criticism* (Philadelphia and Oxford 1983), and my own evaluation in *Reading the Old Testament: Method in Biblical Study* (London and Philadelphia 1984), pp.77-103 and 140-79, and in *People of the Book?*, ch.3 (see preceding note).

16. J. Barr, *The Bible in the Modern World* (London 1973), p.59.

17. K. Stendahl, 'The Bible as a Classic and the Bible as Holy Scripture', *Journal of Biblical Literature* 103 (1984), pp.3-10; quotation on p.4.

18. G. Theissen, *Biblical Faith: an Evolutionary Perspective* (London 1984). I have discussed Theissen at more length in *People of the Book?*, ch.5.

19. *Biblical Faith*, p.168.

THE INCARNATION AND DEVELOPMENT

Maurice Wiles

Illingworth's essay under this title in *Lux Mundi* is not primarily about the Incarnation – except in so far as, for Illingworth, any discussion of Christian faith had to be primarily about the Incarnation. Its central concern is rather with the accord of Christianity with the findings of science, and in particular with the theory of evolution. That the two are in accord Illingworth was in no doubt. Not for him the subterfuge of emphasising that evolution is only a scientific theory or hypothesis, and then using that fact as an excuse for evading its challenge to religious and theological thought. But the use of the word 'challenge' is misleading. It suggests a defensiveness on the part of the theologian, which is wholly absent from Illingworth's approach. So far from being a threat to Christian thought, the development of the theory of evolution had actually served to enhance Christian understanding of its own most central doctrine, the Incarnation. So the mellifluous tones of Illingworth's prose flow on, giving appropriate expression to his confidently holistic view of God's consistent self-revelation to humankind in creation and Incarnation.

The confident optimism of that unitary vision was a bit much for some of his contemporaries, even some of those basically sympathetic to his general theological stance. Did he, it was asked, in tying creation and Incarnation so closely together give enough weight to the fact of moral evil and the experience of human sin? It is the same question that was so persistently to be put to that twentieth-century visionary of the unity of human knowledge and of the interrelatedness of creation and Incarnation, Teilhard de Chardin. And so it is not surprising that the twentieth century, with its experience of two world wars, of Auschwitz and Hiroshima, should have proved more cautious in the expression of so comprehensive an account of God's dealings with his world. A more dialectical approach, stressing rather the radical disjunction between the person of the crucified and the more general 'development' to which Illingworth's title refers, has been a more dominant characteristic of theological writing in the period between his time and ours. Such theologies, with their determination to take full account of the moral force of protest atheism, must temper the way in which we today might develop a theology in continuity with that which Illingworth adumbrates in his essay. But they cannot be allowed to rule out such an undertaking altogether. For unless we are prepared, with the more extreme exponents of such a dialectical approach, to challenge even the monotheistic foundation of Christian faith, the unitary vision for which Illingworth contested must remain the goal to which the theologian continues to aspire.

But if the century that has passed since Illingworth's essay was published suggests the need not for abandonment but for a less assured presentation of his thesis, on one point at least we might have expected that his work would not need to be repeated a hundred years later. The initial shock caused by the publication of Darwin's *Origin of Species* is not surprising. Writing only 30 years later, Illingworth was himself able to embrace its underlying insights in a wholly positive spirit, while recognizing the need to convince others of the rightness of such an attitude. Another hundred years later on, when an evolutionary outlook has become an integral part of our way of apprehending the world, Illingworth's fundamental approach might seem to be beyond question, whatever doubts may be raised about the detail of its execution. But we know that it is not so. The strength of fundamentalism, and the effective propagation of creationist beliefs in various parts of the world, are remarkable phenomena that provide a perplexing backcloth to the often fierce theological debates between Christians for all of whom such notions, widespread and influential though they are, seem too absurd to be taken seriously.

How then does Illingworth see the general development of scientific knowledge, and the theory of evolution in particular, as not merely compatible with but actually reinforcing a fully orthodox understanding of Incarnation as the heart of Christian faith? And how does the particular reasoning that he employs stand up to critical scrutiny a hundred years later? There are three moves that he makes in the development of his argument, on which I want to concentrate attention. Each seems to me to constitute an appropriate and valuable form of theological reasoning, but one whose precise implications call for review.

The role of experience
'It is not the substantive body of our knowledge', wrote Illingworth, 'but the critical faculty which has been sharpened in its acquisition that really comes in conflict with our creed' (p.207). When that critical spirit sought to extend its hegemony over all human knowing under the guise of logical positivism, the conflict took on an even more absolute character. Today

that critical spirit runs in somewhat broader channels. The dimension of religious knowledge is less confidently excluded. But a *prima facie* conflict with the propriety of many of the more particular affirmations of 'our creed', such as the Incarnation, remains.

For Illingworth there had to be a congruity between science and religion, not only in terms of the absence of incompatibilities at the substantive level, but positively in how they function as ways to knowledge. It could not be otherwise, since the possibility and the process of discovering in both cases derive from the one divine Logos. The two ways to knowledge are not, of course, identical, any more than there is an identity between the ways in which the various particular sciences function. But there are analogies between them. And most importantly there is an analogy between the indispensable role of experiment in science and the role of experience in religion (p.197). Indeed 'now, as ever, the real burden of the proof of Christianity is to be sought in our present experience' (p.208).

The implications of giving this crucial role to experience need to be pursued both negatively and positively. When Illingworth puts the burden of proof of Christianity on present experience, he is arguing against those who would place that burden of proof on the appeal to miracle. His acceptance of the validity of the scientific enterprise and the general tenor of its findings did not, for him, rule out the possibility of miracle. But they did, in his view, qualify the role that miracle could play in the defence of Christian truth. For miracle was not something that could be established independently of any prior conviction about the truth of Christianity, and then used as a stepping-stone for the establishment of a reasoned Christian belief. 'It is not so easy to believe Christianity on account of miracles, as miracles on account of Christianity' (p.208). The distinction is a useful one. It is not always clear, for example, when objections are raised today against those who express doubts about some traditional Christian miracles, such as the resurrection of the physical body of Jesus, whether the objection is that such questioning undermines an essential factor for the establishment of the truth of Christianity, or whether it is that a Christian faith which does not automatically involve the acceptance of such a miracle is *ipso facto* a deficient form of faith. Nevertheless, the distinction must not be overpressed. The kind of cumulative argument that is appropriate to the justification of religious belief does not travel in a straight line from premise to conclusion. So the appeal to miracle, even if ineligible as the starting-point or primary determinant of belief, might still have some contribution to make in the complex process that constitutes an appropriate reasoned grounding of Christian faith.

But the principle that Illingworth is insisting on here is of wider application than just to the specific concept of miracle. In relation to the doctrine of the Incarnation, miracles, such as the resurrection of the physical body of Jesus, figure as one aspect of the scriptural witness. And what was already apparent in Illingworth's day and has become increasingly apparent since is that it is not only the appeal to miracle but the appeal to scripture as a written record that cannot sustain the burden of proof that has so often been put on it in the past, and that so many want to continue to put on it today. Experience will have to play the larger role that Illingworth ascribes to it. But can it in fact bear as heavy a load as is being demanded of it?

Illingworth's own account of how Christian experience provides confirmation of the truth of Christian faith is developed in two main ways. They are important not only because they help to a fuller understanding of Illingworth's position, but also because each points forward to a significant trend in the history of Christian thought between his time and ours.

In the first place, Illingworth stresses that the experience of which he is speaking is nothing partial or superficial. It is experience in which every aspect of what goes to make up the human person has to be involved. 'It is only to the spiritual yearning of the whole personality that He reveals Himself as a person' (p.198). And with respect to the Incarnation, this implies 'revealing the Eternal Word as strictly a Person, in the ordinary sense and with all the attributes which we commonly attach to the name' (*ibid*.). The claim that the knowledge of God is only to be found when the whole person is committed to the search for it is a reasonable and proper claim to make. But it is much more difficult to know how to assess its operation in practice. The whole personality is certainly more than the critical faculties, but it neither excludes nor overrides them. The 'revelation' of which Illingworth speaks is, indeed, an essential grounding of a true Christian knowledge of God, but its contents cannot be as directly self-validating as he implies.

There is an interesting parallel with the basic approach of the theology of Karl Barth, so different though it is in most respects from that of Illingworth. For Barth too, true knowledge of God comes only through the self-revelation of the divine Word to those who are fully open and responsive to what it has to disclose. But it is instructive to observe how different is the content of that self-revelation as Barth receives it, leading him to give it expression in terms of a far more modalist understanding of the trinitarian God. What we have been having to learn, indeed are still having to learn, is how to discriminate between what is valid in such an approach and what constitutes its lapse into a false dogmatism that has put itself beyond the reach of reasoned criticism and assessment. 'Experience' does not happen in a historical or social void. It is grounded in a particular historical tradition and occurs within a particular social context. The content of whatever revelation is apprehended through it inevitably shares in the relativity of that particular context. And that fact must give us pause before we can identify ourselves with the confidence of an Illingworth or a Barth as to the precise doctrinal substance which it can validate for us.

The other emphasis in Illingworth's account of how present experience serves to confirm Christian incarnational doctrine is on the long and continuing history of the Christian experience of sin forgiven. This experience can be traced back historically, he argues, to Jesus who himself described the effective proclamation of the forgiveness of sin as a more impressive miracle than the physical healing of a paralytic. This answer at the level of experience to that moral evil which, whatever his critics may have said, Illingworth describes as 'a fact of such stupendous magnitude as to constitute by far the most serious problem of our life', points inescapably, he claims, to a strictly supernatural energy in the one from whom it derives (pp.208-9). This too is an approach that went on to play a dominant role in twentieth-century theology, of particular importance for those who were most sensitive to the increasing difficulties inherent in any direct appeal to the scriptural record. Its archetypal form is summarised in Tillich's aphorism that 'Christology is a function of soteriology'.[1] To use Tillich's distinctive terminology, it is the experience of faith as 'the New Being within and under the conditions of existence' that guarantees that there has existed a personal life (that to which the scriptural record points) in which the New Being has found full embodiment and has conquered the old being.[2] Again, the line of reflection to which Illingworth points is one which is crucial to the work of the theologian, but the question has to be raised whether it can achieve all that both Illingworth and Tillich claim for it. Illingworth speaks of the experience of Christians for whom 'this problem (that is, moral evil) is practically solved'. There is a nice ambiguity about the word 'practically'. The more colloquial sense, in which Illingworth no doubt does not intend it, is nonetheless an appropriate reminder that our experience of such a solution, our experience of a conquest of the old being, is manifestly partial. However much it may point to a divine power from which it stems, can our partial experience go all the way in justifying that fully divine character of the historical figure from whom it derives, which the doctrine of the Incarnation specifically affirms?

But before we pursue the implications of these questions any further, we must take up the second theme within Illingworth's discussion on which I want to focus attention, namely the significance of other religions.

The significance of other religions[3]

Illingworth is drawn into a discussion of this issue by a slightly indirect route. His starting-point is his whole-hearted affirmation of the contribution of Greek culture to the theological understanding of the Incarnation. It 'is no alien element but a legitimate ingredient in Catholic, complete Christianity' (p.202). It is, for him, an important part of that development which Christians see as under the guiding direction of the Logos. Such a view was not to carry all before it in the ensuing years. Harnack's understanding of Catholic theology as a regrettable Hellenization of the faith and the biblical theology movement's exaltation of the religious superiority of Hebraic thought exercised a powerful influence in the obverse direction in the twentieth century. But here too Illingworth's vision, if in a somewhat less assured form, is surely to be preferred. Such an affirmative attitude to the Greek philosophical tradition, Illingworth rightly recognises, has implications for our attitude to other aspects of the story of the world's religious development. If we are to maintain a positive attitude to classical culture (and if we do not, we would surely be faced with a much more radical reworking of the main Christian tradition than most Christians are prepared to contemplate), we cannot be content to view it simply as a second stream within some radically distinct section of the world's development, called sacred history. The underlying logic of our attitude requires at least a readiness to approach other religious traditions in a spirit that is open to seeing the guiding hand of the Logos at work there too.

Reading Illingworth's treatment of this theme a hundred years later, it is difficult to know whether to be more impressed by his determination to give to other religious traditions a positive role within the story of the world's religious development or by that confident sense of superiority which finds expression in his talk of 'uncivilised man' and 'savage races' (p.203). Certainly the attitude is positive, but from within an assurance of the superior truth of Christianity most clearly demonstrated in the event of the Incarnation. The early religious history of the human race is understood as having a preparatory role in relation to the Incarnation and to Christianity, 'the age-long prayer' to which 'the Incarnation was the answer' (p.205). And the continuing major religions of the present time contain truths, but truths which are to be found in a more complete and satisfying whole within the Christian faith.

Once again the twentieth century has for much of the time seen a far more negative attitude towards other religious traditions flourish, not just as a fruit of prejudice and parochialism but with the highly sophisticated theological justification of a Hendrik Kraemer or a Karl Barth. The attitude in practice of many Christians towards people of other faiths has changed very considerably in recent years, but theological reflection has found it hard to keep pace with those changes in attitude. In theological terms the 'inclusive' attitude, characteristic of Illingworth's approach, which affirms the positive values to be found in other religious traditions while insisting that Christianity incorporates and completes those values in itself, is still widely regarded as a generous theological interpretation, beyond which it is not safe for the Christian to go. It finds its most famous expression in Rahner's concept of the 'anonymous Christian'. From the Christian's point of view to bestow such a designation on the adherent of Buddhism or Hinduism, of Judaism or Islam represents the highest conceivable evaluation that he or she could give of that other faith. But it is unlikely to be heard in quite that way. For it remains an affirmation made from the standpoint of the Christian, a standpoint not shared by his or her interlocutor of the other faith.

Now there is nothing wrong in claiming that one's own position is truer than that of someone else. In fact it is more likely that there is something wrong if one does *not* do so; for if one does not believe that one's own position is the truer, the question naturally arises why one has not already converted and adopted the other person's view. Nor is there anything morally offensive in calling a person of another faith 'an anonymous Christian', provided one is prepared (as Rahner was) to accept as an honour the other person's description of oneself as 'an anonymous Buddhist'.[4] But of course, the Christian's claim is not simply that the Christian is in the right. It is the much fuller claim that whatever truth the other person has is already inherently present in Christian truth. That is a peculiarly Christian claim, deriving directly from the absolute and universal implications of the doctrine of the Incarnation. So the primary question in relation to the understanding of other religions hinted at by Illingworth and developed by Rahner is not whether it is compatible with a proper attitude of mutual respect, but whether it can be satisfactorily supported. It is its epistemology, not its courtesy, that is the heart of the matter.

And here the link with the issue raised in the previous section, the central role ascribed to religious experience, is extremely significant. If the burden of proof of Christian truth were primarily located in the appeal to miracle or to the scriptural record, the comparison with similar claims by other religious faiths would still be difficult enough. But if the appeal is primarily to religious experience, those difficulties are enormously compounded. Within Christianity itself the dangers inherent in the appeal to individual experience are well recognized; it is the experience of the church that is paramount. It is the church, rather than the individual, that is the primary locus of the gift of the Spirit. This emphasis on the experience of the church serves to iron out the idiosyncrasies and distortions that arise from too great a reliance on individual experience. But once we allow that religious experience outside the household of Christian faith is to be taken seriously, does that not at least raise the question that what had seemed to be the inescapable implications of our experience as a Christian community may itself prove to be based on too narrow a range of religious experience and therefore to be in need of modification? Is the position that we have been discussing, the widely held 'inclusive' view of Christianity's relation to other religions (itself in large measure an outcome of the enhanced evidential importance ascribed to religious experience), a possible stopping-place? Or does it point towards the need for some modification in our understanding of the significance of the Incarnation?

Once again further consideration of that question must await the third of the three themes that I want to take up from Illingworth's essay, namely the Christian claim to finality.

The finality of Christianity

Illingworth raises the issue but deals with it only briefly. The concept of the finality of Christianity is not incompatible with 'the doctrine of development or evolution', he argues, since that doctrine 'is not a doctrine of limitless change'. Indeed humankind has such powers of adaptation to its environment, that it may be regarded as 'virtually permanent'. Moreover on the positive side, the Incarnation and the divine life that it has brought can be understood in evolutionary terms as the introduction of 'a new species into the world' (p.207).

But even if we accept such an account as a piece of vivid and fruitful imagery for our thinking about the Incarnation, it is questionable whether it will do the full job that Illingworth is requiring of it. A new species does not normally emerge in the form of a perfect and unsurpassable instantiation on its first emergence. The difficulty of claiming finality for one who appears in the course of our human history, once we come to conceive that history in evolutionary terms, is not so easily dealt with. In the century since Illingworth wrote the problem has been acutely felt, not only in relation to scientific thought which was the context of Illingworth's discussion, but also in relation to the study of history. Those who, like Wolfhart Pannenberg, have shown themselves most determined to combine a wholeheartedly critical approach to historical knowledge with a continued affirmation of the finality of the Incarnation in Christian understanding, have been forced to develop concepts such as 'the proleptic anticipation of the end of history' in their attempt to make sense of the latter in terms of the former. But it is open to question how successful those attempts have been. Does such a concept have any intelligible content or is it just a form of words to cover up an aporia resulting from the conflation of two conflicting patterns of thought? Moreover, even if the concept be allowed to be intelligible, there are still grave difficulties in justifying the affirmation of it for those, who like Illingworth and Pannenberg, want to stress a consistency in the ways to knowledge pursued by the scientist, the historian and the theologian.

But the person who has pursued this question with the greatest assiduity is Karl Rahner, with his famous essay entitled 'Christology within an Evolutionary View of the World'.[5] By stressing a human orientation towards mystery and a divine outreach of supernatural grace as fundamental features of the whole evolutionary process, Rahner prepares the ground for his presentation of the hypostatic union as the natural fulfilment of this combination of human self-transcendence and divine self-communication. But just because he integrates this traditionally expressed understanding of the Incarnation so fully into an evolutionary view of the world, the idea of its uniqueness becomes seriously problematic. It is not that Rahner has any doubts on that score. He affirms it unambiguously. The hypostatic union is 'something which must occur once and only once when the world begins to enter its final phase'. But the grounds of that necessity are not easy to grasp. The hypostatic union is not 'in the first instance...something which distinguishes Jesus from us', for it is the intended climax of human self-transcendence. But nonetheless there is a distinction, because it is also the climax of divine self-communication. And to constitute that offer in definitive and irrevocable form, 'the reality of Jesus' has to be 'not only established by God, but...God himself'.[6] It is a profound development of the ideas so briefly hinted at in Illingworth's discussion. But difficulties remain. The nature of the claimed necessity, which requires that the present (final) phase of the evolutionary process be initiated by so unrepeatable an occurrence is not clear. If the offer of divine self-communication is a universal feature of the evolutionary process, why is a unique and unrepeatable instantiation of it necessary before it can reach its full and final implementation in human lives? Has Rahner achieved a genuine integration of traditional christology with an evolutionary view of the world, or is there at this point a remnant from an earlier style of understanding, which has not been assimilated into his evolutionary view but is retained there as an alien and ill-digested element in deference to the tradition of authoritative teaching?

In my essay so far I have attempted to outline some of the main themes that underlie Illingworth's essay and to suggest how those themes are linked to some of the most important theological concerns of our century. My overall assessment of Illingworth's position has been that its general line of argument is a fruitful one that warrants our attention a hundred years later, but that it is worked out with a degree of confidence about just where it leads, which it is not so easy for us to share. For if there is much in the theology of the twentieth century that serves to enhance our sense of the potential inherent in the way Illingworth sets about the theological task, there is also much to be taken note of there that underlines the difficulty of achieving the goal to which he aspired. From that greater awareness of the difficulty has sprung the tendency for so many twentieth-century theologians to abandon the task as Illingworth conceived it. If traditional Christian truth and modern scientific knowledge are both to be embraced, that can only be done (it has come to seem to many) by rejoicing with the neo-orthodox in the paradoxical character of their relation to one another or by insisting with the neo-Wittgensteinians in the role of traditional doctrine as a grammar of faith which needs no further justification. Illingworth would have had no truck with such escape routes, and nor should we. If there is such a thing as a spirit of distinctively Anglican theology, it should express itself in the repudiation of such alternative approaches and the continued pursuit of a more unitary vision.

But how is that vision of unity to be pursued, if, as I have argued, the unity that Illingworth affirms is asserted too easily? The crux of the matter is the kind of finality that can be ascribed to the life of a figure in history from within the context of an evolutionary view of the world, and the grounds on which such an affirmation can be made in an age which has learnt the need to test its convictions through appropriately critical methods of enquiry. The second question comes first in order of logic. The significance of the appeal to experience on which Illingworth laid such stress lies in the way it permits present experience to mould received traditions and also in the recognition that those traditions themselves emerged through human reflection on experience. It was human reflection that gave rise to those christologies of the New Testament era which saw in Jesus the final culmination of God's address to his people and to those cosmic christologies of the Johannine and later (or deutero-) Pauline writings which Illingworth believed had had new life breathed into them by the advances of scientific knowledge. They were interpetations of an experience of spiritual transformation by people who understood the history of the world in ways very different from ours. It would be surprising if such christologies could be affirmed without substantial modification against the background of so different a picture as that offered by our evolutionary understanding of the world.

What modifications, then, are to be expected? All along I have been stressing the need for a less assured, less confident tone in the picture offered by the theologian. The Christian, who finds the spiritual transformation to which the New Testament bears witness a continuing reality within the community which finds its faith in God through Christ, may still speak of Christ as the embodiment of the reality of God for him or her. The difference is indicated by the words 'for him or her'. They do not imply religious solipsism. If it were not evidently true for others also, it could not be for him or her. Indeed the depth with which a person's experience of Christ speaks to him or her may lead that person to the expectation that Christ is one through whom God's saving word can be spoken or heard universally. But no one has a standing point in space or time from which that hope can properly be expressed as confident assertion. The immensely varied range of human experience and the apparently open future of our evolutionary world require a more modest style of affirmation. Christ, and the interpretation of his person in terms of Incarnation, may remain the symbols through which we relate our experience of faith to all the varied disclosures about the nature of our world to which the diverse forms of human learning give rise. In that way Incarnation seen in relation to development can, as Illingworth claimed, gain in richness of meaning. But the shifts in understanding of that symbol already effected by the changes in our contemporary ways of understanding the world should not be played down – still less the shifts in understanding to which future discoveries about the working of the natural world and deeper appreciation of other faiths may bring us.

Notes

1. P. Tillich, *Systematic Theology* Vol.2 (London 1964), p.174.
2. *Ibid.* p.131.
3. The argument of this second section is more fully developed in my 'Christianity and other faiths: some theological reflections', *Theology* (July 1988), pp.302-8.
4. See Karl Rahner, *Theological Investigations* Vol.16 (London 1979), p.219.
5. *Theological Investigations* Vol.5 (London 1966), pp.157-92. The same title serves as the heading for a section of his less technical *Foundations of Christian Faith* (London 1978), pp.178-203).
6. Karl Rahner, *Foundations of Christian Faith*, pp.181 and 202.

THE INCARNATION AS THE BASIS OF DOGMA

Rowan Williams

For Moberly in 1889, the question of the legitimacy of dogmatic statement is, ultimately, a question about whether or not the Church is committed to making truth-claims about its Lord. 'Is it true that he was very God? It is either true or false...If it is not absolutely true, it is absolutely false' (p.237). 'For the dogmatic position of the Church and her Creeds, we claim that it is the true and simple expression upon earth of the highest truth that is, or can be, known' (p.260). Such truth is not discovered merely by attending to the profundity of the heart's affections; it asks to be tried at the bar of reason. It is established by processes familiar to the exact sciences, and rests its case firmly on historical evidence – though we should beware of supposing that such 'proof' or 'evidence' speaks to some abstract logical intelligence. 'That intelligence, as adequately trained to apprehend and give judgement upon religious evidence, is in some respects other, and more, than that intelligence which can deal with evidence into which no element of spiritual consciousness enters' (5th ed., p.232). This, however, is said from the perspective of a mature faith; in the first instance we must appeal more partially to the open ground of history – above all, to claims and counter-claims about the resurrection (pp.234-5). The settling of questions to do with this history is where dogma begins; and it is necessary if faith is not to be irrational. Faith in Jesus Christ is empty if it is incapable of answering the question of *whom* it believes in (pp.243-4), and any definite answer, 'Arian' no less than 'Catholic' is *dogmatic*.

Moberly – rather like that very different writer, Bonhoeffer – is plainly not concerned with the 'How?' of the Incarnation;[1] indeed he does not, at any point in his essay, begin to explain what this term means to him beyond the assertion that Christ is *verus Deus* and *verus homo*. He has no *theory* of the Incarnation, simply the conviction that the Church must be able to give a response it holds to be true to the question, 'Who is it that is the object of your faith?' The facts of the Church's history forbid an answer to this simply in terms of pointing to a man called Jesus of Nazareth; one way or another, we have to deal with what the human story of this figure means – what is the identity of Jesus in the framework of a reality whose whole structure is held to be significant? Where does he belong in a story of the world as coming from God and relating to God? My sympathies are with Moberly (though not without qualification); and what I propose to attempt here is a reworking of the idea that dogma reflects a commitment to truth that grows out of a particular set of historical relationships, at whose centre lies the narrative of Jesus – not a theoretical construct, but the abiding stimulus to certain kinds of theoretical question. And unless one believes that questions about theory are necessarily idle and abstract, such issues will be closely bound up with what the Church thinks it is, and is doing and hoping.

The trouble is that Moberly himself gives way to a certain abstractness when he discusses the way in which Christian commitment to Jesus actually takes shape. We are told that the dogmatic definitions of the early centuries added nothing to the already existing faith of Catholic Christianity except a new facility in 'distinctions and com-parisons...definitions and measurements' (p.239). But what is elided here is the specific nature and origin of that faith within a frame of reference some way removed from Chalcedon; and if that *is* elided, we shall misunderstand at least some of what Chalcedon is itself about. The confession of Jesus as Lord and Anointed in the New Testament is intelligible chiefly against the background of Israel's hope for final restoration, as we are regularly reminded by New Testament scholars: Jesus of Nazareth proclaims and anticipates this restoration, and, in the resurrection appearances, which in some way establish a definite community and tradition around him, he is shown as having achieved this restoration of God's people. He it is, then, who both during and after the days of his flesh determines entry into and membership of the people of God. He is the assayer, the judge; when the renewal that has begun in his resurrection comes to its consummation, it is he who will preside over the tribunal to which the nations must answer for their impenitence. It is in this sense that the resurrection 'designates' him as Lord, King, God's son; and in at least one strand of the New Testament it can also be said that he has received this authority because he is a human being (John 5:27), a judge who knows the human heart as no other heavenly or eschatological figure could, and who, perhaps, also represents the plain human suffering and witness of God's chosen against the monstrous beasts of idolatry and oppression – though it is debatable how far John 5:27 deliberately alludes to this Danielic theme.[2]

The judge to whom all shall answer, who is also 'son of man': the christological paradox begins here. But the point I hope to draw out is the significance of *judgement* in this primordial cluster of responses to the story of Jesus. All – the disciples, the people of Israel and their rulers, Herod, Pilate and the Kings of the nations (Acts 4:27-8) – are to stand before the crucified prophet to know their fate, to know where they belong in the new dispensation; or, as the fourth evangelist would more profoundly see it, to discover what is *true* of them, what they have made themselves to be. The finality of Jesus' authority is simply this, that all must ultimately come to *this* light and this presence for their final place or destiny to be made known. To some extent, the preaching of Jesus as Lord is a kind of parabolic drama: this is what has happened, and you must discover where you stand as you discover your response to this. Nathan's 'You are the man' is obliquely echoed in the apostolic kerygma in the early chapters of Acts – 'This Jesus, whom *you* crucified...' – just as much as in the more sophisticated invitation of the fourth gospel to come into the light so as to find whether your works are worked in God. It is not only in the Johannine context that the proclaiming of Jesus amounts to a summons to an unprecedented moral and spiritual nakedness in which the truth is given shape.

Dogma about Christ, and the concern for telling the truth about Christ, stems from this primitive sense of a truth being told about *us* as human beings implicated in a network of violence and denial. It is a truth believed not simply because of a contingent set of experiences triggered off by the remarkable insights of a human being, but because the proclamation of Jesus invites us to commit ourselves actively to a concrete community, in which we are liberated from the dominance of violence and denial; our work and hope are sustained by the conviction that Jesus' invitation into God's people continues to be renewed on the far side of his death – which is a conviction that nothing can remove the authority of the invitation, and thus the authority of the one who invites. As risen from the dead, he is established as the one from whom we may learn where we stand in respect of the reality of God. If the telling of Christ's life, death and rising does not put to us that kind of question and offer us that kind of discovery, the 'dogma' surrounding the story will have failed to do its job. Or, to put it more polemically, the dogma will be misunderstood to the extent that it has ceased to connect with any awareness of a new identity and a new historical humanity formed in confrontation with the story of Jesus.

We should recast Moberly's title. It is not 'the Incarnation' that is the basis of dogma, but judgement and conversion worked out through encounter with the telling of Jesus' story – because 'the Incarnation' in itself is in danger of being just a rather baroque formulation relating to the origin of Jesus' 'earthly' career. Recent theological controversy has amply shown the ease with which the doctrine of Incarnation is confused with the question of the mechanics of Jesus' conception. There is no sense in thinking that we can talk about the Incarnation without talking of the whole course of Jesus' life, the whole historical identity of Jesus, including the ways it is received or rejected by those with whom he comes into contact. I take it that part of the force of the doctrine of the hypostatic union is precisely to deny that 'Incarnation' is an isolable event in or prior to the biography of Jesus, and that 'divinity' is some *element* in that life; but that is a larger question. A phrase like 'The Incarnation as the Basis of Dogma' begs a fundamental question by assuming that the fact of God's taking human flesh is the fundamental theological datum, intelligible (at some level) in abstraction from the realities of truthfulness and finality, encounter and judgement, in the presence of the entirety of Jesus' story, which I have been trying to characterise as the source of the pressure towards dogmatic utterance. That the language of God's taking flesh remains a crucial part of the exposition of the judgement of Jesus' history needs to be argued, and argued with conscious attention to the particularity of the 'flesh' involved – which does not mean a wistful searching for the pre-dogmatic Jesus of history (another abstraction, insofar as it suggests a picture of Jesus which is nobody's in particular), but a grasp of how *this* story begins to speak of the decisive work of God in its specific historical setting.

If this approach is defensible, Moberly is right to see dogma as representing the Christian concern with truth; but this concern is less to do with rationality or comprehensive elucidation, more involved with the need to preserve the possibility of the kind of encounter with the truthtelling Christ that stands at the source of the Church's identity. This is, in Moberly's terms, the truth appropriate to the 'intelligence trained to apprehend and give judgement upon religious evidence'; but it assumes that being religious in a Christian way is irretrievably bound up with the themes of judgement and repentance – or, to put it less negatively, with conversion and transformation. There is a basic 'shape' to being Christian, determined by the fact that its identifying narrative is one of *peripeteia*, reversal and renewal. If the paschal story is, as a matter of bare fact, the bedrock of Christian self-identification, that which is drawn upon to explain what the whole project is about, there is no escaping the pattern there defined of loss and recovery. Faith begins in a death: the literal death of Jesus for sedition and/or blasphemy, which is also the 'death' of the bonds between him and his followers, and the 'death' of whatever hope or faith had become possible in his presence prior to Good Friday; so that what becomes possible in his renewed presence after Good Friday has the character of a wholly creative, *ex nihilo*, summons to or enabling of, hope and trust and action. To say this, I should add, does not commit us to speculation about the psychology of the Eleven on Good Friday or Easter Eve: it merely recognises that the New Testament narrative presents us with *Christian* faith as that which the resurrection creates, in that all the discernible strands of the gospel tradition insist upon the dissolution of the apostolic band before the crucifixion, and preserve the tradition of Peter's betrayal. Thus Easter faith is what there is beyond that faith and hope which exists prior to or apart from the cross of Jesus; what there is left after the judgement implied by the cross upon human imagining of the work of God aside from the *ex nihilo* gift of the risen Christ. In the face of the cross, there is a revelation of a fundamental lack of reality in our faith and hope, and we are left with no firm place to stand. The 'shape' of Christian faith is the anchoring of our confidence beyond what we do or possess, in the reality of a God who freely gives to those needy enough to ask; a life lived 'away' from a centre in our own innate resourcefulness or meaningfulness, and so a life equipped for question and provisionality in respect of all our moral or spiritual achievement: a life of *repentance in hope*.

Nothing is more promising and nothing more difficult. That the Church repeatedly seeks to secure a faith that is not vulnerable to judgement and to put cross and conversion behind it is manifest in every century of Christian history. But in so doing, it cuts itself off from the gift that lies beyond the void of the cross, and imprisons itself in the kind of self-understanding it can master or control. In such a perspective, the question about dogma becomes a question about how the Church retains a faithful sense of the accessibility of God's promises; though the (obvious) paradox is that dogma has so often been understood as precisely the sign of the Church's command of the data of revelation, the sign of something being 'done with' and settled rather than of a challenge left open. Because of this misperception of the function of dogma, the Church's dogmatic activity, its attempts to structure its public and common language in such a way that the possibilities of judgement and renewal are not buried, must constantly be chastened by the awareness that it so acts in order to give place to the freedom of God – the freedom of God from the Church's sense of itself and its power, and thus the freedom of God to renew and absolve. This is why dogmatic language becomes empty and even destructive of faith when it is isolated from a lively and converting worship and a spirituality that is not afraid of silence and powerlessness. The more God becomes functional to the legitimizing either of ecclesiastical order or of private religiosities, the easier it is to talk of God; the easier it is to talk of God, the less such talk gives place to the freedom of God. And that suggests that there is an aspect of dogmatic utterance that has to do with making it *harder* to talk about God.

'Do you mean', the sceptic may impatiently say, 'that the complexities or apparent contradictions of traditional dogmatic formulations are simply there as deliberate insults to the intellect, a deliberate muddying of the waters? Because if so, that seems at best a rationalisation of endemic conceptual muddle, and at worst mystification.' But the difficulty I am here thinking of is not that of the conceptual structure of creeds and definitions, but rather the way in which a dogmatic tradition sets before us, when working as it ought, large and strange images ('regeneration', 'sin', 'beatitude', or, for that matter, 'Incarnation') that indicate a wider world of understanding than mere functionalism and subjectivism about religious language allow for. And this holds even if there remain elements in such a tradition that we can't make sense of: we have to ask how far our conception of religious seriousness can be broadened by living with other models and idioms. Above all, though, it is important to learn the degree to which we do not yet understand even words that are familiar to us. Bonhoeffer's famous and unheeded remark in 1944 has to be recalled: that we talk all too glibly of redemption and regeneration when the life of the Christian community manifests a radical unawareness of what such words mean. And to recover what they mean, we may need to make them strange, to cease to take them for granted, so that we can ask, 'Why should such words ever come to be, and why should they plausibly claim to be concrete good news?' Bonhoeffer's attack on the jargon of 'religion' is far from being a liberal reformist proposal that hard words be made easy or strange words familiar; he is concerned that the real moral and spiritual strangeness – and thus the judgement – of the gospel should again become audible. If we should now learn a greater reticence in talking fluently about 'Incarnation' and 'atonement', it is because they have become the familiar words of professional religious talkers. They no longer bring the Church to judgement, and so no longer do the job of dogma. They have become simply ideology, in the most malign sense.[3] And, of course, 'conversion' and 'judgement' are easily conscripted for the same ends, if the theologian is interested primarily in a truth-telling that is confined to systematic explanation and comprehensive conceptualities.

So part of the theologian's task in the Church may be to urge that we stand aside from some of the words we think we know, so that we may see better what our language is *for* – keeping open the door to the promises of God. The question, 'Do you believe in "the Incarnation"?' is a quite futile one in itself unless it has something to do with the serious question, 'How do you proclaim, and how do you hear proclaimed, the judgement of Christ?' Anglican theology, with its long-standing enthusiasm about the incarnational principle, has often risked blurring the outline of this second question, because the *image* of Incarnation, the fusion of heaven and earth, the spiritualising of matter, has proved so wonderfully resourceful a tool for making sense of a sacramental community with a social conscience and a cultural homeland. This is not wholly mistaken; but the slippage into ideology is perilously close, to the extent that such theology can lose sight of that element underlying the history of incarnational definition that is to do with the radical testing of human 'sense' before the tribunal of Jesus, which is the tribunal of the last days. As Don Cupitt warned in a provocative essay some years ago, the doctrine of the Incarnation may be a device for uniting what needs to be kept in 'abrupt juxtaposition' and 'ironic contrast'.[4]

When the Church seeks to make definitions – whether in conciliar formulae or in terms and expressions (like 'beatitude' and 'regeneration') canonised implicitly by ages of use and official endorsement in worship and discipline – it is at least recognising what I have elsewhere described as the 'responsible' character of its faith,[5] its nature as 'answering' to a gift and a pressure beyond its own life at any one moment or in any one place. If it lacked the confidence, the sense of *authorisation*, to do this, it would lack that sense of a distinctive identity, rooted in a distinctive call, that grounds its being. It would not see itself as a community existing by gift and grace, entrusted with a mission for whose fulfilment it is answerable. 'The Lord did not set his love upon you, nor choose you, because ye were more in number than any people...But because the Lord loved you...hath the Lord brought you out' (Deut 7:7-8). The theologian's task is to remind the Church both of this fundamental motive and motif in dogma, *and* of that concurrent and inevitable temptation to treat dogma as a solution, a closure. In this, the theologian will share the concern of those who want the Church's liturgy properly to open up a congregation to wonder and newness of life, and will also understand the reticence of the contemplative. The theologian, in fact, can help avert that fatal divorce I mentioned earlier between dogma and worship – not by a piously uncritical defence of dogmatic formulae on the grounds of liturgical use or adherence by holy people, but in helping to articulate the critical dimension of worship itself (so well explored in Timothy Gorringe's essay in this volume). It is not a theologian's business first and foremost to defend this or that dogmatic formula, but to keep alive the impulse that animates such formulae – the need to keep the Church attentive to the judgement it faces, and the mission committed to it. If the theologian is engaged in the critique of certain traditional formulae, or the Bonhoefferian bracketing out of familiar jargon, this should arise not from the anxious attempt to clarify according to canons of general rationality (though these canons are not irrelevant; there is such a thing as recognisable nonsense and slipshod argument in theology), but rather from a concern that the question of the gospel is in danger of no longer being put in this or that piece of dogmatic speech. Bultmann's point stands: we need always to ask whether we have rightly understood where the offence, the *skandalon*, of the gospel *now* lies, and to beware of thinking that this offence is identical merely with the contingent strangeness of an unfamiliar cultural idiom.[6]

It may also be part of the theologian's job to offer examples of 'good practice'. I want to turn now to a specific case in which 'dogma', the Church and the theologian interact in something of the way I have been sketching in general terms. One of the few occasions in the twentieth century when a church has consciously volunteered a definition of its own limits is the celebrated Barmen Declaration of the Confessing Church in 1934.[7] This is, I suggest, a 'dogmatic' act in just the sense I have tried to explain – an acknowledgement of the gospel of Jesus Christ as a call to judgement. And it certainly illustrates the essentially christological character of dogma (though it does not speak of 'the Incarnation' in particular), in its repudiation of any 'other source of its proclamation, apart from and besides this one Word of God' (art.1), and in its insistence that the gospel cannot be put at the service of either ecclesiastical or secular projects that have not passed under the judgment of the one Word (arts. 3 and 6). Yet Barmen itself has proved problematic in more recent years. It is, notoriously, silent on the Jewish question, even though this, as it affected the Church, was so significant a part of Barmen's agenda; it appears to block out any serious interaction on the part of theology and preaching with other faiths and cultures; its reserve in the face of the messianic claims of the Nazi state could be generalised into political pessimism or indifferentism; and its rhetoric has been seen as patriarchally authoritarian. All these reservations reflect ways in which Barmen has actually been used in the post-war German churches: the 'dogma' of a liberating allegiance to Jesus Christ alone has become the ideology of a religious *status quo*, and 'it is understandable that its critics should regard it as a product of "false consciousness", an elitist document concerned about the privileged position of the church but not about the persecution of the Jews and other minorities.'[8] Thus the suspicion of dogma as a tool of control and defence *against* judgement is raised; do we then repudiate the statement, or indeed the *possibility* of any such statement?

The South African theologian, John de Gruchy, whom I have just quoted on the criticisms made of Barmen, argues that the denial of Barmen would be a grave error, because it would ignore the central theological motivation of the Declaration, and, more significantly, would ignore *what Barmen makes possible* in the hands of a theologian and preacher who is both wholly committed to Barmen's side of the struggle, *and* fully aware of the ambivalence of dogmatic statement. Bonhoeffer remained committed to Barmen, despite his growing awareness of the compromised situation even of the Confessing Church, and of the sufferings of the Reich's victims in all sorts of ways of which Barmen was unaware; and despite that sensitivity to the potential emptiness of religious terminology that found such powerful expression in his prison letters. What matters is not that Barmen turned out to be the orthodoxy of people who, for all their courage, had the limitations of their class and profession, but that a church gathering believed itself empowered to act in such a way as to refuse a particular kind of idolatry, a particular evasion of the judgement of Christ. As Barth insisted, Barmen's affirmations and denials alike are a word for a particular crisis, and outside that context they are not simply to be uncritically repeated. But this does not mean that they have only antiquarian interest: if we want, in another context, to identify with Barmen's refusals, we may also need to 'liberate' its affirmations from the past, and set them to work in other ways, aware of the post-history of Barmen – what it made possible, beyond the limitations of those who actually drew it up.

De Gruchy writes that, properly understood, 'Barmen's insistence upon the Lordship of Christ is not inimical to our contemporary concern for the liberation of the oppressed, or to dialogue with other faiths and the doing of theology in diverse cultural contexts.' He elaborates this further:

> For Gentile Christians, the fact that Jesus the *Jew* is Lord should mean a total openness towards and solidarity with the Jewish brothers and sisters of Jesus. For Christians the fact that Jesus is *Lord* should mean a rejection of all ideologies that dehumanize or destroy any sister or brother of Jesus, whether Jew or Arab, black or white. For Christians the fact that Jesus is Lord must mean that he is also *Liberator*, and this requires commitment to his liberating Word and deed...For Christians the fact that Jesus is Lord means *freedom* for the church to be the church in the world and not the captive of any ideology...But this freedom has a particular form (*Gestalt*) because the fact that *Jesus* is Lord means that lordship can be exercised only in service, self emptying, suffering, and costly discipleship. [9]

In this passage, de Gruchy demonstrates precisely what the theologian's job is in relation to the Church's public taking of positions. 'Dogma' is tested and interpreted in the light of the question, 'How does the Church become free to hear and to do the Word of God, free to be its distinctive self?' It is assumed that somewhere in the Church's struggle for self-definition there is a genuine concern to find what it is that keeps it faithful to itself and its Lord (though the seriousness of that concern needs constant testing), so that it is possible to think through the language of dogmatic utterance in such a way as to renew that fidelity, not in bland repetition or in sceptical hostility, but with a sense of an answerability to the judgement of Christ that is shared between the theologian and the dogmatic text. There is a particular kind of hermeneutical charity appropriate here, an assumption that dogmatic utterance is grounded in some sort of concern for the liberty of the gospel, so that there is something to look for. A past dogmatic definition may not necessarily be where we must now begin; but that does not mean we are absolved from the attempt to 'locate' it in the task of witnessing to the basic nature of faith. To repudiate or ignore it would be – as de Gruchy suggests in the case of Barmen – to lose a possible resource for effective proclamation now, as well as to lose sight of the kind of conflict that draws out specific dogmatic pronouncements.

But if it is, as I have argued throughout this essay, the judgement of Christ, our 'dramatic' being caught up into the paschal parable, brought to nothing and brought to life, that is the true basis of dogma, what specifically should we say about those historic formulations of Nicaea and Chalcedon that constitute the heartland of incarnational dogma? Do they have a specially-protected status because they articulate the conditions for all other theological definition – so that Moberly is correct after all? I suspect that something like this may be true, but find Moberly's expression of it unhelpfully positivistic. His robust 'true or false?' in respect of *verus Deus, verus homo* short-circuits the details of doctrinal discussion in a way which I think many a patristic writer would have found alarming. More to the point, it needs to be emphasised that it is harder than Moberly makes it sound to find a single brief formulation that intelligibly expresses *the* doctrine of the Incarnation. We do not find in the early Church debates over the truth or falsity of a phrase like *verus Deus, verus homo* in isolation, but a number of conflicts turning upon and issuing in a set of liturgical and disciplinary conventions, decisions about what may and may not publicly be said in the Church's name about Jesus Christ. If we try to work these into a single coherent theory, we invite trouble; and in fact every reasonably sophisticated christology in the history of Christian doctrine has in practice exercised great flexibility as to the status and 'register' of agreed formulae. To ascribe the name 'Jesus Christ' to the pre-existent Word *sans phrase* is theologically problematic for the strictest Chalcedonian, yet it is a form of words enjoined in the texts of Nicaea and Chalcedon; all serious patristic and mediaeval exegesis of Chalcedon took it for granted that this was not a strict and literal usage from which deductions could be drawn. In other words, discussion of the classical formulae has normally, in the history of doctrine, worked with what the formulae have made possible rather than with a notion that they have closed the debate for ever. In effect, it has been the negative and regulative aspects of patristic dogma that have been most faithfully observed, while the meaning of phrases like *verus Deus, verus homo* has been the subject of careful and context-sensitive discussion.

As a matter of plain syntax, the novel dogmatic expressions of Nicaea and Chalcedon were elaborations of an introductory 'We believe in one Lord, Jesus Christ'; as in the very different case of Barmen, we are dealing with the implications of commitment to Christ as Lord. But that does not mean that it is a matter of pure indifference how *et in unum dominum* is to be elaborated, or that this elaboration claims only a regulative force. At the very least, the extension of the simple statement of belief in one Lord raises the question of what things are or are not consistent with this confession – in Christian language, Christian practice, and the life of humanity at large. If the confession of Lordship has its roots, as I have argued, in the imagery of the apocalyptic tribunal, if it sets before us, narratively and liturgically, a set of transactions in which we are invited to find our role and our truth, if it is inseparable from the belief that the community has a distinctive *Gestalt* and a distinctive human hope to offer, we have some resources for dealing with the question of what is and is not consistent, and thus with what is or is not a fruitful elaboration of the basic confession. It will not do, clearly, to think of Jesus as one in whom fleshly vulnerability is merely adjectival to an inner supranatural power and identity: he is vulnerable, says the story, in spirit and flesh to the ways in which human beings like you and me betray and kill each other in spirit and flesh. And we may again recall John 5:27: here alone is the judge who sees the human heart 'from within', and whose authority and commission depend upon how he lives through the dependence and risk of mortality. Equally, though, it is not enough to say that here is a man who by exemplary achievement manifested a fresh possibility of living. This ignores the crisis and failure of the cross, and the divine reversal of human judgement at Easter; and, in setting before us an exemplary achievement, it fails to break through the imprisoning cycle of struggle, error and guilt from which we need release, absolution, a righting of the past as well as a project for the future. It does not free us to receive renewal of life as sheer gift. Are we to say that Jesus is a man transparent in an exemplary but intermittent fashion to the communication of God's grace? But how then are we to avoid saying that God's self-communication depends on the intermittent receptivity of Jesus – his 'good moments' – so that this appears only another version of the exemplary achievement model? Or is his significance in the bare fact that he stands at the origin of a new style of experiencing God? If so, what matters is what is being transacted in our interior lives, the religiousness that we find important and interesting; there is nothing perceptible beyond our interiority to which we are answerable. Do any of these options, in short, articulate what it is to be drawn into cross and resurrection and to find there (the Barthian echoes are unavoidable) at once a decisive No and an everlasting Yes to our selves?

The plausibility of these options may be argued, and I have done no more than set them out schematically, so as to indicate where they may become problematic in trying to do justice to a faith which struggles to see the entire human identity of Jesus as divine gift. If these options are indeed as vulnerable as I have suggested, what is left? The story of Jesus is not one of a miraculous suspension and interruption of the human world, nor is it a story of human moral and spiritual heroism; it involves us in a self-declaration and a self-discovery. To be judged by the proclamation of Jesus in his ministry, death and resurrection is to find oneself in a particular human relation – parables judge us effectively because they are about relations,[10] and their judgement invites a changing of relations. And it is to cross a boundary that effort, will, imagination and achievement cannot cross, into new life.

> He stands on the boundary of my existence, beyond my existence, but still for me. This expresses the fact that I am separated from the 'I' that I should be by a boundary which I am unable to cross. This boundary lies between me and myself. I am judged in my encounter with this boundary. At this place I cannot stand alone. Here Christ stands, in the centre, between me and myself, between the old existence and the new.[11]

For Bonhoeffer, this mapping of the 'geography' of the encounter with Jesus is part of dealing with the question 'Who?' which he believes to be the only legitimate theological question to put to Jesus. It is the nature of this encounter in the preaching of the gospel that prompts christology to foreswear the solutions both of a 'gnostic' supernaturalism and of the teacher-pupil, hero-emulator scheme. And when we have said that, when we have come to the point of seeing Jesus at the frontier of our existence and understanding in the way Bonhoeffer proposes, we have come to the point at which the Chalcedonian problematic still faces us. How shall we speak of Jesus in a way that is faithful to the fact that it is *human* existence in which he meets us and to the character of what we meet as judgement and gift? The Chalcedonian question will not go away just because we find the terms of its resolution difficult or indigestible.

We have here the kernel of the problem of dogma: it is not a natural starting point for theological enquiry today, and Moberly's blunt confidence in our ability to treat it as straightforward propositional truth is rather rare; yet we must continue to ask how such language was seen to serve the imperative of the gospel, and what sorts of developments in our theological thinking it makes possible. We must ask whether, given the terms of the historic debates, we should be any the better for this particular determination not having been made. If we want to be faithful to the fundamental impulse of dogmatic speech, we may well, I believe, have to say that the classical dogmatic tradition has served to keep the essential questions alive. What would have happened to the Church had other styles prevailed – an Arian or a Nestorian theology – is not possible to know; what is important is that, to some degree at least, the Church's reasons for making the declarations it did have a discernible interest in preserving the scope and comprehensiveness of the work and presence of Christ, against ways of talking that were (rightly or wrongly) seen as limiting or compromising the creative radicality of the person of Jesus, and his authority to renew the nature of men and women in the material and historical world.

I have proposed as a refinement of Moberly's title something like 'Conversion and Judgement as the Basis of Dogma', since I cannot see the full weight of the doctrine that God united a human individual decisively and wholly to the divine life as intelligible outside this context. The language of Incarnation is a secondary move in this theological discourse – precarious, yet unavoidable as one central way of doing justice to what Christian conversion means; a dogmatic utterance without which it is significantly harder to witness clearly to the *freedom* of the Church to hear and to preach the gospel. But as itself the *basis* of dogma...?

> Like rafts down a river, like a convoy of barges,
> The centuries will float to me out of the darkness.
> And I shall judge them. [12]

That is the beginning – and the end – of dogma.

Notes

1. Dietrich Bonhoeffer, *Christology* (London 1966), pp.29-37 especially on the difference betweeen 'How?' and 'Who?' as christological questions.
2. Among Johannine commentators, Hoskyns and Barrett are disposed to see a reference to Daniel; Bultmann is not. Bultmann and Barrett are also cautious about taking 'son of man' here as having any reference to Jesus' human condition, despite the oddity of the lack of an article in the phrase.
3. On the complex relation between theological definition and ideology, see Nicholas Lash, 'Ideology, metaphor and analogy', in *The Philosophical Frontiers of Christian Theology*, ed. Brian Hebblethwaite and Stewart Sutherland (Cambridge 1982), pp.68-94,

and Rowan Williams, 'What is Catholic Orthodoxy?' in *Essays Catholic and Radical*, ed. Kenneth Leech and Rowan Williams (London 1983), pp.11-25, especially pp.12-15.

4. Don Cupitt, 'The Christ Of Christendom', in *The Myth of God Incarnate*, ed. John Hick (London 1977), pp.133-47, especially p.140.

5. James Atkinson and Rowan Williams, 'On Doing Theology', in *Stepping Stones. Joint Essays on Anglican Catholic and Evangelical Unity*, ed. Christina Baxter (London 1987), pp.1-20, especially pp.1-4.

6. See Bultmann's contributions to *Kerygma and Myth* I, ed. H.W. Bartsch (London 1953), and his response to Karl Jaspers in *Kerygma and Myth* II, ed. H.W. Bartsch (London 1962) ('The Case for Demythologizing', pp.181-94): 'The purpose of demythologizing is not to make religion more acceptable to modern man by trimming the traditional Biblical texts, but to make clear to modern man what the Christian faith is...the *skandalon* is peculiarly disturbing to man in general, not only to modern man.' Thus the task is 'clearing away the false stumbling blocks created for modern man by the fact that his world-view is determined by science' (*Kerygma and Myth* II, pp.182-3).

7. Text in A.C. Cochrane, *The Church's Confession under Hitler* (Philadelphia 1962), pp.238-42, and J.W. de Gruchy, *Bonhoeffer and South Africa* (Grand Rapids/Exeter 1984), pp.146-50.

8. De Gruchy, *op.cit.*, p.127. On the use of Barmen in post-war German discussion, see Barth's remarks in 'An Outing to the Bruderholz', *Fragments Grave and Gay* (London 1971), pp.71-94, especially 71-81, and also the abundant material on the early debate about atomic weapons in the German churches in *Theologische Existenz Heute*, 1958 and 1959, especially nos. 64 and 70.

9. De Gruchy, *op.cit.*, pp.128-9.

10. See, e.g., Sallie McFague, *Metaphorical Theology. Models of God in Religious Language* (Philadelphia and London 1982), pp.42-54, especially 53; although I have some reservations about the characterisation of classical christology in this section, it expresses much of what I regard as crucial for christological method.

11. Bonhoeffer, *Christology*, p.61.

12. Boris Pasternak, *Doctor Zhivago* (London 1961), p.539 (from Zhivago's poem, 'Gethsemane', pp.537-9).

THE ATONEMENT

Trevor Williams

The setting of the question of atonement

Why should the life and the cruel death of a Galilean holy man two thousand years ago have any significance today in our vastly different world? How can it do any good to me, let alone to humanity in general, in the face of all the disruptive and destructive forces let loose in the world? Paul spoke of it at the time as a scandal to Jews and foolishness to Greeks (1 Cor. 1:23). It has now become highly problematic for historians, a source of indignation to cultural pluralists, and to many others a matter of supreme indifference. In the last case, it is not because our world is any less threatened or disordered than it was in Jesus' day. It must rather be because the connections between his life and ours have somehow been lost. It is left to a few who are seemingly out of touch with the world as it 'really' is to harp on about Jesus, while those who are in touch feel, with more or less regret, that questions about Jesus are not now worth pursuing seriously.

The Rev. and Hon. Arthur Lyttleton argued in his chapter in *Lux Mundi* for the inter-connection of doctrine:

> Theological doctrine, describing as it professes to do, the dealings of an all-wise Person with the human race, must be a consistent whole, each part of which reflects the oneness of the will on which it is based. What we call particular doctrines are in reality only various applications to various human conditions of one great uniform method of divine government which is the expression in human affairs of one Divine will. (5th ed. p.275)

Such confidence in divine government might have carried more conviction in the nineteenth century than it would for many now, but on one point at least Lyttleton is correct. No doctrine can be properly understood in isolation, least of all the doctrine of the atonement, precisely because the word means 'reconciliation'. It has to with interaction, the drawing together of what has fallen apart. That used to mean, primarily, humanity and God. But few are bothered now about Adam and Eve's disobedience or the God that they offended. Far more real is the anguished experience of one's own life, of relationships falling apart, of society divided and nations in conflict. Humanity itself seems to be at war with the natural order. The values and beliefs that once guided us and gave meaning to life are, it seems, broken beyond repair. The stories that used to enchant us are now so much bric-a-brac around our feet like children's toys; we cannot bring ourselves to throw them out and yet do not know what to do with them. The question of atonement is whether these and the many other scattered fragments of existence can be drawn together into wholeness – a wholeness that is not a plaything but life-enhancing power.

Lyttleton notes that 'In the course of religious controversy this doctrine [of atonement] has become separated from the rest, at one time neglected, at another over emphasized, till in its isolation it has been so stated as to be almost incredible' (*ibid*). His worthy aim was to restate it in a manner consistent with its wider doctrinal setting and in terms that could make sense to the beliefs and experiences of his day. Precisely because the question of atonement is so remote from the beliefs and experiences of so many in our day, it is tempting to settle for the narrower task of relating it simply to its wider doctrinal setting. For people who are still at home in its traditional setting, this remains a useful and necessary undertaking. Those who have no difficulty with the idea of God as an 'all-wise Person' are rightly still concerned to exclude what is incredible and unworthy of God in Christian doctrine. A firm basis for this undertaking is provided by the beliefs that Jesus Christ is the incarnate Son of God and that the sacred scriptures are the inspired witnesses to God's revelation in him. Yet it is beliefs such as these in their traditional formulations that for many raise an impenetrable barrier between Jesus and themselves, between Jesus as he is portrayed and talked about and the world as we experience it and perceive it in a scientific age. The tension between the two has contributed to the collapse of doctrinal confidence which renders the wider doctrinal setting itself as shaky as a partly dismantled scaffolding – no longer the secure framework in which to reset the doctrine of atonement or any other doctrine.

Ways of proceeding

In these circumstances, two basic options are open. One is to fend off the modern world and modern thought at every point and to declare in God's name that nothing ever can or ever will disturb the frame of traditional doctrine. Only time will tell if this is so; discussion is fruitless. The second option is to embark on the difficult task of doctrinal reconstruction, in which each attempt to reformulate one doctrine may, indeed must involve reformulations of all the others, if they are to fit together coherently. This means that the second option is not a single option at all, because every attempt to reconstruct will give rise to a different framework. Since the value of each cannot be settled until the different possibilities have been tried and tested, it follows that a time of doctrinal reconstruction must be a time of doctrinal pluralism.

Pluralism as such is not new in the case of the atonement, since the Church never ascribed dogmatic authority to its teaching on this subject; what is new is not only the need to reformulate it within the wider setting of doctrinal reconstruction, but to do so in the context of very different understandings of the function of language. Recognition of the pictorial and symbolic function of language (not only in theology) loosens the hold of rigidly defined propositions. This opens up possibilites of repicturing and resymbolizing the realities with which theology is concerned in a way that is at once more tentative and less exclusive than were the formulations of the past. Those who yearn for unshakeable security may see the loosening of language and diversification of frameworks as a sign of weakness. For others it is a sign of strength and courage. Whatever their value, it is not structures or terminology that matter, whether doctrinal or otherwise, but human beings. A framework of belief and understanding within which a person can grow becomes a prison or a cage when it cannot be changed or enlarged. In the process of change mistakes may be made, but human beings open to each other and to the quest of truth can help each other to keep such mistakes to a minimum. In other words, within the option of doctrinal pluralism, argument, mis-understanding, and indeed passionate disagreement may arise, but from it truth may be hammered out, not as a finished product but as a way of life. For all the variety, the connecting thread will be the conviction that this way of life is not a merely speculative possiblity or purely human achievement, but something made real for, and available to, all human beings through the life and death of Jesus.

Given that the task of formulating a single fully adequate doctrine of atonement is ruled out, one can with some relief settle for the lesser task of trying to show how the story of Jesus and the events surrounding him may still speak with transforming and integrating power to ourselves and our world, in terms that are compatible with, though not necessarily determined by, modern perceptions of the world. It may also emerge that ways of understanding and responding to that story today do in fact express the underlying intentions of earlier interpretations. Though the temptation to find present thinking in the past for the sake of doctrinal respectability must be resisted, this does not mean that a continuity of experience and understanding has to be ruled out. After all, it would be surprising if this were totally lacking in human beings in any age whose lives are orientated on Jesus, even if deep gulfs of time and thought separate them.

Facing up to the difficulties

The problem for many today in relation to the doctrine of the atonement is that key words have lost their power. Sin is out of fashion, the Devil a joke, and God irrelevant. Of course that is not universally the case, but even where such terms have not lost all seriousness, they are often used ambivalently or superstitiously. Problems have long been recognized within traditional theological discourse. How is it that a loving omnipotent God could have allowed the Devil such scope for destruction for so long? How can victory be claimed when evil is still so rampant in the world? Again, if God is loving, why could he not have offered us free forgiveness without demanding satisfaction on our behalf, or the punishment of his innocent Son in our place, or a sacrifice for sin – whatever that may mean; and why is there so much suffering?

Apart from attempting to reinstate such language and imagery with all its problems, we may try to meet the difficulties in two ways. One is to accept this traditional terminology but to reconsider its function. The other would be to abandon it in favour of other terms that may better express for us what is at stake.

Taking myth seriously

The first solution to the embarrassment caused by the bizarre imagery of the atonement is to stop being embarrassed and to acknowledge unashamedly its mythological character. 'Myth' must be understood here not as a fairy tale or outdated pre-scientific *explanation* of how things are, but in the very positive sense of a story that *declares* how things are and by so doing makes them what they are for the hearer who receives it. Thus myths function positively as reality-constituting stories.

A myth can be false if it portrays things wrongly and so misleads. A myth is true if it discloses and communicates to the hearer what is real; in so doing it illuminates even if it does not explain. The point can be illustrated from Kipling's *Just So* story about the Elephant Child and the crocodile, even if this is only a pseudo-myth. The fact is that elephants do have long trunks and crocodiles long jaws, even if there was no tug-of-war on the banks of the Limpopo river at the dawn of history. The story is simply untrue if regarded as history, or as literal description of events, or as scientific explanation. But it communicates truths in its conclusion which might be of more value to a child living by the Limpopo than any amount of theoretical knowledge about Darwin and evolution.

A story, whether told out of imagination or derived from historical events, acquires mythological power when it serves to impart and so create an understanding of reality in the mind of the hearer. Fundamental myths not only declare what the world is like, but where human beings belong within the totality of things. The myth that matters to me is the story that tells me where I am in the vastness of reality – who I am and what I might be. Seen from outside, it is just one of many stories that jostle for attention in the crowded bazaar of reality seekers. Whether these stories are labelled political, ideological or religious, they are all addressed to similar needs. Seen from inside, the story I grasp, or rather that grasps me, is the one that makes me and my world, my visions and my hopes, what they are. Though vital to me it cannot be my private property; rather it is shared by and communicated to me by the community I belong to, whether I was born into it or drawn or driven into it in later life.

The stories Christians told of old and still sing about declare that we as human beings have grounds for hope and joy because there is something or rather someone ultimately real and powerful who is on our side. It is indeed no accident that these stories are most powerfully evocative in the setting of the cult, rather than in the lecture hall. They celebrate the 'truth' that is believed and lived within, against the backdrop of what might have been otherwise. God might have been helpless against the power of evil, the Devil; or he might not have been on our side, but a demon or cosmic joker playing cat and mouse with human beings before destroying them; or he might ultimately have been a God of Law who could not or would not revoke the penalties due to law breakers – eternal damnation. Indeed, there might be no ultimate God, only an empty void in which the cry of humanity is no more than momentary disturbance of infinite silence.

Stories that end with the declaration that there is God and that he is as he is seen to be in Jesus, and that what is ultimately real is the relationship we have with God through Jesus, are Christian myths, in the most positive sense of myth as the story that declares who we are and where we stand. To accept it as true is to believe that the story does not simply make things what they are by merely saying it, but that by saying it, it imparts and makes true and real for the hearer what is real and true in itself. Grasping and being grasped by the story is faith in its twofold character as grace (or gift) and decision. However bizarre the imagery sometimes used in the story, the crucial point is that things are as the final conclusion declares them to be. Whether there is a devil or not, whatever the forces of evil may be, God is not powerless against them, nor is he against us.

Moving from what seems more obviously mythological, such as conflicts with the Devil, one might also say that many ostensibly rational theories of atonement – of satisfaction or penal substitution – are mythologically valid, that is, truth-imparting, if in their conclusion they impart a message of hope through Christ, however logically inadequate or morally repugnant they may appear in the telling. The worst mistakes follow from treating them as proofs or explanations throughout, rather than as declarations in their conclusions.

Demythologizing – the existential way

However, it will not do just to take myth seriously and leave it at that, for two reasons. First, the Christian story is not simply an imaginative account of what might have been, but is about things that really happened to real people – a story grounded in history, in a personal life, and in the impact of that life on other human lives. The fact that this story acquired mythological – reality-constituting – power can be fully acknowledged, but unless the manner in which mythological significance was woven into the account of historical events is clearly perceived, serious and dangerous distortion can result, as when historical elements are mistaken for mythological, and vice versa.

The danger of transposing historical actors on to the stage of mythological drama can be illustrated by the traditional portrayal of Cowboys and Indians. Historically, there was conflict between European immigrants and indigenous peoples in North America. The story of their encounter and conflict served mythologically to help forge the identity of white Americans, as brave heroes conquering a hostile environment. But casting the indigenous peoples of America in the mythological role of demonic forces opposed to the triumph of virtue grotesquely misrepresented their humanity and distorted history.

We may now see that a similar fate befell the Jews when the story of Jesus acquired mythological significance. Their role in history was to be members of a society that reacted variously and ambiguously to the challenge presented by the appearance of a fellow Jew called Jesus. If they have any role in the mythological presentation of the ensuing drama, it is as representatives of humanity, not excluding Christians, when confronted by the truth of God. When the mythological and historical role of the Jews is confused, the consequences have been and still are appalling. (It is no accident that the danger manifested itself in the earliest writings to dwell on the historical events of Jesus' life, i.e. in the gospels, and is less evident in a writer who dwelt more on its aftermath, namely, Paul.)

Secondly, to treat doctrines as myth and no more is in any case to do them less than justice. It may safeguard them as declarations of faith, and yet simply of blind faith, without any explanatory value or rational appeal. To leave faith unsupported by any rational or intellectual framework is to leave it liable to collapse or open to unwitting absorption into portrayals of reality fundamentally at odds with the origins and intentions of Christian faith.

To recognize the unsupported character of faith and to do nothing about it may initially be mistaken for heroic reliance on faith alone; in fact it is evidence of laziness and a refusal to face up to the struggle of seeing how faith must relate to our understanding and experience, if it is to enhance and not exclude human reason. To exclude human reason would not only result in split consciousness, but would be an insult to God's creation.

In any case, the fact that the story of Jesus had a before and after in the flow of history means that the conclusion of his story cannot be totally divorced from the structure and setting of the whole. The problem for us, as we have seen, is that the original conceptual framework of that whole was a pre-scientific picture of reality which inevitably clashed and still clashes with modern scientific perceptions of the world. It is these considerations that drive us towards the alternative route proposed above.

The route we have explored was that of accepting traditional language and imagery but of re-evaluating and restricting it to a mythological function. The alternative to be pursued now is that of finding different terms and imagery that point to the disruption and disorder in the experience of individuals and society, but which have emerged within and so are compatible with scientific perceptions of human life and the world in a way in which many of the old images are not. Such terms are 'alienation', 'estrangement' and 'inauthentic existence'. The task then for the doctrine of atonement will be to try to show how Jesus' life and death has or somehow can overcome these things and put humanity right, drawing together the scattered aspects of life.

Those who pursue this line will face two questions. First, how truly is 'God' in word and reality involved in the situation that is analysed in 'ungodly' language? Is God being adapted to fit into the human reconstruction, or does the human reconstruction and the analysis of human experience in fact help to disclose where and how God is actually at work?

Secondly, is 'sin', too, being adapted to fit into the human reconstruction? or does the reconstruction based on the analysis of human experience in fact help to disclose something of the true quality and character of sin? The question then arises as to how far other terms can function adequately as synonyms for 'sin', or whether that word signifies something distinct which cannot be set aside in theology.

A familiar word for this transposition of imagery, though one that has often proved misleading, is 'demythologization'. It is misleading here because it employs 'myth' in a sense contrary to that which was offered in the previous section. Bultmann commonly used the word 'myth' in a derogatory sense (similar to 'discourse' in Heidegger's philosophy) for a way of speaking which objectified dimensions of reality which were not objects, such as human existence, God, life as a continuing open process, love itself. His programme of demythologization was therefore an attack on false objectifications which barred the way to the real encounter between human beings and the will of God disclosed in Jesus. This has nothing to do with the idea of myth explored above as a reality-constituting story. To avoid the risk of confusion arising from different meanings of 'myth', Paul Tillich preferred to speak of 'deliteralization' rather than 'demythologization', and so to preserve 'myth' as a possible vehicle of truth rather than inevitably of untruth, as usually in Bultmann's usage. Whether the word 'myth' is abandoned or reinterpreted, the intention here is the same, to escape from the literalistic quasi-scientific objectivist understanding of traditional imagery, and in the case of atonement language, to recover its value as the symbolic declaration of renewed relationship with God and the recovery of human wholeness.

However, Bultmann's aim was to go further than this and to engage in the task of transposing traditional Christian doctrine into contemporary language, in particular into the terminology and to some extent the conceptuality developed by Heidegger. For this reason, his project has sometimes been described as an exercise in remythologization or doctrinal reconstruction, using the tools of existentialist philosophy developed by Heidegger to recover the truth-imparting quality of the story of Jesus, where truth has to do with life and meaning, rather than with objective facts.

This is not the place to give an elaborate account of his reconstruction, but some key elements of it should be mentioned. For a start, though Bultmann is commonly spoken of as an 'existentialist', both he and Heidegger may be better described as phenomenologists in so far as they analyse the concrete experience of human existence and reflect upon the conditions that make it possible. Such reflection discloses human beings as existing uniquely between the sheer givenness of things and the freedom of decision – within the polarities of facticity and possibility. It thus discloses human finitude and confronts the human being with the challenge to accept his or her freedom in the face of death, to accept finitude. In Heidegger's words, human existence is being-towards-death.

To recognize this fact is to live authentically. But human beings are tempted to run away from the fact of death – the limitation on their freedom – and to hide from the responsibility and guilt which their freedom confers. In short, they fall into inauthentic existence. The question of salvation, then, is the question of the power to live authentically, of how to escape from the loss of self in the irresponsibility of the collective, from the loss of subjectivity in the world of objects. For Bultmann, in opposition to Heidegger, this power is not innate in the call of conscience, but is given, a gift of grace through the preaching of the Word of God. In that preaching two possibilities of human existence are disclosed, of turning away from or of turning towards Jesus as the revealer of the will of God. In making the cross of Christ their own, believers discover liberation from the powers of this world, the law, sin and death. The experience of the gift is in effect a pre-emptive victory over death, and entry into true authentic life. Traditional Christian imagery of fall, sin, damnation, of the Devil, and of Christ's atoning work and resurrection can all then be reinterpreted along these lines, no longer as descriptions of objectified beings or external events, but as the symbolic representation of existential experience, the transposition from inauthentic to authentic existence through encounter with the Word of God. For many this approach has breathed new life into outworn symbols and made sense of the (at face value) unbelievable accounts of God's dealings with forces of sin and disorder in human experience.

Two things stand out of this brief summary: first, the intervention of God in the world is narrowed down to the impact of the Word on the depths of the individual. This may appear to have advantages and disadvantages. On the one hand, no embarrassing competition arises between God and the structures of causality open to empirical scientific observation. On the other hand, it may seem that too much has been sacrificed for such a gain – the sense of God's providential guidance and of his being the one who answers prayer and is present in a loving relationship. Secondly, in the nature of the existentialist approach, the emphasis is on the individual. It is this that offends the proponents of the view that human life is best approached and understood in terms of the solidarities and structures of corporate existence, not in its isolated particulars. It is to reconstructions from this perspective that we now turn.

The social way

The Bible witnesses to the continuous warfare of the prophets against idols and false gods from the time of the golden calf. It has often been remarked that Karl Marx stands in this tradition, extending the campaign against idolatry from constructs of wood and stone to the constructs of society, both its political and economic structures and its conceptual systems. His analysis was subsequently developed in two related but distinct directions, put simply, the political and the sociological – in particular, in the sociology of knowledge.

It can be argued that in the task of doctrinal reconstruction theologians today have as much right to draw on Marxist analysis as Paul had to draw on Judaism, the early Christians on Plato, Aquinas on Aristotle, or Bultmann on Heidegger. The biggest difference perhaps is that, in the nature of the case, an analysis utilizing Marxist tools is likely to hit traditional views where it hurts most, by bearing not merely on theoretical constructions, but on the power base and material interests of the constructors or defenders of those systems, especially since analysis alone is deemed invalid unless it is the fruit of action, or praxis, of a kind likely to impinge directly on vested interests. It will also hurt theoretical constructions when it radically challenges their absolute or revelatory status, and hence the authority of whatever systems they have hitherto served to legitimate.

Thus doctrinal reconstruction in the light of Marxist analysis, not least the reconstruction of the doctrine of the atonement, has had an unavoidable practical and political impact, as seen in South America, where it has emerged most strongly in liberation theologies. It is threatening to traditional ecclesiastical authorities, not only because of its political character, but because it stems from a rejection in principle of the traditional doctrinal structure of those authorities.

Again, this is not the place to go into the details of Marxist analysis, or liberation theology, but in brief, a central feature is the belief that socio-economic and political systems are not natural, neutral or God-given phenomena, but the result of the modes and relations of production which in turn give rise to the class structure and the conflict of class interest. In the struggle for advantage between the classes, ideas and belief systems, not excluding religious belief systems, become the ideological tools of those in power; in other words, they serve to protect and legitimate their particular interests. Whether one thinks of the proletariat or the powerless in a broader sense, the underdogs in the class struggle are denied the achievement of truly human existence and thus experience alienation in its harshest form.

The victims of alienation are enslaved in this situation as long as they suppose their condition to be natural or God-given, in other words, unchangeable and not the result of human activity. The first step to liberation, wholeness, and salvation is to know that the alienating and enslaving system is not absolute. What humans have made they can unmake. The god revealed as an idol can be overthrown, its demonic power broken. But this discovery comes about through challenging action and not merely by theorizing.

What 'liberation' or 'salvation' means in this context is a crucial question for the Christian theologian. Are such concepts transposed into sociopolitical terms without remainder in such a way as to part company with the Christian tradition? This is the fear of many, and one reason for opposition to Latin American theology. On the other hand, it can be argued that any insight into the causes of dehumanization and into ways of overcoming it belongs by right to the religion of Incarnation and redemption and can even recall it to its proper task when it has failed.

Before exploring how these ideas might contribute to a Christian doctrinal reconstruction, we should consider the other stream of thought flowing from the same original source, the sociological.

The crucial insight of the sociology of knowledge is the recognition that not only sociopolitical systems but conceptual systems, world views or cognitive structures, are human social products and not autonomous or God-given. In fact, the belief that any world view is absolute or God-given is taken to be a symptom of alienation. Human beings have forgotten that it is the product of society – of many generations interacting with their environment and searching for order and meaning. The resultant cognitive structure confronts the community in the present as something given to it from outside, hence 'alien' and not the fruit of its own labour. But the function of a world view in establishing order and meaning is vital; the price of challenging or overthrowing it can seem too great to contemplate. It becomes the task of the authorities, supported by the guardians of sacred tradition – the priesthood – to defend it against any challenge. Yet in so far as any given world view is not absolute or perfect, its relation to the realities of existence will be increasingly strained as time passes in a changing world. The attempt to maintain its authority will prove increasingly destructive for human society, however sincere the motives of its defenders. But that sincerity may well be doubted if on closer examination it turns out that it is the defenders' interests and power that is legitimated by such a system and threatened by the loss of its divine or quasi-divine authority.

In so far as inauthentic existence or alienation in a political or conceptual sense is dehumanizing, the overcoming of these conditions must clearly be a first step on the path to humanization. What follows will then depend on what is meant by truly human, or what sort of quality, value or goal is presupposed in the project of becoming human. It is here that Christianity may prove to be distinctive, even if it employs the analysis of non-Christians in arriving at an understanding of what it is to be somehow less than truly human and why that state has come about. If the story of the fall of Adam and Eve is not taken literally, an answer to the latter question – why we are less than fully human – must at least be attempted. In so far as the questions concern the actual condition of all human beings, one may reasonably look to one's fellow human beings for a contribution to the answer, even if more adequate understanding awaits the discovery of the true solution to the problem. It is here that the paths may and do divide over the question whether human beings individually or corporately have it within themselves to right themselves, or whether they in fact depend on some source beyond themselves for the possibility of being righted. These questions are too big to be settled here, but our next step will be to examine how Jesus' life and death may be understood against the framework of thought briefly summarized in this section, and how the traditional imagery of atonement might be understood in a reconstructed framework.

Jesus – the odd one out

In terms of the account of alienation given above, Jesus stands out strikingly as a man without a power base, not representing or defending group interests, unless one can say he defended the 'group interest' of the poor, social outcasts, and the weak, but their plight was in large part not to be a group. In what sense would a rich quisling tax official count himself in the same group as a leper? – a successful insider dealer with an AIDS victim or starving refugee? (Some recent theology has perhaps been too ready to align Jesus with the poor as a group.) Further, he lacked recognized legitimation. Yet he spoke with authority and by so doing presented an inescapable challenge to the existing range of recognized legitimations, whether religious or political or both.

He posed a threat to the imperial Roman procurator who had reason to fear the appearance of a Messiah, i.e. any nationalist leader who challenged the power of Rome. Jesus, who denied the absolute authority of any wordly power, could easily and however misleadingly be lumped in with the Jewish nationalists and enemies of Rome, whose policies of violence posed a serious threat to Roman interests. At the same time, a Jesus who challenged the authority and status of the Pharisees and Sadducees could easily be cast in the role of enemy of God and the Torah (or 'Law of Moses'), which they claimed to defend and which legitimated their authority. If Jesus truly spoke for God, his authority would have to be acknowledged. It is not surprising that many considered this unthinkable; it was much easier to suppose he was a blasphemer, who should be treated accordingly.

These were not the only group interests that failed to control Jesus or hitch him to their cause. He slipped out of the clutches of public opinion as much when it tried to make him king as when it was trying to lynch him. He declared himself free from family ties in a way that was remarkable for a Jew. He pursued what he saw to be his own vocation even when pressed to do otherwise by his closest friends and advisors.

He accepted what in historical terms one could see as the inevitable outcome, his rejection by all vested and group interests, and finally a cruel death.

It is a profound paradox that what in worldly terms is the final *denial* of freedom was in the case of Jesus the final manifestation of freedom. Death came to him because he refused to become anyone else's property or tool; he was his own man, or should we say God's man? It might be objected that to mention God here is to reintroduce the old doctrinal structure from which we are trying to escape, but that is to go too far. The task of doctrinal reconstruction is not to deny God but to ask how we may conceive of the relation of God, as the ultimate ground of life and reality, to our own world and existence as we now perceive and experience it.

To be confronted by one who is free, who is true to himself in the face of the forces of alienation and inauthentic existence, is to be challenged by the question, How could he be like that? Was his freedom and humanity the fruit of the heroic exercise of his own innate resources? Or was it because his refusal to put his trust in unreliable worldly powers (to worship idols) left him open to the life-giving power from which all existence ultimately derives and by which it is sustained? In other words, we might be able to say that by not aligning himself with anything or anyone else, he was able to be and to remain perfectly aligned with God, and in doing so to be free, authentic, unalienated, able to demonstrate how death and all that corrupts and dehumanizes can be defeated by the power of life, which even the fact of physical death could not overcome.

The sheer phenomenon of Jesus challenges us with these questions, however sure or unsure we may be of the answers. Luckily, we do not need to have all the answers in order to make a choice. The choice indeed is unavoidable. Confronted by Jesus' way of being in the world, as conveyed to us by the gospel stories and the lives of his followers, do we align ourselves with him or not? No one can dictate the choice to anyone else, but one can spell out the implications.

Defeat of the Devil and accomplices

To align oneself with Jesus, to respond to his way of being human in the world, is *ipso facto* to withdraw recognition from the claim of anyone or anything else to be absolute or determinative. In so far as we ever regarded anyone or anything else explicitly or implicitly to be absolute, we recognize now that we were worshipping an idol, a false god, and so were guilty of sin against God. In contemporary terms, in so far as anything we once regarded as absolute is now seen to be a worldly phenomenon or a human creation, whether a political, cultural, religious or conceptual construct, then in principle the state of alienation is overcome and its destructive consequences are held in check. In practice, the followers of Jesus are unlikely to achieve or experience immediate and complete release from alienation and its subtle hold upon their lives (as Paul knew well), and they are no more exempt than Jesus was himself from the externally destructive power of individuals and societies still in the grip of alienation in the world. It means rather that the power of alienation to take hold of and corrupt our innermost being and to drive us towards the corruption and destruction of others, is ultimately broken.

It is in these terms that the traditional imagery of victory over the Devil can be understood. The Devil here is not an autonomous agent of evil whose interference in the world is problematic on every count, but the symbol and symptom of human godlessness, the destructive power unleashed when human beings make what is less than God their God. God's apparent failure to destroy the Devil proves to be an act of grace when the destruction of the Devil could only mean the destruction of human freedom to turn *from* God, and hence equally, the loss of human freedom to turn *to* God in love. We may hold that the freedom of human beings to turn to God in love is co-extensive with their freedom to turn to each other in love and thus the precondition of becoming human in community.

The question for Christian faith

The greatest challenge of all faces religious people; they are familiar with God-talk and recognize the unqualified seriousness of claims made for God and of claims believed to be made by God on human beings. The hardest false God of all to overthrow is the one we have always believed to be the true God. Easygoing agnostics are not bothered; the price to be paid for principled not bothering is to deny seriousness to existence. The price to be paid by those who do bother is taking the wrong thing too seriously. It is no accident that in his day those who bothered most about God were most bothered about Jesus. Yet we need to remind ourselves that bothering too much about God can all too easily become a cloak for bothering too much about oneself.

To take Jesus' side is to deny the claim to absolute seriousness, in other words the name of God, to anything else, but Jesus. Yet Jesus addressed another as God. Here lie the roots of Christian reflection about God that leads ultimately to the doctrine of the Trinity. That is not an issue to be pursued now. We ask rather, if God is truly seen in Jesus, what follows?

The negative side, as we have seen, though it is hardly negative, is release from false absolutes of our own or society's making. Both are important. The desire in all of us to give content and shape to the ultimate mystery of being results in a cottage industry of God production, of little dolls grandly dressed and cherished too long after we should have grown up and come to grips with reality. Whatever an individual thinks or believes about God needs to be constantly challenged, tested against the words of the Scripture, the formative insight of tradition, the experience and perception of fellow Christians and our fellow human beings. Even if it stands the test for a time, no single product or expression of human thought about God can claim to be absolute and eternally binding without becoming an idol, and imposing the shackles of alienation upon us. For creating our own idols we are responsible. God is always more than we can say.

But we are part of a society or societies that are engaged in the same enterprise. And here often more is at stake; the gods of society offer security and power to their worshippers and defend their interests. To challenge these, as Jesus knew well, is a dangerous exercise. Those who are aligned with him are committed to deny all other absolute claims, and to challenge the powerful who enforce those claims, wherever they conflict with that vision stemming from Jesus of what it means to be human in the world. To spell out that vision adequately here or anywhere is impossible, it is still in the process of being worked out in history, but it has everything to do with life and freedom, with drawing human beings out of the narrow confines of subhuman, degrading, fettered conditions (whether of body or spirit) into the maturity of personhood bonded by love and enhanced by self sacrifice.

This can never be a perfect state on earth, but confronts humanity as a project always to be pursued, whatever the cost, because it conforms with the purpose of creation.

The vindication of such sweeping statements does not lie in the quality or otherwise of the language in which they are expressed but in the actualization, even if imperfect, in living experience of what is so described. It is to the extent that such a vision becomes a reality in the lives of those who respond to Jesus, and can be seen to be real by others, that the claim to truth may be vindicated.

The question of other faiths

The claim to possession of a truth that is valid and significant for all human beings raises one of the most challenging questions facing Christianity today: how does it stand in relation to the great religions of the world and their claims to truth? In the confines of this chapter only two brief points may be made.

First, nothing said thus far would preclude acknowledgement of truth and value in other faiths. It cannot possibly be denied that they have provided ways of life and contexts of meaning within which much of the rich and varied potential of human beings has been realized. Within them too there has been a recognition of human finitude and openness to transcendence. More than that, from the perspective of Christian faith there is no difficulty in believing that the Spirit of God has been present and at work in these other traditions of faith, evoking and responding to the human quest for the ultimately real and holy.

In the second place, in terms of the argument proposed in this section, there is no reason to suppose that any religion or ideology anywhere has successfully escaped the pitfalls of idolatry or the tendency to mistake the medium or channels of grace for the source. The escalation of fanatical cults and fundamentalist movements provides all too much evidence of this tragic tendency today. One can therefore suggest that all religions (including Christianity) just as much as individuals, stand in need of redemption, of liberation from self-created idols that stand between them and God, if they are to be brought or brought back into relationship with that which, or rather the one who, is ultimately real. If Jesus does in fact make possible such reconciliation, then he will be significant for all, though how that works out in practice for different people in different contexts and traditions cannot be anticipated.

Sacrifice for sin

We have seen how the traditional and problematic imagery of Christ's victory over the Devil might be reinterpreted in terms of liberation from alienation. One other image has always stood at the heart both of the worship and the teaching of the Church, namely sacrifice. The next question is how this image might be understood in terms of the line of interpretation that has been explored here.

Traditional animal sacrifice is remote from most people's experience in the West today, but the language of self-sacrifice is still meaningful. The report of people sacrificing their lives to rescue victims of some disaster can be powerfully moving. It can evoke in those directly affected, and also in those affected imaginatively, a sense of gratitude and commitment to similar service. But taken in isolation, sacrifice in this sense fails to express adequately the significance of Jesus' life and death. As has often been pointed out, unless it can be shown that by giving up his life he has done something good for us, the grounds for responding in gratitude, love and commitment are lacking.

Traditional so-called objective theories of the atonement attempt to spell out what Jesus has done. 'Sacrifice' then features in its traditional sense as the offering to God of a perfect victim whose blood serves to wipe out the sins of humankind. It is here that difficulties arise. The appeal to scripture to justify the necessity of blood sacrifice simply does not convince those who accept a critical approach to scripture and recognize its historical conditioning. Even if the idea of a flawless victim is interpreted in profoundly moral and spiritual terms, the problem of the need for his sacrificial death is not resolved.

One solution may be to turn the language round, or more precisely, to start with the user rather than with the referent of the word.

Whatever else the word 'sacrifice' might mean in the rich history of its development, one thing is clear: in the context of Judaism it signified an offering which would be, or was intended to be, acceptable to God. Confronted with the fact of Jesus' death, witnesses to it faced a choice. Was it the death of one who deserved to die, a blasphemer, an enemy of God, rightly punished? Or was it the death of someone not in fact estranged from God?

The former response was more likely and reasonable, especially in view of the judgement passed on Jesus by the authorities who could claim to be the guardians and rightful interpreters of God's law, the Torah. Right or wrong, to regard his death as punishment by God was in effect to distance God from that death and from the life of the one who suffered it. To distance God from it was to distance oneself from it.

In contrast, to call that man's death a sacrifice had cataclysmic implications. Rather than explaining anything, one might suggest rather that it simply said everything. It said first that his death was acceptable to God, but it was not an isolated physical act as the death of a sheep would be; it was the outcome of a life of words and action that led to death, not as an accident but as its inevitable culmination. To call the death of the person who lived that life a sacrifice was to say that that whole life, that way of life was acceptable to God.

The same point had been made in principle of other deaths, not least those of the Maccabean martyrs nearly two centuries before Jesus. They died for a shared cause, the Torah and the community of the Torah, in the face of apostasy and persecution. To call their deaths a sacrifice was to say that their lives and the cause for which they died were approved by God. But as we have seen, it seems that Jesus was amazingly independent of any existing cause. His death was for what he saw to be God's cause, but his contemporaries had nothing to go on, to discover what that cause was, other than Jesus himself, his person and life story and death. Confronted by these, the witness could either conclude they stood opposed to God, or were in themselves the true manifestation of God's cause. Hence to call Jesus' death a sacrifice was to declare him to be the revelation of God. In so far as in his life he had reached out to the fallen, the outcast, the sinner, and had challenged the power and authority of worldly rulers, he revealed God to be against the power and authority of the world, and free to reach out to and raise up life's failures and villains, the marginalized and the dehumanized; he revealed God's freedom to affirm the humanity of human beings, however much that was lacking in the eyes of the world.

To see Jesus' death as a sacrifice, to respond to him as the place where God was seen and at work, had to mean more than merely theoretical assent. The question of God meant nothing if the answer did not imply total commitment – the whole history of Judaism from Abraham to the prophets to the Maccabean martyrs witnessed to that. To call Jesus' death a sacrifice is thus to align oneself with his life, to deny the claim of any power or authority to exceed him, to be prepared to suffer the consequences as he did. It is at the same time to accept the affirmation of one's own humanity and the freedom and hope this brings, and to affirm the human worth of all one's fellow human beings. This cannot be merely a matter of words, but as in the case of Jesus, must be made real in actions – actions that cannot help but engender conflict wherever human value is denied, but which will help create truly *human* life wherever that goal is pursued.

It can at least be maintained that by focussing less on the word than on the one who uses it, we escape many of the difficulties raised by an objectified external view of sacrifice – how it 'worked', why God insisted on 'it'. Our attention is concentrated instead on human response and decision, on the fundamental decision that confronts every person faced with the story of Jesus' life and death, whether to distance oneself from it, or to engage and be engaged with it and with all that it means and can mean. This is nothing other than the question of faith, and maybe it is only in faith that the mysterious final episode in the story of Jesus can begin to be grasped, the discovery of new life out of death – resurrection.

The question of forgiveness

At the beginning I suggested that one reason for opposing doctrinal reconstruction was the fear of denying the reality of God as a person in loving relationship. A criticism of the interpretation I have offered might be that nothing is left of God outside the relationships of human beings to each other. One might reply that the freeing of human beings to become persons, and to be persons in loving relationship, might be not only God's way of working in history, but his way of meeting us in this world, not alongside but through relationships with other persons. If the doctrine of the Incarnation means that God was encountered in a human person, then to suggest that God is still at work in the bringing into being of truly human persons, and is to be encountered through our response to persons – our loving and forgiving – may not be as radical a reconstruction as it at first appeared.

Yet the objection may still be raised that human loving and forgiving is inevitably flawed. How can we be sure of unconditional love and forgiveness unless our relationship to God and God's to us is something more than the mutuality of human relations? There is force in this objection, but far less in the obstacles often raised against God's freedom to forgive. The question, How can we be sure that God forgives us? is no different for those who stand in faith from the question, How can we be sure Jesus forgives us? Faith starts from the discovery and conviction that he does. Love is always free to forgive and to bear the pain of the offense that needs forgiveness. To forego one's rights in retrospect out of love for the offender is what forgiveness is, whether human or divine. Too many theologians have imposed absurd limitations on God's freedom to forgive, as though God had problems which somehow Jesus did not face. But the love that forgives is on its own not enough to restore. Forgiveness has its own logic, it cannot be received by those who cannot or dare not recognize their offence. They need not only to see the truth about themselves but to accept the truth about themselves. That is not easy or even possible outside a relationship of trustworthy love, where the promise of restored relationship is given. It is only within such a relationship that the reality of sin emerges as something more deeply personal than the language of alienation and inauthentic existence can convey, however useful such language is in the analysis of the workings of sin. It is only where the promise of restored relationship – reconciliation, atonement – is given that we may dare to acknowledge the reality of sin. Thus faith sees in Jesus the true quality of human being, which itself discloses the truth about ourselves. But faith also receives from Jesus the promise of trustworthy love that makes it possible to accept that truth, however hard it is to bear, and so to be open to forgiveness. Where forgiveness is received, the stranglehold of the past is broken and a new future opens up.

But yet, the simple declaration of trustworthy love is not enough, and interpretations of Christ's atoning work which reduce it to such a declaration are inadequate, because the fruits of love and forgiveness cannot be fully enjoyed unless the power of sin is broken, whether it is at work in the individual or in society. The individual cannot be a person totally apart from society, and cannot be restored to wholeness apart from the restoration to wholeness of society. The reality of trustworthy love is itself confirmed through the gift of the power to defeat sin, in the individual and in the structures of society. These pages have concentrated mainly on how we can recognize the reality of this gift and appropriate it in terms of our perceptions of our world today. Unless the Christian doctrine of the atonement can embrace the individual and society, and not only promise the reality of love and forgiveness, but show how the power to overcome sin and demonic forces is in principle available to us, it must be inadequate and unable to offer hope to the world we live in. But it does embrace the solidarity of human life, offer the power of transforming it, and give grounds for hope, however incomplete or inadequate this attempt to convey the fact may be.

The life and cruel death of a Galilean holy man two thousand years ago is profoundly significant for our world today, which in terms of human conflict, frustration, fragmentation, guilt, and failure, may not after all be so very different from what it was before, however much our perceptions of the world outside ourselves may have changed.

THE HOLY SPIRIT AND INSPIRATION

John Muddiman

Charles Gore's essay 'The Holy Spirit and Inspiration' was central in the original *Lux Mundi*. He was the general editor of the volume and alone seems to have had a clear perception of its overall strategy, that is 'to put the Catholic faith in its right relation to modern intellectual and moral problems'.[1] It was his contribution that identified the most controversial issue of the day and encountered the most immediate resistance.[2] By modifying the notion of inspiration to allow critical inquiry in Old Testament studies, he steered Anglican Catholics away from that blind alley which was to lead the Roman Catholic church via the encyclical *Providentissimus Deus* of 1893 to the dead end of the anti-modernist purges. His reassurances that there was nothing to fear from biblical scholarship released the energies and confidence of a generation of Anglo-Catholic clergy for work in overseas mission and social action at home. In *Lux Mundi* he began the development of a 'free, biblical Catholicism', which within only a few decades was to become an unquestionably legitimate, if not the actually definitive, form of Anglicanism as such.

I

Gore's essay has been described as 'restrained, innocuous' and 'almost unreadable'.[3] Since the unreadable is not always carefully read, it may be useful to give a full summary, introducing some initial points of reservation but also indicating why it may still be worth reading. In three sections, Gore discusses 1) the work of the Spirit; 2) the traditional doctrine of the Spirit; and 3) the inspiration of scripture, particularly of the Old Testament. His main argument is thus contained in the structure of the essay itself. Instead of asking the circular and anachronistic question[4] 'What account does the Bible give of its own inspiration?' he asks 'What do we know of the Spirit (from experience, tradition and doctrinal formulation) so as rightly to conceive his role in scripture?' By re-ordering the question in this way, Gore was able to achieve two immediate objectives, to demonstrate firstly that 'the Religion of the Incarnation' as expounded in *Lux Mundi* was not at all a substitute for biblical revelation; and secondly that the flexibility needed to accommodate the in any case unavoidable challenge of current Old Testament criticism was theologically justifiable.

Regardless of its results, Gore's method is surely correct and permanently valid. The doctrine of scriptural inspiration should not be detached from the doctrine of the Spirit in the church and the world, upon which it is dependent. Nor should the doctrine of the Incarnation, with its special emphasis on personal revelation in Christ and the living tradition of the church, be allowed to become detached from the scriptural inheritance. And failure to follow this method inevitably opens an unbridgeable gulf between conservative and liberal forms of Christianity.

In the first section, Gore appeals to 'experience' as evidence for the work of the Spirit, but he warns that this must not be understood as something emotional or eccentric but as 'that wherein God touches man most nearly, most familiarly, in common life' (p.230). His primary concern is with 'normal' human experiences, particularly the consciousness of sin and the desire for fellowship with God, for without them the facts of the gospel, however well attested, would remain remote and 'lack the power to compel belief' (p.247). In passages like this, the thoroughly rational nature of Gore's approach is apparent, and we begin to sense his almost pathological fear of the 'irrational', – a fear which underlies his very selective characterisation of the work of the Spirit, and his lack of curiosity about the phenomena of prophecy and the poetic imagination – the very omissions which are likely to strike us as most obvious as we read his discussion again today.

The data for 'experience' used in this section is, somewhat surprisingly, the writings of the Fathers; and it is here also that we find a lengthy passage on the work of the Spirit in the life of Jesus (pp.234-5). Clearly, for Gore there is no tension between experience and history, indeed history is the best sourcebook for experience; and the human life of Jesus is the perfect paradigm for the Spirit's work in human nature. Nor does he feel any threat at all to orthodox christology from this direction,[5] for he is describing only the human nature of Christ, and not his divine nature. In other words, the Spirit effects the gradual preparation of what Christ 'used'; it is not involved in what he 'revealed' (p.264). This distinction between final revelation through the Incarnation and gradual revelation through the Spirit is a recurring motif in the essay. It is also the point at which today we begin to feel distinctly uncomfortable with Gore's argument. For the way he speaks of Jesus' divine and human natures appears to keep them in sealed compartments; and one has to ask whether, on this account, the Incarnation involved any serious degree of risk on God's part, or any possibility that what it revealed could be misunderstood. We shall return to this problem a little later. It is only fair to note, however, that, at the time, the effect of Gore's 'less wooden and less purely conceptual'[6] treatment of Jesus' humanity was entirely positive. By associating the life of Jesus with the work of the Holy Spirit in human nature, English theology was able to avoid that sudden, and for the most part destructive, retreat from the historical Jesus which was to become typical of German theology in the twentieth century.

The next step is to identify four characteristics of the work of the Spirit in the church. First, that it is *social*. The redeemed humanity in Christ is a society, the church, bound together by the sacraments as social ceremonies, preserved through time by an apostolic succession of ministers and preserved in the truth, again by a social instrument, the common apostolic tradition embodied in scripture and perpetuated by the teaching church.

Second, and conversely the Spirit *nourishes individuality*. On this characteristic Gore spreads himself a little, possibly because neglect of the rights of the individual leads to 'the Romanist system of proscribing free inquiry and making appeal to antiquity to test the present teaching of the church a "treason and a heresy" ' (p.279). Against this, the 'developed Christian' can claim the right use his own judgement (1 Cor. 2:15) for the benefit of the community as a whole. It is, therefore, possible for freedom to coexist with the exercise of ecclesiastical authority, as long as the latter is properly understood as having an educative function, its aim being to school the values of undeveloped Christians until their judgement becomes enlightened and independent. And there is a special role for gifted individuals in bringing about reform in the church, by 'reverting to type', by recalling the church to the original apostolic teaching.

Third, the Spirit *consecrates the whole of nature*. The Spirit does not annihilate, but perfects nature. Thus, the Montanist (and pagan) notion of inspiration as ecstasy, and any kind of Gnostic dualism are to be rejected, and also, by implication, any doctrine of scripture which bypasses the natural attributes of its human authors.

Fourth, the Spirit's method is to work *by gradualness*. Gore cites the Old Testament as a prime example: the developmental understanding of Old Testament revelation is, he says, self-evident to 'modern Christians' but we need to be reminded that it is also a thoroughly traditional view, receiving venerable support from the Cappadocians and John Chrysostom. Another example of the gradual operation of the Spirit is the church itself. Against perfectionists who claim that ordinary Christians are 'vulgar, ignorant, imperfect, sinful', the church replied that 'what she represented was a hope, not a realization; a tendency, not a result; a life in process, not a ripened fruit' (p.242). This latter example makes it clear that Gore is not using 'gradualness' in a simplistic way to denote the idea of progressive revelation. The history of the church, no less than the chronology of the Old Testament documents, shows that earlier insights can be obscured and distorted by later developments. The gradualness of the Spirit's work belongs, rather, to its function of co-operation with nature.

However, there is one important exception to this rule: 'It is the essence of the New Testament as the religion of the Incarnation to be final and catholic' just as 'it is of the essence of the Old Testament to be imperfect and gradual' (p.240). Because of this statement, Gore is often accused of failing to carry through his own best insight, and of trying to erect a dogmatic barrier to protect the New Testament at least from the ravages of critical enquiry. There is some truth in the accusation, but it requires qualification. Certainly, Gore failed to anticipate the extent to which tradition-historical methods were going to prove applicable to the New Testament. He also turned a blind eye to evidence of its 'gradualness' which must already have been apparent to him. Do the gospels, in the order of their composition, not imply gradual movement and the deepening of theological understanding? Does comparison between the earlier and later epistles of Paul not imply the same in the case of one individual? If Gore had wanted, he could have turned such points to his own advantage. For scholarship has often assumed gradualness in the opposite direction, and read the New Testament as a chronicle of decline from pure vision to clouded compromise; but it is precisely in the interests of a Catholic understanding of the New Testament to argue that this is not invariably the case, and that sometimes later means better. And it would have been perfectly logical for Gore to claim the finality of Christian revelation, and yet be willing to admit that the New Testament reflects the gradual growth in understanding of that revelation in the post-Easter church.

The reasons for Gore's inhibitions in this area only become clear in a later section. The New Testament is true, he claims, not so much because of its inspiration – that is merely an additional guarantee – but because it was written by Apostles or their assistants who had had the benefit of 'prolonged training' from the Lord: and 'If Jesus Christ both was, and knew Himself to be, the Revealer of the Father, it almost stands to reason that He must have secured that His revelation should be, without material alloy, communicated to the church' (p.254). This argument is clearly based on a rational and dogmatic *a priori*. Gore does not trouble himself to deal even with the obvious objections to it: why, in that case, are the disciples portrayed in the gospels as such poor trainees (and indeed why was Judas Iscariot selected at all!); where does this leave Paul, who did not have the advantage of prolonged training; and what if the traditional attributions of the gospels are incorrect, and so forth? Even more seriously, on his own terms, Gore fails to ask why the Third Person of the Trinity should be content to co-operate with limited and fallible human nature, whereas the Second Person must have 'secured' the truth of his revelation, free of any 'material alloy'.[7]

Nevertheless, the customary accusation of dogmatism requires some qualification. For Gore does allow a possible way of verifying the truth of the New Testament, namely by examining 'the unity of testimony' among its various writers, and especially their testimony to the doctrine of Christ (p.255). And it is important here to recall the context in which Gore was writing. Nineteenth-century theology had already encountered in the Tübingen school the most thoroughly and dogmatically developmental interpretation of the New Testament conceivable;[8] and against that assault, the Cambridge scholars, Westcott, Lightfoot and Hort, had already demonstrated, to Gore's satisfaction, that the principles of historical enquiry could be used to substantiate the reliability of the New Testament record and the originality of its apostolic ministry and sacraments.[9] His conservatism on the New Testament was, therefore, to a considerable extent, *a posteriori*; and academic integrity demanded that the same critical principles which had so successfully vindicated the New Testament be employed also in Old Testament studies.

The second section of Gore's essay is no more than a brief outline of the classic doctrine of the personality and divinity of the Spirit, in relation to Incarnation and Trinity. He quickly presses on to apply his understanding of the work of the Spirit to the problem of scriptural inspiration.

He begins this task in the third section by noting as a commonplace that 'the scriptures have suffered greatly from being isolated' (p.247). The isolation he has in mind is that caused by the separation of history and experience, by treating scripture *either* as the record of historical revelation *or* as inspiring, revelatory address to the individual. He proposes to end this false dichotomy by appeal to the corporate nature of Christian faith. We should not know what to make of the New Testament as historical record, he remarks, 'if it were simply contained in some old manuscripts' or had been recently 'unearthed out of the Syrian sand'. Without the continuous life of the church, mediating the essential facts summarised in the creed and placing them in context as parts of an intelligible universe of faith, there would be no revelation in the New Testament. But equally, when anyone approaches the New Testament as inspiring personal address, he needs to be sure that he is not doing 'an eccentric, abnormal thing' but something which belongs to 'the best and richest movement of humanity' and produces 'the strongest, most lasting, most catholic sort of human character'. And again, it is the continuous life of the church that alone can deliver such assurances. This passage (pp.247f.) is a rather impressive anticipation on Gore's part of the course of twentieth-century debate on the hermeneutical problem, steering its way through salvation-history and existentialism and ending up with the church.

He goes on, furthermore, to make some acute observations on the corporate nature of the New Testament documents, which deserve to be remembered, since they would also receive endorsement from subsequent scholarship. Thus, 'The apostolic writings were written as occasion required, within the church, and for the church. They presuppose membership in it and familiarity with its tradition. They are secondary, not primary, instructors; for edification, not for initiation' (p.248). So, the New Testament was written – as we should learn to say, later – 'from faith to faith'. Or again, 'Nor, in fact, can a hard and fast line be drawn between what lies within and without the canon.' It was the church that defined the boundaries of the canon.[10]

Having shown that scripture, whether as record of history or as direct address from the Spirit, cannot be separated from the church, the argument proceeds in six theses:

1. Belief in the inspiration of scripture arises out of Christian faith; it is not its basis.

2. Nevertheless, the fact of inspiration is the *communis sensus* of the church.

3. The exact meaning of inspiration , however, is to be discovered by examining the different biblical writings themselves. For their inspiration varies both in degree and kind.

4. This recognition does not diminish the equal authority of differently inspired works for practical purposes.

5. The Old Testament contains occasional errors of fact, pseud-onymous writings and elements of myth, which are not incompatible with belief in its inspiration.

6. The church is not prevented, either by an existing definition of inspiration, or by anything Jesus said, from admitting the critical study of the Old Testament.

By sharpening the points in this way, we can perhaps more easily appreciate how well the argument hangs together. The theses are in pairs, on the fact of inspiration, its meaning and its relevance to Old Testament criticism respectively, with an appeal to reason in each case followed and balanced by an appeal to tradition. Just as the thesis that inspiration is not a basic doctrine (1), does not involve the denial, that it properly belongs to Christian faith (2); so also the thesis that inspiration varies (3) does not imply the denial that every part of scripture is equally inspired and useful in practice (4). Reference to the examples Gore uses in developing points (3) and (4) helps to elucidate them. The inspiration of a prophet is 'direct, continuous and absorbing', while that, say, of Ecclesiastes is quite different, expressing itself in tortuous, faltering exploration. There is variation in the degree of inspiration, because there are varieties of human media through which it operates. Gore seems to be saying, not that Ecclesiastes is less inspired than the prophets, but that inspiration could only take the form it did in him, if it were to avoid annihilating his human nature. This is why Gore can go on immediately to speak of differences in the kinds of literature which are inspired: poetry, history, philosophy, and of the particular aspect of certain books in which inspiration is to be located; for example, it is what differentiates the early chapters of Genesis from other ancient cosmogonies; it is the 'point of view' from which the histories are written; it is 'those piercing, lightning-like gleams of strange, spiritual truth' in the Psalms and so forth. In the New Testament also, inspiration takes different forms. 'In St John's gospel, for example, we have an account of our Lord which has obviously passed through the medium of a most remarkable personality.' In the case of Luke's writings, on the other hand, inspiration consists, as its prologue indicates, chiefly in careful investigation.[11]

Since the Spirit always co-operates with human nature and does not override it, there are bound to be such differences between the inspired books of the Bible, but 'every inspired scripture is profitable for teaching, reproof, correction and instruction in righteousness.' Only at this point does Gore allow 2 Tim. 3:16 into his discussion. For practical purposes there is an equality of inspiration, and 'We are to put ourselves to school with each in turn of the inspired writings.' The 'ecclesiastically disposed' should read Romans; those who 'most value the freedom of the gospel' should read the Corinthians, the Pastorals and James. Even material like the imprecatory Psalms have their own special value, when they are understood to reflect the stages of spiritual education through which every believer has to pass in practice in order to be brought to perfection. It is not the case, therefore, that Gore's theory of varied inspiration depreciates certain writings or sets up a 'canon within the canon'.

To the findings of current Old Testament criticism, Gore makes some mild concessions: despite the general atmosphere of truthfulness and even self-deprecation in Israel's literature, there are the odd 'narrative idealisms'; certain works like The Song of Songs, Deuteronomy, Jonah or Daniel may be 'dramatic compositions'; and one might legitimately use the word 'myth' to describe 'the earliest mode in which the mind of man apprehended the truth' in the time before Abraham (p.262). For all the delicacy with which he expresses them, Gore was well aware that the impact of his comments, in the context of 1889, would be considerable. The first Principal of Pusey House had betrayed Pusey, and switched allegiance to Wellhausen and Driver.[12] As Gore, soothingly but not without a touch of historical irony, puts it: 'We are being asked to make...no greater changes than were involved in the acceptance of the heliocentric astronomy'(p.261).

In his final thesis, Gore claims that neither the church nor her Founder forbids free critical inquiry. For the church has never officially defined the meaning of inspiration, and has in fact allowed several different schools of Old Testament interpretation to flourish, some more allegorical and some more literal. Nor do the words of Jesus foreclose certain critical positions, like the historicity of Jonah's whale or Noah's flood or the Davidic authorship of Psalm 110. If the Lord had wanted to convey instructions on such technical matters, which do not affect his fulfilment of these types and prophecies, he would have made his purpose plainer. And there is nothing to indicate that Jesus was 'departing from the general method of the Incarnation, by bringing to bear the unveiled omniscience of the Godhead to anticipate or foreclose a development of natural knowledge' (p.265).

With a final appeal for free and frank discussion, and for the legitimacy of more than one school of opinion on certain questions of exegesis, Gore the pastor and missionary ends on an optimistic note: historical criticism of the Old Testament is 'removing obstacles from the path to belief of many who want to believe and do not exhibit any undue scepticism' and 'will ultimately not diminish but enrich our reverence for its inspiration' (p.266).

II

The second half of this essay ought by rights to provide a constructive statement on biblical inspiration, based on the preceding analysis of Gore's article in *Lux Mundi*. It should take account of all significant developments since, and offer a word in season to Anglican Theology today. But in fact, the following pages will, more modestly, try to explain why such an undertaking is extraordinarily difficult, why it is nonetheless urgently needed and why it would probably be premature to attempt it.

It has often been pointed out that the term 'inspiration' is not itself scriptural; the closest approximation to it is the reference at 2 Tim. 3:16 to the Old Testament (or at least certain books of it) as 'God-breathed'. Despite this and other good reasons for avoiding the term, it is nevertheless the conventional way of expressing the claim that scripture in some sense results from the activity of God. An alternative way of making the same claim – and one more popular in liturgy and devotion – is to call the Bible 'the Word of God'. But since this phrase is also used to refer to the Person of Christ, and to the transcendent action of God in creation and revelation, and since it is more appropriate to prophecy and law than to other biblical genres, it is even less helpful.

'Scriptural inspiration' is a very broad concept, including several different elements. It is used (a) to guarantee the truth and accuracy of the contents of the Bible; (b) to justify the supreme authority of the canon over everything outside it; and (c) to point to certain features of the biblical literature claimed as unique and distinctive, whether the intensity of its religious experience, the depth of its theological insight, or the artistic power of its imagery. But broad as it is, the concept is not broad enough; for (a) cannot be discussed without considering the methods and results of historical criticism and comparing them with the philosophical presuppositions, apologetics and hidden theological agenda[13] of Fundamentalism; similarly (b) is only one of a whole set of issues concerning the structures of authority in the church, the function of the liturgy and the history of interpretation; and the features listed in (c) draw their criteria from disciplines as widely spread as the psychology of religion, systematic theology, and literary theory. Thus, the question of inspiration quickly reduces into discussion of one or other of its components, or else expands to embrace other departments of theology and church life.

Another peculiarity which makes our subject unwieldy is that it is both a highly reactive and at the same time astonishingly static field of theological interest. Since the topic of scriptural inspiration cannot be slotted neatly into one place in the theological syllabus, it fails to receive continuous attention and regular restatement from theologians. Indeed, it can lie hidden in obscurity for whole periods, eclipsed by other concepts that seem to cover the same area but with sharper definition, such as historical revelation, the authority of scripture, biblical theology, hermeneutics or the use of the Bible. However, it is also liable suddenly to be revived, if inadequacies begin to be detected in the prevailing alternatives, or sufficient popular demand builds up in the church.[14] So, inspiration is not a bare fact but a whole cluster of different meanings, and while many theologians prefer not to use the term except by default or in emergencies, Christian believers continue to assume some position or other on the question, as they need to for the purposes of private devotion, public liturgy and the making of moral and pastoral decisions.

In the late nineteenth century, as we have seen, it was possible to take a very different view. Gore drew a distinction between the commonly agreed *fact* of inspiration and its as yet undefined *meaning*. But scriptural inspiration is just not the sort of fact that can be agreed without having some prior notion of its meaning and consequences. He also thought he had detected a kind of 'providential vacuum' in the church's teaching on the subject, waiting unoccupied until such time as 'the state of knowledge admitted of the question being legitimately raised' (p.263) – a convenient, if rather limited space, into which moderate critical scholarship could fit without disturbing the structure of traditional faith. Even at the time, this argument was somewhat pedantic: that the church had not defined its position on inspiration was only true on an Anglo-Catholic definition of the church which chose to ignore the churches of the Reformation and post-Tridentine Catholicism; and the ancient church had not defined the inspiration of the Bible chiefly because, from the time of Marcion onwards, it was simply not in dispute.

In the more limited case of the Church of England, it is true that there is an odd reticence in her historic formularies on the doctrine of scripture. The Articles assert that 'Holy scripture containeth all things necessary to salvation' (VI) and that 'both in the Old and New Testaments everlasting life is offered to Mankind by Christ' (VII) but they do not explain how scripture as sourcebook for doctrine is related to scripture (both Testaments) as offer of salvation. Some Anglican scholars continue to claim this reticence as either a happy accident,[15] or as the result of deliberate policy.[16] But the course of Anglicanism in the twentieth century makes these views difficult to sustain. There never has been a doctrinal vacuum, not even in the Church of England: the absence of official definition has simply allowed many different understandings of inspiration to run on and to jockey for position, from the most rigid to the most tenuous. At the official level, as a result, there have been sudden changes of emphasis. Thus, at Lambeth 1948 a concept of 'dispersed authority' was explicitly defended, with scripture as one element among 'many which combine, interact with and check each other'.[17] At Lambeth 1958, by contrast, scriptural supremacy, as understood by the Biblical Theology movement, was reasserted.[18] The awareness that Anglicanism is weak in this area has gradually dawned in the context of ecumenical dialogue. Theologians representing the Communion expound their own personal views with sincerity and conviction, but are quite unable to appeal to any consensus in the church they represent.[19] Similarly, recent reports to the General Synod of the Church of England on controversial ethical questions handle the biblical material but in different ways, and they are uncertain both about the weight it should be given and about the way arguments based upon it will be received by their readers.[20] Only on a view of the church which sees it as little more than the means of transmitting a symbol system, which individuals are at liberty to appropriate as they see fit, can official Anglican vagueness on the doctrine of scripture be considered anything other than a defect.

Even the much acclaimed advantage of official reticence on biblical inspiration, that it has allowed Anglican biblical and theological scholarship to flourish without interference from church authority and in a genuine atmosphere of mutual respect and co-operation, is becoming a liability. As Professor Adrian Hastings has recently commented: 'The Church of England is particularly vulnerable to collapse due to intellectual bankruptcy just because – far more than most – it has long been a thinking Church.' [21]

What we have been calling the 'providential vacuum' approach to the rise of historical criticism has proved to be unsatisfactory. It has led to a false hope in the church that critical scholarship can be kept within tolerable limits; and when it goes beyond these limits, as it periodically does, to impinge on some aspect of traditional faith or practice, it can drive even Catholic Anglicans back into their own form of Fundamentalism.[22] It has also tempted biblical scholars into thinking that inspiration was outside their province; and this has left them without a base of continuous research and reflection to work from, when the question is raised again.

A quite different approach, rather more like that of *Essays Catholic and Critical* of 1926 than *Lux Mundi,* would understand criticism and catholic faith as distinct but mutually inter-active dimensions of the same reality.[23] Critical scholarship, by its very nature, is autonomous; its findings cannot be controlled by external authority. But this is not to say that it is uncontrollable; the views of one scholar are held in check by the criticism and alternatives put forward by another. On the other hand, Christian faith is not required to wait patiently upon the outcome of long-drawn out and self-correcting critical debates. It is already in possession of the legacy on which such debates feed. As the living faith of a whole community, it is entitled to express itself uninhibitedly, here and now; and to fail to do so would be an abdication of its practical responsibilities. Although faith and criticism are both autonomous, they interact. Well founded criticism gradually changes the corporate consensus among believers; and faith proposes to critical scholarship the particular issues that are most worth discussing.

Anglicanism is only just awakening to the fact that it needs an articulated doctrine of scripture. Without this, it will continue to be harassed and frightened into immobility by facile appeals to the Bible.

It might prefer to let sleeping dogs lie, but when they are already up, and barking 'biblical morality' to prevent the development of a workable and compassionate sexual ethic, or 'biblical revelation' to prevent the entry of women to the ordained ministry, or 'biblical supremacy' to prevent ecumenical rapprochement with Roman Catholics, it has no alternative but to pronounce. And the issues which require clarification are precisely those which form the components of the idea of inspiration listed earlier.

Anglican biblical scholars are also just waking up to the fact that they cannot ignore the question of inspiration for very much longer: it is a piece of unfinished business. The direct line of theological development from Gore led, as is well known, to the Liberal Catholicism of Hoskyns and Temple,[24] and thereafter to figures like A.M. Ramsey and Alan Richardson. In alliance with the Biblical Theology movement, it emphasised revelation in history to which scripture bears witness – inspired witness, certainly, but there was a distinct reluctance to examine inspiration at all closely for fear of masking the immediacy of saving event with a layer of human subjectivity. On the fringes of this development, however, there are perhaps two major critical attempts to render the notion of inspiration comprehensible which deserve mention. The classic treatment by William Sanday in his Bampton Lectures for 1893,[25] has led many Anglican theologians, liberal Evangelicals and others, down to the present[26] to reject the verbal, mechanical and propositional under-standing of inspiration, and to insist instead on the personal nature of the encounter between the Spirit of God and the minds of the biblical writers, with the prophetic experience as the typical and defining case. This view succeeds in making inspiration a credible phenomenon; but it leaves many questions unanswered; what is the resulting status of the majority of the biblical material which does not recount direct personal experience of God; what are the criteria of authenticity for this experience; and how much of this view survives historical analysis of the prophetic role, or redactional analysis of prophetic tradition.

A.M. Farrer's Bampton Lectures of 1948[27] were a conscious reaction to the prophetic, personalist model. He also tried to give a credible account of inspiration. But, rejecting on philosophical grounds the notion of unmediated knowledge of God through 'an inward colloquy', he proposed instead a poetic-textual model, arguing that the 'stuff of inspiration' is living images existing in the minds of the sacred writers, as they write, 'with their pens in their hands'.[28] With one or two exceptions[29] Farrer's approach did not command much support. As with the earlier model, it seemed to illuminate only one part of the problem, and to depend essentially upon the plausibility of the particular case-studies (Mark's Gospel and Revelation) in which he expounded it.

The differences between these two models of inspiration not only remain unreconciled; they represent tendencies which currently threaten to fly off in opposite directions. The latest fashions in biblical scholarship, the sociological approach[30] and the new literary critical approach[31] are quite prepared to discuss the phenomenon of inspiration, but in a reductionist way, without any concern for the question of the truth of what is inspired. Sociologists of the New Testament portray a first century Christian charismatic sect and analyse the social function of its inspired speech. New literary critics treat scripture as an artistic creation, whose inspiration i.e. poetic, rhetorical and narrative power, may be appreciated by any modern reader quite apart from the beliefs of the community that produced it or the intention of the authors who wrote it. These movements have almost nothing in common; and in this situation, the coherence of biblical criticism as a theological discipline is at stake, unless the question of inspiration is reopened.

We have warned of impending crisis on two fronts, both within Anglicanism and within biblical scholarship. We can do no more, in the space that remains, than list some points for discussion in any future debate. By way of counterbalance to Gore's preoccupation with the Old Testament, we shall pay particular attention to the question of the Spirit and inspiration of the New Testament.

1. The proper theological method, as outlined by Gore, is to move from the work and doctrine of the Spirit to an understanding of the inspiration of scripture. But the list of characteristics he identified - that the Spirit is social, nourishes individuality, consecrates nature and proceeds by gradualness – is highly selective and excessively 'rational'.

2. In the New Testament, the Spirit is more than an impersonal endowment, or enhancement of natural human qualities. He is the Spirit of the Risen christ who is the Last Adam (1 Cor. 15:45); he remains with Jesus throughout his ministry (John 1:32) and is the form of his abiding presence in the church (John 14:16-17), the guarantor of faithful remembrance and witness (John 14:26,15:27). When the Spirit is understood in this way, as the link between the earthly Jesus and the risen Christ, we may begin to explain why inspiration, in the sense in which it applies uniquely to scripture, ceases with the New Testament.

3. In the New Testament, the Spirit is also understood distinctively as the foretaste and assurance of the approaching end (e.g. 2 Cor. 5:5). The pressing imminence of eschatological hope is the main feature that distinguishes canonical from post-canonical literature. Despite what must have been a strong temptation to abandon hope when it failed to materialise and to rewrite its foundation documents (witness second century Gnosticism), Christianity, nevertheless, insisted on retaining its

original vision. It did this by lowering the status of the interim period, the post-apostolic church, and marking off the time of the first generation with a 'scriptural boundary'. If the Spirit who inspires scripture is understood eschatologically, we may be able to offer another reason why uniquely inspired scripture ceases with the New Testament.

4. Recognition of the eschatological character of the Spirit also helps to solve a problem we found in Gore's treatment, the distinction between gradual and final revelation, between the Old Testament and the New. The effect of this was to make the inspiration of the New Testament almost redundant, merely an additional support for the unalloyed direct communication of truth from Jesus to his well trained Apostles. Understanding the Spirit eschatologically, we may be able to say how scriptural revelation can be both final and at the same time gradual and still unfolding. For 'finality' would then be thought of as essentially 'proleptic', the anticipation of a future hope. Alongside the strong notion of God's perfect self-revelation in the life, death and resurrection of his Son, the early church retained the dimension of openness to God's future. Thus Paul could write, 'Now I know only in part, then I shall know even as I am known!' (1 Cor. 13:12); and the author of 1 John, similarly: 'It does not yet appear what we shall be, but we know that when he appears we shall be like him' (1 John 3:2).

5. The variety and diversity of the Spirit's operation (1 Cor 12:4-6) imply that inspiration is going to mean different things in the case of different scriptural genres and authors. The attempt to define inspiration in only one way or in one typical way is therefore bound to fail. In the New Testament, for instance, there are several kinds of epistles (communal, personal, pseudepigraphical, homiletic etc.) and more than one type of gospel; and in each inspiration will need to be evaluated differently.

6. Both the prophetic-personal model and the poetic-textual model can throw light on some of the processes of inspiration, and make them more comprehensible by analogy with mystical experience and artistic creativity respectively. However, such models are appropriate only to a proportion of the biblical material; they also tend to concentrate too much on the individual. But the Holy Spirit, as distinct from religious or literary genius, stands for the idea of personality-transcending individuality, the corporate activity of God creating a community of faith, worship and service. As the most recent report of the Church of England Doctrine Commission expresses it: 'It can never have been true to the nature of Scripture to regard it solely as the medium through which a succession of uniquely inspired writers has conveyed the truth about God

to later generations...Scripture is also, and perhaps chiefly, the distillation of those perceptions of the reality of God which came to a...community.'[32]

7. Since much of the Bible consists of historical narrative, which cannot be translated without loss of its essential character, into terms of personal encounter or poetic imagery, inspiration here must take a peculiarly narrative and historical form. And while this cannot be expressed as inerrancy, we need to discuss what would be involved in claiming biblical indefectibility, especially – for the Christian church – in the case of the gospels.

8. Finally, in face of all the complexities surrounding the formulation of a doctrine of scriptural inspiration, there is an understandable tendency in modern theology to locate inspiration in the reader, rather than in the original experience, intention or text of the writer. This tendency is fed from several different sources, theological objections to apologetics, philosophical attacks on the alleged idealism of the historical-critical method, and reader-response theory in literary criticism.[33] Although problems attend each of these sources, the activity of the Spirit in the production of scripture cannot ultimately be detached from the activity of the Spirit in inspiring its reception. But the proof that the Spirit is present and active in this way is to be found, not in idiosyncratic or esoteric interpretations of scripture, but in the responses of obedience and faith; for the chief work of the Spirit who caused scripture to be written is the inspiration of prayer (Rom. 8:26f.) and good works (Gal. 5:22f.).

Notes

1. Preface p.vii; all references are to the 15th edition,1890.
2. See D.G. Rowell, *The Vision Glorious* (Oxford 1983), ch. X.
3. A. Richardson, *The Bible in the Age of Science* (London 1961), p.66.
4. See J. Barr, *Holy Scripture* (Oxford 1983), p.14 and *passim*.
5. Contrast G.W.H. Lampe, *God as Spirit* (Oxford 1977).
6. J.L. Houlden, *Connections* (London 1986), p.112.
7. Contrast the eloquent comments of A.E. Harvey in *Believing in the Church*, The Doctrine Commission of the Church of England (London 1981), p.36, 'If scripture is "inspired", it is inspired by the same God who accepted the constraints of the incarnation. It is not invested with an other-worldly, totally self-authenticating power; as with the incarnation itself, its uniqueness and authority can be glimpsed only through the limitations imposed upon it...'
8. See p.265, 'We shall probably be bidden to remember Tubingen.'
9. Cf. preface to the 10th edition, p.xvii.
10. Gore illustrates with the example of Hebrews and I Clement, and his incisive, if somewhat polemical, remarks are worth recalling. Since the line between them was drawn by the church, 'how irrational' is the attitude of a certain kind of unecclesiastical Protestantism, 'to interpret Clement in a sense hostile to Hebrews, which represents

exactly the same stream of apostolic tradition only one short stage lower down. For Clement interprets the high priesthood of Christ in a sense which, instead of excluding, makes it the basis of, the ministerial hierarchy of the Church' (p.249).

11. Compare A. Plummer, *A Critical and Exegetical Commentary on the Gospel according to S. Luke* (Edinburgh 1896), p.5. And on Gore's influence on Plummer, see J. Muddiman, 'Alfred Plummer - New Testament Commentator' in R. Boudens, *Alfred Plummer - Conversations with Dr Döllinger 1870-1890* (BETL LXVII) (Leuven 1985), p.xliii.

12. See John Rogerson, *Old Testament Criticism in the Nineteenth Century: England and Germany* (London 1984), chs. 17 & 20.

13. See J. Barr, *Fundamentalism* (London 1978).

14. A.E. Harvey, *op. cit.* (n.7) p.36, writes: 'The Christian will certainly continue to feel that there is some inherent quality or power in the Bible...which gives it unique authority for him, and he will encourage theologians in their efforts to achieve an adequate and intelligible formulation of it.' Evidently, contemporary Anglican theologians do not yet feel sufficiently 'encouraged' to have done anything about it, but for recent responses to this demand in the USA from Roman Catholic, Lutheran and Methodist theologians, see respectively: B. Vawter, *Biblical Inspiration* (London 1972); P. Achtemeier, *The Inspiration of Scripture: Problems and Proposals* (Philadelphia 1980); and W.J Abraham, *The Divine Inspiration of Holy Scripture* (Oxford 1981). For an Anglican example from an earlier period, see J. Burnaby, *Is the Bible Inspired?* (London 1949).

15. Thus, R.H. Fuller, in his excellent contribution, 'The Authority of Scripture in Anglicanism', to *Lutheran-Episcopal Dialogue: Report and Recommendations* (Cincinnati 1983), p.93: 'There was cause to be thankful that it [the Anglican Church] was never committed to a definition of the nature of inspiration...the way was left open for the acceptance of critical methods in the latter part of the 19th century.'

16. Thus, D.E. Nineham, in 'Wherein lies the Authority of the Bible?' in L. Hodgson, ed., *On the Authority of the Bible* (London 1960) reprinted in his *Explorations in Theology* I (London 1977), p.68: 'In so far as it [The report of the Lambeth Conference of 1958] constituted an attempt to bring this matter within the sphere of dogmatic definition, it was undoubtedly something of a novelty, so far as the Church of England is concerned.'

17. See R.H. Fuller, *op.cit.* (n.15), pp.102, 105.

18. Comparison of the Church of England Doctrine Commission reports of 1976 (*Christian Believing*) and 1981 (*Believing in the Church*) reveals an even more dramatic change of direction.

19. See *Towards a Church of England Response to BEM and ARCIC* (London 1985), which rejects the accusation, presumably from Anglican conservative evangelicals, that the ARCIC Final Report fails to give a good account of the primacy of scripture, but then lists a series of unanswered questions 'which in the future Anglicans and Roman Catholics will need to explore together'(p.82).

20. For further searching observations, see J. Barton 'The Place of the Bible in Moral Debate', *Theology* LXXXVIII (May 1985), pp.204-9.

21. A. Hastings, *A History of English Christianity*, 1920-1985 (London 1986), p.663. He illustrates his point thus: 'The theology of Gore, Temple, Ramsey or Farrer was most certainly one the Church could live and thrive with. The same cannot be said for that of Nineham, Hick, or Cupitt.'

22. As e.g. G. Leonard, 'The Ordination of Women: theological and biblical issues' in *Epworth Review* xi (January 1984), pp.42-9.

23. See further, J. Muddiman, *The Bible, Fountain and Well of Truth* (Oxford 1983), pp.6-18.

24. See A.M. Ramsey, *From Gore to Temple* (London 1960).

25. W. Sanday, *Inspiration* (London 1894), the Bampton Lectures for 1893.

26. E.g. C.F.D. Moule, *The Holy Spirit* (London 1978), pp.56-64.

27. Austin Farrer, *The Glass of Vision* (London 1948); see also his essays 'Inspiration Poetical and Divine' and 'On Looking Below the Surface' reprinted in *Interpretation and Belief* (London 1976).

28. *The Glass of Vision*, pp.7, 44, 54.

29. Most notably L.S. Thornton, *The Dominion of Christ* (London 1952), on whom see D.H. Kelsey, *The Uses of Scripture in Recent Theology* (London 1975), pp.57-64.

30. See e.g. B. Holmberg *Paul and Power* (Philadelphia 1980), ch.5; and more generally, W.A. Meeks, *The First Urban Christians* (New Haven 1983).

31. See the survey by N. Petersen, *Literary Criticism for New Testament Critics* (Philadelphia 1978); and R. Alter and F. Kermode, eds., *The Literary Guide to the Bible* (London 1987).

32. *We Believe in God*, The Doctrine Commission of the Church of England (London 1987), pp.53-4.

33. See, respectively: K. Barth, *Church Dogmatics* I/2, (Edinburgh 1956), pp.514-26; A. Louth, *Discerning the Mystery* (Oxford 1982), pp.29-43, 102f.; W. Iser, *The Act of Reading* (Baltimore 1978).

THE CHURCH

Peter Hinchliff

The ninth essay in *Lux Mundi*, the chapter on the church, was by Walter Lock. When the volume appeared he was a fellow of Magdalen and subwarden of the new Keble College where he had belonged to the original group of founding tutors. At 43 he was one of the older members of the 'Holy Party' and on the verge of a distinguished career in the university. Six years after the publication of *Lux Mundi* he was elected to the Dean Ireland chair which he combined, for nearly a quarter of a century, with the wardenship of Keble. He only relinquished the latter office after he became, in 1919, the Lady Margaret professor of divinity which carried with it a canonry at Christ Church. He was then already 73 but was not to retire for a further eight years. He died in 1933, not long after the death of Charles Gore himself.

Benjamin Jowett, master of Balliol and the grand old man of theological liberalism in Oxford, greeted the publication of *Lux Mundi* with the comment that it was the 'same old haze and maze' that High churchmen tended to indulge in, though more friendly than usual to the liberal point of view. 'The point on which the High church party tend to give way,' he added, 'is the Scripture and especially the Old Testament. They feel that as the Bible is seen more and more to be like any other book, the greater the need for the Church, an aspect of the question which is not displeasing to them.'[1] In retrospect, of course, it does not seem to require great acumen on Jowett's part to perceive this particular thrust in the argument of *Lux Mundi*. The Anglo-Catholic case was that the authority of the Bible depends upon the prior authority of the church. The church, after all, had taken over the Old Testament from Judaism and had created the New Testament out of its own tradition. Therefore the true authority behind Christian teaching is the authority of the church rather than the Bible. This point was made, repeatedly though not explicitly, in Lock's essay.

Jowett's comment, however, was rather more significant in 1889 than it might seem now. In the generation before *Lux Mundi* the great debate between the ecclesiastical parties, at least in the University of Oxford, had centred upon a question which was almost methodological. The question may be formulated as, 'How is one to arrive at the truth in matters of theology?'

The Tractarians adopted an essentially conservative approach on this issue. They were not, of course, uncritical of the university any more than they were uncritical of the Church of England or of its relationship with the state. Their great desire was to *restore* the ideal of the university as the handmaid of the church, an ideal expressed in theory in many of its regulations and practices but hardly a living reality. For them theology was to be taught on authority – the authority of the teacher, of the church which authorised him, of the Bible which enshrined the divine revelation, and so of God himself. Those of a more 'liberal' persuasion believed that theology ought to be a subject for rational enquiry. In other disciplines, after all, this was an age when the acquisition of right answers from authority had come to matter less. Truth – even truth about God – was what the mind arrived at after a critical, though often speculative, enquiry.[2]

The debate had been going on for a long time. The Oriel Noetics in the 1830s had argued whether doctrinal formulations possessed the same authority as the 'facts' of revelation and nature of which they were thought to be interpretations. Thomas Arnold had argued in *Principles of Church Reform* that theological issues, by their very nature, were open to a variety of interpretations because they, 'lying out of the reach of demonstrative science, are through the constitution of man's nature, peculiarly apt to be regarded by different minds differently'.[3] Baden Powell had come to devise a clever theory about the relationship between reason and revelation, maintaining that God had revealed only those truths which the unaided human mind would never be able to arrive at. Therefore if rational enquiry discovered some new truth about the origins of man, for instance, the statements of Genesis which it seemed to contradict had never been part of divine revelation.[4]

In the 1840s the reform of the university became the great issue. Closely linked with it was this other question of the nature of truth in theological matters. Benjamin Jowett and A.P. Stanley, then just beginning to be known as leading young liberals, published an anonymous pamphlet early in 1848 which argued that any projected reform of the university should include the creation of a school of theology.[5] They pleaded for a syllabus that would, in a phrase which Jowett was later to make notorious in *Essays and Reviews* and to which he harked back in his comment on *Lux Mundi*, treat the Bible 'like any other book'. Such an approach, they believed, would revitalise theology.

Pusey was determinedly against introducing theology as a purely academic study. He objected to any kind of critical approach to the Bible since that seemed to him to threaten its authority as the account of the divine revelation. But he objected also to treating the history of dogma as a subject for study because that would seem to imply that the faith had not been once and for all delivered to the saints.[6] This was an essentially static concept of theological truth – and particularly significant when one remembers that only a few years previously Newman, on ceasing to be an Anglican, had argued for a very different understanding of authority and truth in his *Essay on the Development of Doctrine*.

Throughout the 1860s and 1870s Pusey and Jowett continued their long struggle, taking opposing sides on virtually every religious issue which disturbed the university. Obstinate and terrifying though both could be in controversy[7] each came to shift his position somewhat on the subject of a school of theology. Pusey still regarded the 'heretical' Professor Jowett as a painful embarrassment foisted on to the university by an uncaring state.[8] But he was also aware that the liberals were losing ground in the university and he began to believe that it would be possible to ensure that teaching and examining was controlled by the orthodox. When Pusey started to argue in support of the creation of a theology school, however, it was Jowett's turn to argue that the discipline was too sacred a matter to examine undergraduates in.[9] When the school had been introduced, Jowett (by that time master of Balliol) appointed a theology tutor who would ensure that no Tractarian views were taught to his young men. He also continually snubbed the new tutor's attempts to draw attention to the fact that theology was taught at Balliol.[10]

Newman had been the leader of the earliest phase of the Oxford Movement almost in the sense of being its embodiment. Whether Pusey was ever, in that sort of sense, the leader of those who came popularly to be called 'Puseyites' has been a matter much debated. It is difficult, however, to escape the impression that it was his indomitable opposition, at least so far as Oxford was concerned, which held back the tide of new theological ideas. Descriptions of his funeral, the enormous procession of friends and admirers from all over England, speak of the devotion he had evoked from others and, by implication, of the authority he could exercise over them. 'The procession of clergy, five or six abreast, reached round three sides of the Great Quadrangle [of Christ Church].'[11] (If literally true this must mean that some three thousand priests were present.)

Once Pusey had gone, however, it was almost as if, with a sigh of relief, even those who had regarded him as their mentor and hero began to relax some of the rigid positions that he had imposed upon them. He died in the autumn of 1882 and his successor as professor of Hebrew, S.R. Driver, a critical but moderate scholar, met with little opposition and was very soon widely regarded as typifying moderate good sense. Almost at once the theology school for which Pusey had been largely responsible began to admit the thin end of the critical and historical wedge. In the early days of the school, the 1870s, the emphasis had been on a knowledge of the *subject matter* of the Old and New Testaments. Questions in the examination had been of a factual kind; about what *urim* and *thummim* were and how they were used; about the geography of Palestine; about the design and contents of Solomon's temple; even about 'The private life and arrangements of St Paul during his journeys'.[12] Apart from an occasional question which admitted doubt as to whether Paul had written the Epistle to the Hebrews, 'higher' critical questions were simply ignored, though candidates were sometimes asked to *controvert* the claims of the critics.

In that first decade of the school's existence the examiners were often chosen from among the ranks of the generally conservative non-resident clerical masters of arts who still exercised considerable power in the university and whose influence the reformers were anxious to limit. Many of them were Tractarian incumbents of parishes. Those examiners who were actually teachers in the university tended to be either language specialists or men like Rawlinson, the professor of Ancient History, who had delivered the Bampton Lectures of 1859 (the year of Darwin's *The Origin of Species*) in defence of the 'truth of the Scripture records'.

In the very year of Pusey's death, however, it is possible to detect a loosening of the 'orthodox' grip on the theology examination. One of the examiners was the eccentric but critical Old Testament scholar, T.K. Cheyne, and candidates were invited to discuss such daring topics as whether the fourth gospel and the apocalypse were by the same author.[13] Another question, asking candidates to defend the authenticity of the Pauline epistles, specifically excluded Hebrews and the Pastoral Epistles.[14] By early in the next decade the examination had come to reflect a much more radical outlook. In 1891 candidates were asked questions which required a knowledge of the various critical theories about the relationship between the synoptic gospels.[15] A question was also asked which seems to assume familiarity with F.C. Baur's views about the Acts of the Apostles.[16] It is significant that in that year one of the examiners was J.O. Johnston, the principal of Cuddesdon. Johnston had been one of Liddon's assistants in the work of preparing the life of Pusey and was himself subsequently to be Liddon's biographer.

Liddon died in 1890, the year after the publication of *Lux Mundi*. Although the mantle of Pusey had fallen upon him after 1882 and he had done his best to exert the same conservative influence as his master, he had never been so powerful or so effective. He had tried, when *Lux Mundi* appeared, to destroy Gore's moderately critical approach to the

Old Testament[17] by virtually repeating the argument he had used against Bishop Colenso in his Bampton Lectures of more than twenty years earlier.[18] In both cases he took the line which had, perhaps, originally been forced upon him by Pusey himself[19] that either our Lord was free from all human ignorance and error or he was not divine. But times had changed. In the 1860s every right-thinking Tractarian had found the argument convincing. In 1890 Gore, in spite of his reverence for Pusey and for Liddon himself, was simply not prepared to be bullied out of his position by the posing of what he regarded as a false dilemma.

For this change in Anglo-Catholic attitudes to critical scholarship *Lux Mundi* itself is often given the sole credit. Gore's own account of the aims of the contributors was quite clear. He told Mrs Illingworth that they wished 'to conciliate the claims of reason and revelation, and so to interpret the ancient Catholic Faith as not to lay an intolerable strain upon the free action of the intellect.'[20] And it is usual for this to be represented as a revolutionary breaking of new ground in sharp contrast with the views of the earlier Catholic figures.

> The older Tractarians had preferred dogmatic certainty to liberty of thinking, and their immediate disciples, of the type of Liddon, held tenaciously to the old lines of defence. Dr Gore...had come to realise that these lines could no longer be maintained.[21]

It may be, however, that the process was a more gradual one and not confined to members of the 'Holy Party' alone. Many younger Anglo-Catholics may possibly have been thinking along these lines. The fact that Johnston was able to approve such relatively radical examination papers by 1892 (for the examiners had to take collective responsibility for all the papers) suggests a more general change of view among Tractarians. And Gore himself was to maintain that he had become convinced as early as 1876 that a less than conservative view of the Old Testament was 'reconcilable' with the creeds.[22]

It seems to be widely held, indeed, that the early 1880s were precisely the time when a new and critical approach to biblical scholarship was becoming widely acceptable in the Church of England as a whole. Frederick Temple's Bampton Lectures on science and religion were delivered in 1884 and have been described by Owen Chadwick as making Darwin's evolutionary hypothesis respectable.[23] The following decade has been identified as the period when the 'scientific revolution' in the writing of history took place[24] and when the majority of scholars and a fair proportion of educated laity in each of the British churches accepted the general idea that a critical approach to the scriptures was not incompatible with faith.[25] Jowett himself had become vice-chancellor of Oxford almost as Pusey died and he does not seem to have found that theological issues at all disturbed his term of office. And there seems to have been a growing together of Tractarian and 'liberal' strands of scholarship. Jowett's description of *Lux Mundi* as 'more friendly' can be construed as recognising this. Even more significantly for one who had so disapproved of Tractarian theology in the 1870s, he felt able to urge a young Anglo-Catholic – Cosmo Gordon Lang – to become chaplain of Balliol in 1893.[26]

It may be, in other words, that Tractarians were not immune to the new attitude towards critical biblical scholarship and that the 'Holy Party' merely reflected a widespread change in thinking generally. There is certainly clear evidence that the climate of opinion had changed in Oxford itself since Pusey's death. Therefore *Lux Mundi* ought not to be seen as quite so independently revolutionary as the conventional account makes it appear. It may simply have been typical of the general liberalising of theological opinion.

But if, in this respect, one ought to revise the conventional account and treat *Lux Mundi* as being a less significant landmark than has been sometimes supposed, there is another and less obvious sense in which it set out to be an important contribution to thought. The contributors to the volume proposed to attempt their task of reconciling 'the free action of the intellect' with 'the ancient Catholic Faith' by making the Incarnation – the classic Christian statement of the ultimate relationship of the human to the divine – the key concept in the book. This was something which they were passionate about. 'The truth about our Lord's humanity,' Gore said, 'came to us with a fresh thrill of delight.'[27] And it was a kenotic understanding of the Incarnation which enabled them to experience this 'fresh thrill'. A school of thought which maintained the presence of the divine within the human, yet without in any way diminishing the reality of the human, might hope to reconcile the two ways of approaching theology which had divided Oxford since the 1840s, the Tractarian and the liberal. A kenotic approach would allow one to give due significance to human knowledge. A faithful adherence to the traditional belief in the divinity of Christ would allow one to attach a proper weight to authority. And it would not be surprising if the contributors to *Lux Mundi* believed they could justify a position which recognised the validity of human reason *and* maintained the divinely guaranteed truths of the catholic faith. Gore (the editor of the volume) and Scott Holland (the founder of the 'Holy Party') had, after all, both been pupils of Jowett's.[28]

But it also has to be said that the *Lux Mundi* group as a whole failed to make the most of their own creative theological theme. Gore's essay distinguished between the religious truth of scripture, which by implication he related to Christ's divine knowledge, and the unscientific and unhistorical content of Old Testament narratives which Christ, because of the limitations of his humanity, did not question. In this way he may be said to have used a kenotic understanding of the Incarnation as the basis for theological enquiry. But even he developed this theme most fully in his reply to Liddon's criticisms rather than in the essay itself. Apart from Gore's contribution, the point in the volume where the theme comes closest to the surface is at the beginning of Moberly's chapter on the Incarnation as the basis of dogma, where the contrast between speculative (i.e. liberal) and dogmatic theology is discussed. On the whole one is left with a feeling that, though they claimed that the Incarnation was central to all their theology, the contributors to the volume had not really built their theology upon that central doctrine.

A year or two after *Lux Mundi* Illingworth published a volume of sermons containing an address entitled 'The Incarnation of the Word' which reinforces this opinion. It begins with the exciting sentence, 'The Incarnation of our Lord has a bearing upon the problems of science and philosophy, the history of matter, and the history of mind, as well as upon the personal hopes of the individual soul.'[29] But the sermon does not really show how the Incarnation has this bearing. It becomes a sort of meditation upon the phrases of the prologue to the fourth gospel.

Lock's essay in *Lux Mundi* is disappointing in precisely the same way. Quite early in his chapter on the church, having argued that ideas can only survive within corporate societies and that knowledge of God had been revealed in the history of the people of Israel, he said:

> It must be from considerations such as these that we approach the foundation of the Christian church and the Incarnation of our Lord Jesus Christ on which it rests. We approach it with the expectation that we shall find these principles embodied in it, for Christianity sprang directly out of Judaism, and so would naturally inherit its principles: and to go deeper still, the very essence of the Incarnation lies in the consecration of human life and human means. He who before had been acting invisibly upon the world as the Word, implanting life and light in man, now entered visibly into human flesh. All tendencies which made for the fulness of life and truth before His coming, all that tended to enlighten, elevate, combine men, had been His unknown working: now they are known to be His. The Infinite appears in finite form; the spiritual takes the material in which to express itself; human media are consecrated to deeper ends, and charged with a fuller meaning than before: so that, in Hooker's words, 'We cannot now conceive how God should, without man, exercise Divine power or receive the glory of Divine praise.'[30]

It looks as if the main theme of Lock's chapter will be that the church reflects the Incarnation and must, therefore, be both a truly divine institution yet a genuinely human one. And it is true that he takes as the framework of the essay the three points which he believes were derived from the history of the Jewish nation and passed into the life of the church through the Incarnation – that the church is an organisation for spiritual life, a school for truth and the home of worship. Occasionally, as he works his way through these three points, he seems to pick up the idea enunciated so strongly at the beginning. When dealing with the sinfulness exhibited in the church, for instance, he argues that 'the ideal is never thought of [by St Paul] as something different from the real; the ideal is not simply in heaven nor the real simply on earth; the real is the ideal, though not yet completely developed; the ideal is the actual basis of the real as much as the goal to which the real is tending.'[31] And again 'The idea of an invisible Church to express the body of true believers, who alone are the Church, to whatever community they belong, so that the visible Church becomes an unimportant thing, is an idea entirely at variance with Scripture and all pre-reformation teaching.'[32]

One begins to believe that the theme of genuine humanity indissolubly linked, in spite of its weakness, with the truly divine, will develop into vigorous argument for a particular understanding of the church. This never quite happens. The essay is, for the most part, a very simplistic and jejune presentation of conventional, moderate Anglo-Catholic opinion. Indeed, almost the most important point in the first passage quoted above turns out to be the reference to Hooker. For the heart of the essay is a sustained assertion of the continuity of the Church of England with the church of the apostolic age. It begins in the section devoted to the church as a spiritual organisation, where this argument about the relationship of the real and the ideal belongs, and it goes on into the section on the church as a school for truth. In it Lock's summary of Irenaeus plays a crucial part:

> Truth is essentially a thing *received*; it was received by the Apostles from Christ. He *was* the truth Himself; He revealed it to His Apostles; they embodied it in their writings and handed it on to the Bishops and Presbyters who succeeded them; hence the test of truth is to be sought in Holy Scriptures and in the teaching of those churches which were founded directly by the Apostles.[33]

This is the point at which Lock, by implication at least, adopts the line which Jowett thought distinctive of the *Lux Mundi* position. By enhancing the teaching authority of the church one is able to protect oneself from the loss of certainty caused by the recognition that the Bible may be treated like other books. Moreover, Lock's emphasis upon the truth as something *received* puts him firmly in the Tractarian tradition of Pusey. Even though he claims simply to be summarising the teaching of Irenaeus, his own sympathies seem clear.

At least Lock has got Irenaeus right at a point where Catholic sympathies might have led him in another direction. He does not represent him as an exponent of a 'hands-on-heads' apostolic succession. It is the apostolic witness which guarantees the continuity of the church. The church is primarily a witness to the central truths ('the Fatherhood of God, the Person and work of Jesus Christ, the Redemption of all mankind, the origin and purpose of human life'.)[34] There are other truths which are open questions – a rather curious notion – and the test of truth is defined by Vincent of Lerins though not in the usual form but as prohibiting additions to catholic truth though permitting some element of 'development'.[35]   This simplistic view of the continuing church is repeated again and again in the essay. Christ founded the church by choosing his apostles; they appointed bishops; the Church of Rome has added the distorting 'test of communion with itself';[36] the reformers have 'rejected the whole principle of historic continuity'.[37] By implication only the Anglican church remains faithful.

It may be unfair to caricature Lock's essay in this way. He does recognise some of the difficulties faced by anyone who writes theologically about the church. He does make a passing reference or two to the fact that the events of history are capable of being interpreted in ways other than those he uses himself. But it is extremely difficult to avoid the feeling that he has evaded all the really crucial questions and, in doing so, has failed to meet his own challenge to present the church as the extension of the Incarnation, both human and divine.

Part of the explanation may be that Lock himself was simply not an exciting theologian. His writings are, in a sense, the more significant as they are less professional. His first professorship, the Dean Ireland, was a chair for the exegesis of scriptures. But Lock's work on scriptural exegesis, including commentaries on the pastoral epistles published in 1924, is now totally disregarded. His life of Keble is an attractive but hardly an objective historical account. His *Oxford Memories* which appeared in 1932 is a collection of brief, graceful thumbnail sketches spread over almost seventy years of Oxford's history. Some of the 'memories' were pieces he had written much earlier. Three of them are about members of the 'Holy Party' (Moore, Illingworth and Scott Holland). But none of them aims to convey factual information – they are about how the subjects seemed to the author – so they do not help in trying to understand the ideas behind *Lux Mundi*.

Illingworth himself once admitted that 'there is a tone of "fortyness" about *Lux Mundi* which has made it duller than I hoped.'[38] It is not entirely clear from the context what he meant by 'fortyness'. He may simply have meant that the volume displayed a more middle-aged mentality than he had hoped. But if he meant that the ideas expressed had not moved much beyond the 1840s, then Lock's essay certainly deserved the criticism. For all the notice he takes of the problem of authority, Lock might never have heard why Newman became a Roman Catholic in 1845 (the year before Lock himself was born). For Newman the problem had been that, though the Church of England could claim descent from the church of the apostles and though he and his friends could validate their teaching by appealing to apostolic authority, it came to seem that they were always looking to a dead past instead of to a living teaching authority.

One of Newman's biographers has paraphrased his doubts in these words – 'a Revelation from God given in history required a living authority in every age, guaranteed to keep it immune from error.'[39] And Wilfrid Ward's *Life* made the same point by saying that Newman, by his study of Augustine's controversy with the Donatists who claimed to be faithful to antiquity, had come to realise that 'the mere appeal to antiquity had been disallowed'.[40] Yet Lock's appeal is simply to the continuity of the church from the apostolic age to the Church of England of the late nineteenth century. It is the 'mere appeal to antiquity' all over again, with no attempt to say what constitutes the authority of a living church. Lock even mentions the possibility of a development of doctrine and then fails to deal with it properly, though Newman's revised edition of the *Essay on Development*, so extensively revised as to be virtually an entirely new book, had appeared just a decade before the publication of *Lux Mundi*.

Lock cannot have believed that the theory of continuity that he claimed to have derived from Irenaeus – Christ was the truth; he revealed it to the apostles; they wrote it down and handed it on to the bishops who succeeded them; therefore truth is to be found in the scriptures and in the churches founded by the apostles – could be applied in some simple form to the long and complex history of Christianity from the second century to the 1880s. But he simply ignored the problems of history and, with them, the whole question of what authority the church possesses to adapt the tradition to a different age. And, because his essay was part of a book intended to relate traditional faith to the modern intellectual world, the omission is particularly surprising. The Anglo-Catholic Sunday school lesson which he provided instead hardly even attempts to apply to the church the same critical historical methods which Gore was applying to the Bible.

The dangers of this failure of the younger leaders of Oxford Anglo-Catholicism were to be demonstrated in the next decade. Lock and his friends cannot be blamed for not knowing the future. But the Anglo-Catholic movement was about the enter the 'Church Crisis' of the 1890s when ritualism became the focus of controversy and the authority of the church was the central issue. The Public Worship Regulation Act of 1874 had attempted to suppress ritualism by legislation. It was too rigid to allow the bishops any latitude for negotiation with the ritualists. Anglo-Catholics defied the law and the bishops were unwilling to make a new generation of martyrs by sending recalcitrant clergymen to prison. Those Anglo-Catholics who were still, in some sense, linked to Oxford had hardly developed any theory of the catholicity of the church beyond the 'branch' theory of the early nineteenth century. They believed that the Church of England possessed an authority of its own to which Anglican clergy owed an obedience.[41]

But the 'London, Brighton and South Coast' Anglo-Catholics could not recognise that the Church of England had any existence except as two provinces of the Catholic church. Those two provinces could claim no independent authority at all. In order to find some form of authority which ritualists would obey absurd devices were resorted to. The most popular was the 'ancient' episcopal *ius liturgicum*, unknown to history or to canon law,[42] but supposed to give a bishop the right to order any aspect of worship within his diocese. And those 'Oxford' Anglo-Catholics who tried to mediate between the bishops and the ritualists had no sensible alternative ecclesiology to urge against such extravagances. Even Charles Gore as late as 1900 was still doing little more than re-echo the ideas of the 1840s.[43]

Part of the problem was that different parties within the Church of England had different ideas about the relationship between tradition and authority. It was difficult to devise a doctrine of the church because the nature of the church was itself in dispute. A time when there is furious controversy is always a bad time for developing a theory of authority for ending disputes. This may explain why, a hundred years later, when issues relating to authority are once again disturbing the Church of England, very little in the way of a theology of the church is being developed.[44]

Most of the issues which have been troubling the Church of England in recent years and have attracted even the attention of the popular press – dissatisfaction with the General Synod, demands for a 'strong lead' in matters of (sexual) morality, complaints about 'interference' in social and political affairs, controversy over proposed departures from tradition, particularly the ordination of women – are implicitly questions related to authority in the church. Some of these issues were on the agenda for the Lambeth Conference and hopes that firm decisions would be taken there were widely expressed. Such hopes were unlikely to be met for, in the very nature of things, large conferences tend to produce compromises. And, even if firm decisions had been taken, there was still less likelihood of their being supported by theologically based statements about the authority of the church. None of the preparatory material had seemed to indicate that there would be a serious consideration of the subject.

Among the unofficial publications that were produced in the hope of having some influence on the thinking of Lambeth was one which appears to relate directly to the subject of this essay. It is a study by Francis Penhale of the contribution of 'Catholics' to Anglicanism in the past and of their present position and hopes.[45] The book deals briefly with some of the ideas of authority that have existed among Anglo-Catholics in the past but is surprisingly reticent about present problems connected with the issue that has haunted the movement since 1845.

The same silence has been noted elsewhere. Reviewing the conference papers published in connection with the 150th anniversary of the Oxford Movement, John Sharp of the Pontifical Beda College in Rome pointed out that:

> The real weakness of the Oxford Movement was in its distaste for the Protestantism of the reformed Church of England and its failure to develop a proper ecclesiology beyond the 'branch theory' of the high churchmen, with the result that the Tractarians had no living tradition to which to make appeal. It is difficult to see how 'a renewed ecclesiology', derived from Newman's Anglican sermons, can 'prove to be our most precious inheritance from the Oxford Movement' ...without acknowledging Newman's later assertions on the subject...[46]

Inevitably one begins to wonder whether Anglo-Catholicism has ceased to be primarily concerned with *catholicity*, since it seems so consistently to evade the questions related to it, and has simply become a movement for preserving ritualist practices such as benediction, which occupies a large place in Penhale's work.

Yet it is a curious fact that exactly the same problem has disturbed the Roman Catholic church in recent years. Archbishop Lefèbvre's claim that he represents the true traditional *Catholic* church as against the liberalism of recent popes, raises precisely the same question – whether there can be a truly catholic authority other than the institutional authority of ecclesiastical bodies as they actually exist – as was raised by Anglican ritualists of the 1890s. And many of the particular issues connected with authority which have been raised since Vatican II have been those which, broadly speaking, are also found within Anglicanism. The place of women in the church, matters of sexual morality, the church's role in politics, are all problems which are common to Anglicans and Roman Catholics.

The work of Hans Küng[47] and the writings of the liberation theologians[48] have been only a part of a wide range of new thinking about the church. Both have tended, in effect, to transfer at least some of the teaching authority of the hierarchical *magisterium* to the communities where the actual ecclesiastical grass is growing. And one very significant Roman Catholic contribution to ecclesiology has been that of Karl Rahner who sees the church primarily as sacrament – divine grace and outward human structure.

> ... the Church is not a mythical entity to be hypostasized or personified in a false way. By the will of Christ her founder she is the organized community of the people of God, established through the incarnation in the unity of the one human race....the Church, as the continuance of Christ's presence in the world, is the fundamental sacrament of the eschatologically triumphant mercy of God...[49]

The church, conceived of as a continuation of the union of the human and the divine in the incarnate Christ, is a very obvious theme here.

It is not surprising to discover, then, that the work of the Anglican Roman Catholic International Commission (ARCIC) has been concerned with the question of authority not just in the traditional form raised by the divisions of Christendom but in a much more contemporary style. At the present moment, admittedly, the dynamics of ecumenical relations seems to discourage much direct engagement with the theology of the church itself. These 'dynamics' seem to operate in a strangely anti-climactic way. A group of theologians is appointed by each of the participating churches. They meet and live and work together over a considerable period of time. Even if the individual participants were originally chosen to represent a wide variety of opinion in their own church, not by any means always entirely sympathetic to the other bodies involved, the group inevitably develops a kind of common life. Praying and eating and talking together, the members come to understand how others in the group will react to ideas and how those ideas can be made to seem intelligible and acceptable to them. A common shorthand develops and, by the time the report comes to be written, the group finds itself able to record a surprisingly large amount of agreement. But the report, which enshrines so much of their common shorthand, can only be presented to the churches at large in the cold printed form of the words themselves. The process of participation by which the words came to be a common expression cannot be communicated. The report is explained by the original participants and each time the explanation is given, it tends to move away a little from the common intention. Eventually the official reaction of the church seems to pour cold water on the enthusiasm and optimism of the original report.[50]

Yet the ARCIC statement 'Authority in the Church I' (1976) must count as one of the most important contributions to ecclesiological thinking in recent years. Though it needs some careful concentration to penetrate the typically bland 'ecumenical' language in which it is written, the whole of the argument of the report is built upon the opening paragraph:

> The confession of Christ as Lord is the heart of the Christian faith. To him God has given all authority in heaven and on earth. As Lord of the Church he bestows the Holy Spirit to create a communion of men with God and with one another. To bring this *koinonia* to perfection is God's eternal purpose. The Church exists to serve the fulfilment of this purpose when God will be all in all.[51]

It is plain that the participants shared a vision of the church as an institution both human and divine. The unity of these two aspects of the church's existence underlies its authority, its life in the Spirit, its character as *koinonia*. It also defines its purpose.

The response of the Faith and Order Advisory Group of the church of England (FOAG) to this document, and to this paragraph in particular, reflects the next stage in the ecumenical dynamic. It has a mildly carping tone, as though FOAG felt obliged to demonstrate that it was not going to be easily persuaded to accept the ARCIC statement. Instead of dealing with what ARCIC said, it fastened upon what it had *not* said:

> The Commission cannot have been unaware of the difficulties of speaking at all about authority within the secular social climate where all forms of authority are under constant question. Criticism and challenge are features of modern 'pluralist' societies...authority becomes more accountable as it is more widely questioned.[52]

This very reservation, however, led FOAG to make a very important point. Pointing out that any concept of ecclesiastical authority needs to be founded firmly on the scriptural understanding of the authority of God himself, it argued that a most important characteristic of that understanding was 'the doctrine of God as at once powerful and yet giving his children freedom to challenge him...' And it then immediately alluded to that most crucial passage for all kenoticists, Philippians 2:7. The sentence quoted above continued with the words, 'of God who in Christ took the form of a servant and suffered, thereby demonstrating power as of the powerless in worldly terms (it is the power of the crucified that is lodged in the Church); and of God whose authority is exercised in enabling his creatures to respond freely.'

The Church of England scholar who has written most about authority in the church is Stephen Sykes, the Regius Professor of Divinity at Cambridge.[53] Sykes believes that the Anglican – and proper – model of ecclesiastical authority is a 'dispersed authority', exercised through several organs rather than a single *magisterium* and for that very reason implying the continual possibility of conflict. He founds this view on a statement made in the report of the Lambeth Conference of 1948. Sykes says:

> In respect of Anglicanism, the report claims (with perhaps, at this point, too little explanation), this authority is reflected in adherence to episcopacy as 'the source and centre of our order' and the Book of Common Prayer. But it is significantly stated that the crucible in which these elements of authority are fused [is] liturgy, the offering and ordering of the public worship of God in the power of the Holy Spirit and in the presence of the living and ascended Christ.[54]

Sykes then proceeds to provide an explanation himself in which he maintains that it is in and through the church's worship that the authority is exercised. His conclusion is perhaps surprising.

> ...the dispersal of authority in Anglicanism is rooted in the conviction that Christians to whom the scriptures are read in their own language are able to judge of the essentials of the faith. Because it is a liturgical provision that the scriptures should be heard, and because the scriptures are contextualised in worship which seeks at once to evoke the fundamentals and induct the worshipper into the heart of Christian experience, decisions made about worship are crucial to the integrity of the faith. And decisions are unavoidable because liturgical arrangements must change. Because the decisions involved in change rest upon judgements, which are necessarily controversial, it is essential to the health of the church that it learn how to conduct controversy constructively and openly. Authority is not embodied, it is dispersed; and the reaching of authoritative decisions is a continuous process involving all the participants.[55]

At first sight this unusual version of the argument that the *lex orandi* and the *lex credendi* are closely related to one another, may seem to be nothing more than an Anglican attempt to justify the state of affairs with which history has lumbered Anglicans. But it is worth noting that there is a sense in which there is a thread that connects Sykes' understanding of authority with the points made by the ARCIC report and the church of England's Faith and Order Advisory Group. ARCIC, as we have seen, thought that authority in the church was, in some sense, an extension of the purpose behind the union of the human and the divine in Christ himself. In the Faith and Order Group's response, the same theme reappears but it is now – in a specifically Anglican context – given a kenotic twist. The authority must be exercised, as Christ's was, in a servant-like manner and that implies, in turn, a certain scope for human independence. Sykes makes that independence a virtue: the element of conflict is a vital part of the whole. And, very significantly, by basing his argument on the report of the 1948 Lambeth Conference, he links it to what that report said about 'the living and ascended Christ'. The connecting thread, in other words, is a christological one, which among Anglicans takes a kenotic form. It may be that what Lock failed to provide in his essay in *Lux Mundi* – a doctrine of ecclesiastical authority founded upon kenotic christology – has come to be a staple of general Anglican thinking. It may even be, since Sykes builds his theory upon the report of the 1948 Lambeth Conference with its reference to the presence of the 'living and ascended Christ', that the Ascension has a vital part to play in this 'kenotic' theology of authority.

One has only to examine ecclesiastical authority in constitutional rather than theological terms for a moment, to find that this aspect becomes one of primary importance. In the 1960s, when many former colonies were achieving independence and constitution-making was a common occurrence, it was made very clear that a workable and efficient constitution depended upon there being a clear answer to the question, 'Where is sovereignty to lie?' If the answer to the question was confused or vague, or if attempts were made to protect too many local or historical interests, an effective exercise of authority became impossible. Attempts to entrench the rights of tribal or racial groups or to marry traditions of local rulership with centralised parliamentary democracy, could be self-defeating because they reflected a confusion about where the real authority was thought to be found. One could not say that sovereign authority lay with the people, in a one-man-one-vote sense, and argue at the same time that it must be hedged about with restrictions in favour of some individuals or groups. Such an entrenchment of rights implies the existence of another authority, if only the authority of the constitution, which limits the authority of the supposed sovereign. And a limited sovereign is not sovereign.

If one puts the same question, 'Where does sovereignty lie?' about the church, it is very difficult for any Christian to give an answer other than the answer provided by ARCIC – 'The confession of Christ as Lord is the heart of the Christian faith. To him God has given all authority in heaven and on earth.' The answer must be, in other words, that Christ is the only sovereign authority. The problem with this answer, however, is that there seems to be no way in which that sovereignty can be exercised in a direct and immediate sense. And this is where the reference to the Ascension in the report of the 1948 Lambeth Conference is so significant. The reason why Christ's sovereignty cannot be exercised immediately (in its strict and original sense of 'without mediation') is that Christ is both 'living and ascended'. Because Christ is living, his authority cannot be thought to have passed absolutely into other hands: because he is ascended, he does not exercise it in his own person.

Whether ARCIC perceived this point or not, the very words which come after its ascription of authority to Christ do, in fact, follow the course which such an argument would have to take. For ARCIC goes on to say, 'As Lord of the church he bestows the Holy Spirit to create a communion of men with God and with one another.' From that bestowal of the Spirit there comes the *koinonia* and thus the authority to hold it together. The point is that, if one believes that Christ's authority cannot pass absolutely into other hands but, nevertheless, cannot be exercised in his own person, one is obliged to advance an answer to the next question, 'How is some form of delegated authority to be exercised in the Church?' There have been many answers to that question in the course of history. And it is precisely over the differences between these answers that the sometimes vicious disagreements about the nature of ecclesiastical authority have arisen among Christians.

One may argue, on an implicit analogy with vice-regal delegated authority, that some designated individual ought to exercise Christ's sovereignty over the church. This does not imply that the authority has ceased to be Christ's but it does mean that, to all intents and purposes, he will not revoke or modify the decisions taken by his vice-regent, whose authority is therefore in practice absolute. As a consequence one is more or less compelled to argue that the decisions of the vice-regent are virtually the decisions of Christ himself The vice-regent, at least in matters germane to the exercise of authority, has to be regarded as Christ's spokesman. And in such a case the sending of the Spirit to create *koinonia* becomes a sending of the Spirit to guarantee the accuracy of the vice-regent's interpretation of the mind of Christ.

It should be noted, further, that a theology of this kind, in so far as it is a theology about the relationship of the human to the divine, is, so to speak, parallel to an Apollinarian Christology. It has to insist that the divine authority is exercised absolutely and without any possibility of its being distorted by the humanity of the church. (This need not necessarily mean that such a view constitutes a heresy. It is the parallel rather than whether the understanding is right or wrong which is pertinent.)

One could, in a wholly contrary direction, argue that the fact that Christ is living, even if ascended, means that his authority *cannot* be exercised by anyone else at all. This would imply that the church is a purely human institution, that its decisions are for practical purposes without any divine authority at all. They could not conceivably bind the individual conscience and would merely be convenient decisions like those taken by any human organisation for the practical and orderly arrangement of its affairs. In terms of the parallel with christology that would be like arguing for a purely human Christ liable to all the errors, limitations and imperfection of any other human being.

Or one might argue that, in so far as Christ's authority was exercised at all, it was exercised through those who sought to obey it. Acting as individuals or in a group, through the reading of the scriptures, through prayer or through immediate ecstatic or mystical experiences, they might come to a decision that this or that was the will of Christ. In such a case one begins to have an ecclesiological parallel to an adoptianist christ-ology.

Or one could have a view like that which appears to be the view of Sykes or FOAG, which seems to be parallel to a kenotic christology. This view does not deny that the authority of Christ can and must be exercised in the church. FOAG argued for 'the doctrine of God as at once powerful and yet giving his children freedom to challenge him; of God who in Christ took the form of a servant and suffered, thereby demonstrating power as of the powerless in worldly terms (it is the power of the crucified that is lodged in the Church); and of God whose authority is exercised in enabling his creatures to respond freely'. The authority is real but limited by the humanity of those through and on whom it is exercised. And the same features are to be found in Sykes' thesis. The authority is not doubted but it is to be exercised in a 'dispersed' form and through a necessary, almost a desirable, conflict.

This kenotic ecclesiology shares many of the strengths and weak-nesses of its christological counterpart. In a kenotic christology it is maintained that the divine is present in its fullness but voluntarily limited by a self-emptying so as to allow the existence alongside it of human ignorance, weakness and vulnerability. In that sense it attempts to pre-serve the existence of both human and divine within a union of the two. The weakness of a kenotic christology is well-known. If some of the essential characteristics of the divine are put aside, it is difficult to maintain that the divine exists at all.[56] The same sort of objection could be directed at those who argue for a kenotic theory of ecclesiastical authority. If the exercise of authority is so limited by human inde-pendence and conflict, how can it be said to be Christ's authority at all?

The strength of such an approach is much like the strength often attributed to the British constitutional monarchy. In the 1970s a popular film about the royal family, much talked about as the first attempt to portray its members as ordinary human beings, ended with a voice-over pointing out that, though the Queen exercised little real power, so long as she was the head of state no one else could usurp absolute power. In the same way one might argue that a theory of dispersed authority in the church ensures that no single organ can claim to exercise absolutely the sovereign authority which is Christ's alone. Or, to use a different constitutional model, one might maintain that dispersed authority is like the separation of powers in the American constitution. That was a device intended to prevent the improper concentration of power in any single organ of the state: power which belongs to the sovereign people alone. Dispersed authority, it could be argued, similarly prevents the concentration of Christ's authority in the hands of anyone other than Christ himself. The problem is to show how the dispersed authority actually being exercised in the church derives from the authority of Christ in a positive sense.

At least it can be argued that this dispersed model of authority is better than what appears to be the only rival theory among Anglicans at the present time – the theory that the bishops are guardians of the faith. Like the bogus *ius liturgicum* this theory of the conservative authority of the episcopate seems to have become an axiom without anyone being very clear about its derivation. It exists in two rather different forms. The more 'Catholic' version seems to assume that the bishops have an almost mystical quality, conferred by their consecration, which enables them to maintain the true faith. The more 'Evangelical' version tends to stress the *duty* of the bishops to maintain the traditional orthodoxy.

Neither version of the theory has much to support it. Like the *ius liturgicum* the theory has no basis in history, though Irenaeus and Cyprian are sometimes cited as exponents of it. But Irenaeus's view of the teaching role of the bishops is approached from an almost diametrically opposite point from the way the 'Catholic' version of the theory is usually expounded today. He does not argue that the bishops, by virtue of their consecration, have some infallible ability to distinguish between true and false teaching. He maintains that, as a matter of fact, it is possible to discover that the bishops always have taught the same faith as that which was taught by the apostles. Cyprian, moreover, though he spoke of the bishops as the 'glue' of the church and though he was quite sure that *he* taught the true faith, was often equally certain that other bishops – notably Stephen of Rome – had a pitifully inadequate grasp upon traditional orthodoxy.

The problem about the 'evangelical' version of the theory is, in fact, exactly the same as the problem that was found to exist in the theory of the *ius liturgicum*. It very quickly turned out that the bishops were not always endowed with the desired liturgical expertise. When David Jenkins was appointed to the see of Durham, some 'evangelical' exponents of the theory of conservative episcopal authority maintained that prospective bishops ought to be required to subscribe a statement of faith that would ensure that they would defend traditional orthodoxy.

Amongst the propositions to be included in such a statement was one which asserted that Christ is 'God made flesh'. The bishops of the Church of England would then have been committed to defending a proposition condemned as Apollinarianism at the Council of Constantinople in 381. The absurdity of the theory stood revealed. Who would have the authority to define the faith which the bishops were to guard?

At the same time the controversy revealed precisely why the present unease exists. The General Synod is, in practice, the final authority in the Church of England. When it came into existence there was very little discussion of theological/constitutional fundamentals. There was no agreed theory of authority and therefore no agreement about exactly what authority the synod possessed. The constitutional framework was a pragmatic one. It dealt with such issues as the relationship of synod to the convocations and to parliament. It did not settle the relationship of the synod to the authority of Christ in his church nor did it define how the authority of the synod was to be understood in relation to the rest of Christendom or to what might be called 'the traditional faith'. It is impossible to draw a clear dividing line between doctrinal and practical matters in the business that comes before a synodical body. Liturgical revision, above all else, makes this very obvious. At the same time it seems to many Anglicans that for a synod to pass a measure which appears drastically to alter traditional beliefs is too cavalier a method. They feel instinctively that there ought to be some other authority to appeal to, or some way of slowing things down so that the mind of the church as a whole can come to be expressed. And that, in turn, reveals that a greater clarity is needed about what constitutes 'the-church-as-a-whole' – the laity of the Church of England, the other provinces of the Anglican Communion, or the rest of the Christian world.

Notes

1. E. Abbott and L. Campbell, *The Life and Letters of Benjamin Jowett,* 2 vols (London 1897), II pp.377f.

2. P. Hinchliff, *Benjamin Jowett and the Christian Religion* (Oxford 1987), pp.12ff.

3. T. Arnold, *Principles of Church Reform, with an introductory essay by J.M. Jackson and J. Rogan* (London 1962), p.99.

4. P. Corsi, *Science and Religion: Baden Powell and the Anglican Debate 1800-1860* (Cambridge 1988), p.134.

5.*Suggestions for an Improvement of the Examination Statute* and see L. Campbell, *On the Nationalisation of the Old English Universities* (London 1901), p.74.

6. I. Ellis, 'Pusey and University Reform', in P. Butler (ed.), *Pusey Rediscovered* (London 1983), p.300.

7. A. Livesley, 'Regius Professor of Hebrew', in Butler, p.108.

8. B.M. add. MS 44,281, fos 218f., Pusey to Gladstone.

9. W.R. Ward, *Victorian Oxford* (London 1965), pp.250ff.

10. Hinchliff, *op. cit.* pp.147f.

11. H.P. Liddon, *Life of Edward Bouverie Pusey,* 4 vols (London, 3rd Impression 1898), II, pp.386f.

12. Examination papers of the Honour School of Theology, Trinity term 1873, New Testament II, question 4.

13. Examination papers of the Honour School of Theology, Trinity term 1882, Apologetica II, question 1.

14. Examination papers of the Honour School of Theology, Michaelmas term 1882, Apologetica II, question 4.

15. Examination papers of the Honour School of Theology, Trinity term 1891, St Mark and St John, question 4.

16. *Ibid.*, Acts of the Apostles, question 3.

17. E.g. in *The Spectator*, 5 April 1890.

18. P. Hinchliff, *John William Colenso, Bishop of Natal* (London 1964), p.178.

19. G.L. Prestige, *Life of Charles Gore* (London 1935), p.103.

20. Quoted in G. Crosse, *Charles Gore: a Biographical Sketch* (London 1932), p.24

21. Crosse, *op.cit.* p.25.

22. Crosse, *op.cit.* p.14.

23. O. Chadwick, *The Victorian Church*, 2 vols (London 1966), II, p.23 .

24. V.A. Harvey, *The Historian and the Believer* (London 1967), pp.68ff.

25. D.L. Pals, *The Victorian 'Lives' of Jesus* (San Antonio 1982), p.152.

26. Hinchliff, *Benjamin Jowett and the Christian Religion,* pp.207f.

27. Crosse, *op. cit.* p.26.

28. Hinchliff, *op. cit.* p.167ff.

29. J.R. Illingworth, *University and Cathedral Sermons* (London 1893), p.181. I am grateful to my colleague, the Revd Dr H.D. Dupree, for drawing my attention to this sermon.

30. C. Gore (ed.), *Lux Mundi: a series of studies in the Religion of the Incarnation*, 4th ed. (London 1890), pp.370f.

31. *Lux Mundi*, p.375.

32. *Lux Mundi*, pp.375f.

33. *Lux Mundi*, p.385.

34. *Lux Mundi*, p.387.

35. *Lux Mundi* pp.388f.

36. *Lux Mundi,* pp.380f.

37. *Lux Mundi,* p.381.

38. *The Life and Work of John Richardson Illingworth edited by his wife* (London 1917), p.159.

39. C.S. Dessain, *John Henry Newman* (London 1966), p.82.

40. W. Ward, *The Life of John Henry Newman*, 2 vols (London 1912), I p.67.

41. I am indebted for the information in this and the next paragraph to the Revd Alan Wilson who is preparing a D.Phil. thesis on the church crisis.

42. G. Dix, *The Shape of the Liturgy*, 2nd ed. (London 1945), p.588.

43. C. Gore, *Roman Catholic Claims*, 7th ed. (London 1900), pp.44ff.

44. Since this was written several works dealing with the issue have been published, e.g. G.R. Evans (ed.), *Christian Authority: Essays in Honour of Henry Chadwick* (Oxford 1988); S.W. Sykes (ed.), *Authority in the Anglican Communion: Essays Presented to Bishop John Howe* (Toronto 1987); J. Halliburton, *The Authority of a Bishop* (London 1987). Two lectures and a sermon of the Archbishop of Canterbury's have also been republished in a small volume entitled *Authority in Crisis?* (London 1988).

45. F. Penhale, *The Anglican Church Today: Catholics in Crisis* (London 1986).

46. *Journal of Ecclesiastical History*, 38 (January 1988), p.154.

47. H. Küng, *The Church*, tr. R. & R. Ockenden (London 1967).

48. See e.g. J.L. Segundo, *A Theology for a New Humanity*, tr. J. Drury, 5 vols (Dublin 1980) - the fourth volume is subtitled *The Community Called Church.*

49. G.A. McCool (ed.), *A Rahner Reader* (London 1975), pp.279f.

50. This process can be traced very clearly in *The Emmaus Report: a report of the Anglican Ecumenical Consultation in preparation for ACC-73* Singapore 1987 *and the Lambeth Conference 1988* (London 1987), pp.49ff.

51. *Anglican-Roman Catholic International Commission: Final Report* (London 1982), p.52.

52. *Towards a Church of England Response to BEM and ARCIC* (London 1985), p.82.

53. E.g. S.W. Sykes, *The Integrity of Anglicanism* (London 1978), S.W. Sykes, *The Identity of Christianity* (London 1984), and S.W. Sykes, 'Authority in the Church of England' in R. Jeffery (ed.), *By What Authority* (London 1987), pp.7ff. Sykes also edited, with John Booty, *The Study of Anglicanism,* published in July 1988 to coincide with the start of the Lambeth Conference.

54. S.W. Sykes, *The Integrity of Anglicanism,* p.88 actually has 'are fused in' in this passage but it is clear from reference to the Lambeth report that it should read 'are fused is'.

55. *Ibid.* p.99.

56. See e.g. D. Cupitt, 'The Christ of Christendom', in J.Hick (ed.), *The Myth of God Incarnate* (London 1977), p.137. Curiously, much the same argument - though with the opposite intention - is advanced in K. Barth, *Church Dogmatics*, tr. G.W. Bromiley, vol. iv. 1 (Edinburgh 1956), pp.179ff.

SACRAMENTS

Timothy Gorringe

God engages: the reason there is anything rather than nothing.

The symbol of the Trinity is the attempt to articulate what it means to live within that continuing engagement. Sacramental language developed, and continues to develop, to point up the occasions, events, moments, situations where lesions in the absorption of everyday reveal the mystery of this inventive and subversive engagement.

We turn to the word 'mystery' at once, and for good reason: the term 'sacrament' began its complex theological journey as a translation for the New Testament's *mysterion*. For Mark the 'mystery' of the Kingdom is present in Jesus, hidden from most, made known to the few (Mark 4:11f). Paul focusses this in the light of cross and resurrection, understanding the dialectical power and wisdom of the cross as the truth of the cosmos revealed in a mystery (1 Cor 2:7). Colossians speaks of Christ as 'God's mystery', 'hidden for ages and generations but now made known' (Col. 1:26). This mystery is the continuing secret of history, 'Christ in you, the hope of glory'. The confession of 1 Timothy sums up this witness: 'Great (i.e. Christ?) is indeed the mystery of that which we worship (*tes eusebias*): he was manifested in the flesh, vindicated in the Spirit, seen by angels, preached among the nations, believed in the world, taken up in glory' (1 Tim 3.16). Derivately the word refers back to the apocalyptic sense it had in Dan 2:28, and sometimes refers to the travails which mark the end of all things (e.g. 2 Thess. 2:7, Rev. 17:5).

Adverting to this New Testament usage, where what happens in Christ is the heart of God's mystery revealed, Luther tentatively suggested that the word 'sacrament' might be given an exclusively christological use but quickly reverted to what was by this time convention, retaining the term for 'those promises which have signs attached to them', namely, baptism and bread. Towards the end of his life Karl Barth took up Luther's original suggestion maintaining that 'the death of Christ is the one *mysterium*, the one sacrament, and the one existential fact before and beside and after which there is no room for any other of the same rank'.[1] The Incarnation is without analogy and therefore it is 'the great Christian mystery and sacrament besides which there is, in the proper sense, no other.'[2] But what is the proper sense? The predication of Barth's doctrine of creation, and especially of his doctrine of the human, on an immensely complex *analogia Christi* sufficiently illustrates that we cannot escape analogies with fundamental ways of characterizing the Incarnation. On the grounds of just such an analogy Francis Paget, the contributor on 'Sacraments' in *Lux Mundi*, moved from the Incarnation to a 'sacramental principle' which discerned glory and the means of redemption in and through the physical. And if sacraments are markers of God's engagement then Paget was surely correct to begin from what, for Christians, is the central focus and expression of that engagement, the Incarnation. In the life, death and resurrection of Christ we learn what it is to engage: a commitment and an intervention which is personal, calling, judging, forgiving; which is historical, story creating, community involved and forming; which is fleshly, material, not interpreting merely but changing. All these things must be involved in 'sacrament' if 'sacrament' is to have a Christ-like sense. At the same time engagement means response, for it involves not one party but two, and sacraments are also the free dance of those who hear the Bridegroom's voice, celebrating the 'for nothing' of God's love. They are part of the play of all worship and as such are not to be understood instrumentally. Whilst they are primarily a part of God's initiative, bearing upon and breaking open our situation, in their aspect as human response they have no rationale except the delighted 'thank you' which being met with love always evokes.

The depth and range of the sacramental discussion within the Christian tradition indicates that 'sacrament' is not a word we should seek narrowly to define. With a nod towards Popper's model for understanding the growth of scientific knowledge we can think of moving from tentative understanding, to the awareness of the limitations (and sometimes even downright error) of this understanding to a further tentative understanding. In this particular exploration, which does not aspire to capture but only to sighting of tracks, we proceed in four directions roughly indicated by the terms 'word', 'community', 'matter' and 'hope', corresponding, as it happens, to four great descriptions of what Aquinas called the *sacramentum sacramentorum*: Lord's Supper, Holy Communion, Eucharist, and Mass. Everything which is said about the eucharist applies, *mutatis mutandis*, to baptism but this is obscured by the still widespread practice of infant baptism. When we finally have a renewal of church discipline which makes baptism once again a sacrament of engagement, the meeting of the Confessing God and the confessing disciple, then the nature of baptism as the sign of God's long revolution will again become clear, and no longer stand in need of the desperately unconvincing arguments about the priority of God's grace (as if this could ever be other than prior!) advanced in favour of present practice.

Sacrament and story

Accedit verbum ad elementum et fit sacramentum (when word and element are joined they become a sacrament): this remark thrown out in the course of Augustine's continued wrestle with God's engagement (*Super Joannem* 88, on John 15:2) has proved seminal for all Western Christian traditions. The 'word' in question was from an early date taken to refer to the accounts of the 'Last Supper', read as the *ipsissima vox Jesu*, thus tying sacraments to a Founder christology, and producing forced, if ingenious, attempts to root other sacraments in Christ's life and teaching. Luther understood 'word' more creatively as promise: 'We have said that in every sacrament there is a word of divine promise...for to constitute a sacrament there must be above all things else a word of divine promise, by which faith may be exercised.'[3] But 'word' also included for Luther the exact form of the 'words of institution', the 'is' of 'This is my body' guaranteeing the real presence, whilst the inviolability of the promise functioned as his version of the *ex opere operato* doctrine. To know the transfiguring power of God's Word in the sacraments, however, we do not need to bind ourselves to any particular text in a mantic way.

> For I received from the Lord what I also delivered to you, that the Lord Jesus on the night when he was betrayed took bread... (1 Cor. 11:23 f.)

The Christian community, the community in Corinth, or wherever else it may be, is called into being by the story of what God has done in and through Jesus of Nazareth. Laurens van der Post learned from the Bushmen of Southern Africa that without a story you do not have a tribe or a people or a nation, and though he did not add it, you have no individual either. To translate *verbum* as 'story' is no shallow rationalisation: we see the power of stories to give life to a community and even to call it back to life in Exodus, in Judges, in an appeal such as that of Deuteronomy, and in the prophets, just as we see it in the contemporary search for 'roots', for stories which tell us who we are. If the so-called 'Old' Testament does not consist wholly of stories, nevertheless the stories are the thread on which law and wisdom are strung. Jesus himself seems to have preferred to teach through stories, and what he bequeathed to his followers was no eight-fold path, no body of sacred teaching, but essentially a story in which elements of teaching inhere. As the eucharist did for the community in Corinth, and has done for the church through the ages, so sacraments in general re-present the story, they show it again, they are an effective recalling. 'The Word must make the element a sacrament; otherwise it remains a mere element' (Luther). Without the telling of the story, without the transposing of these actions and these commonplace elements of creation into a new context (transignification?) there is no sacrament. The telling puts the familiar, the everyday, the present, into the context of God's past, present and future engagement: it shows how God worked, the mode and manner of that working, offering it for reflection in the obscurity of the present, shaping what happens there so that the future is not ours only but God's also. The subversion of human confusion by the story telling of Israel and church forms part at least of the deeply wrought providence of the God whose Son refuses the twelve legions of angels. This story telling is itself repeatedly subverted: the sin of the church. But it has a strength which bends and refuses to be broken, reasserting itself against distortion, the resistance of the text against its interpreters, the church *semper reformanda*, and in this process human history moves neither aimlessly, nor in a downward spiral, but slowly towards the future of the Son of Man.

Over the centuries sacramental theology has rightly invoked the category of mystery, especially in connection with the idea of the 'real presence' in the eucharist. Mystery is indeed an essential element in describing the reality of any sacrament but we have to remember that the most fundamental mystery in common experience is our neighbour, and this encounter points us to the mystery of God and of his meeting with us. Barth drew a distinction between the miracle and the mystery of Christmas. No doubt life is full of miracles, and sacraments may be part of that pattern of surprise, but the miracle is only the sign of the real thing, of the condescension, encounter and engagement of the God who is love. From this point of view again to understand 'word' as 'story' involves no bare rationalisation but points to the way in which people try to share and point to the ultimate mystery in their lives by creating and sharing their stories. Both biblical and individual stories speak of the encounter of mystery with mystery and in so doing open up the way to the present encounter of God and human beings. One meaning at least of the term 'Lord's Supper' refers to the reality of this encounter. It is the 'Lord's' supper because in this liturgical act Christ is re-called, re-presented in the self-interpretation in which he sums up his life. This re-presenting is a real presence in which Christ meets and shapes those whom he encounters, those who put themselves in the way of the story.

The mystery, of course, cannot be located in the various sets of liturgical actions usually called sacraments as such, which would be fetishisation. Sacraments rather provide windows on to the reality of the triune engagement with our totality. Segundo puts this well:

> One of the essential principles of the gospel seems to be that the community formed to succeed Jesus is not going to have sacred rites, gestures, or words endowed with divine power...the fact is that...man's whole destiny depends on just and cordial relations with his neighbour

(Matt. 5:21-3). This is so true that the necessity of righting these relations takes precedence over the strictly religious function. In other words, the natural causality which directs human relationships is more important than the extraordinary causality which governs cultic worship... Any and all sacred magic is completely rejected.[4]

The love and wrath of God encountered in the love and wrath of my neighbour: this is the mystery. Sacraments are the prisms which refract this terrible light, revealing the extraordinarily complex beauty under the veil of the mundane, pitching us deeper into God's presence there in the ordinary.

Writing out of a Roman Catholic background, Segundo speaks very properly of the malign effect of a 'pagan insistence on the altar' and we have to add that Protestantism has known an equally 'pagan insistence on the Word', since both Word and altar can become symbols of the human attempt to enclose God within safe and manageable boundaries. But the priority of right human relations, and the rejection of sacred magic, does not lessen but rather increases the importance of sacraments as expressions of our response of praise and celebration. We do not celebrate sacraments in order to love our neighbour better; rather, the more we love our neighbour the better we celebrate sacraments. Again, not that the purpose of human life is liturgy, but that redeemed human life *is* liturgy, and this is anticipated in the eucharist.

It follows, therefore, that the story we speak of is not fantasy, but history (allowing, of course, that there is an indispensable element of fantasy, both interpretative and otherwise, in what is usually called 'history'). It is human history, the totality of human stories, which is, as Rahner has described it, God's liturgy. The true liturgy of the world is offered and celebrated in the entire human history of superficiality, folly, inadequacy and hatred on the one hand, and silent submission, responsibility, reaching heights and plumbing depths on the other. Liturgical sacraments interpret and reflect this engagement of God with the whole of human history; they provide a point from which reflection on it is possible; they are a reminder of that engagement. The eucharistic liturgy is, as Paul Lehmann has put it, 'the dramatic presentation of the reality and the proof of what God is doing in the world.'[5] Therefore this liturgy of God, the fundamental liturgy of human joy, suffering and exploration must be reflected on in church liturgies if these are not to become 'empty ritual attitudinizings, full of unbelief'. And the entering in to the deeper liturgy which is effected through the sacraments must lead to action in love if, at the eucharistic table, we are to avoid occupying the seat of a Judas.[6]

Community and conflict

'When signs or symbolic acts point to divine things, then they are called sacraments' – a second of Augustine's raids into sacramental territory (*Ep*. 138,7) To what divine things do they point? The redemptive story creates a people, a movement, a community. The rule of God which Jesus announced is a call, as the author of the First Epistle of John puts it, to be 'like him' (1 John 3:2), which is to say, to realise the image of the God who is relationship in essence. From the raw material of creation God calls into being and fashions not individuals but persons in relation, a people, a church, a community. For something to be a sacrament is for it to have a part in this divine fashioning and the 'seven' sacraments of Peter Lombard, Aquinas and Trent can all be understood in this community related sense: baptism and confirmation incorporate into the community; eucharist establishes it; penance restores to it; ordination refers to leadership of the community; marriage, as Genesis 2:24 makes clear, is about the fundamental roots of human community; and extreme unction looks to the community continuing beyond death.

The restriction of the number of sacraments to seven is undoubtedly artificial and may owe something, as Moltmann suggests, to the influence of seven as a sacred number. Prior to Peter Lombard a much greater number was sometimes posited – Hugh of St Victor suggested thirty. Luther and the Reformers generally restricted them to two, though with a bad conscience, as confirmation, marriage and penance all seemed to be reasonable candidates. Following Schleiermacher's breaking up of the ground it became fashionable to extend the scope massively: for John Oman, for instance, life itself is 'the one Supreme Divine sacrament' and the sacraments of the Church exist to 'express and, as it were, give the concentrated essence of the sacrament of life'.[7] From a similar background H.H. Farmer speaking, as Paget did, of a 'sacramental principle', thought of 'nature and society' as God's symbols or signs, 'God's language with the personality of man'.[8] Farmer's use of symbol and sign as synonyms indicates a deep-seated confusion which cuts at the root of sacramental thinking. His fundamental distinction was between extrinsic or conventional signs such as words and intrinsic or expressive symbols, which carry their meaning with them. In his view the created order, the situations of nature and society, constituted intrinsic symbols mediating between God and the human. But if everything is a sign, nothing is. It is perhaps true that anything in the created order may *become* a sign: in particular persons become signs of God's engagement to persons, and invest rings, flowers, and other covenantal symbols with sacramental significance. But in the sacraments as the Church has generally understood them we have to do with the freedom of God, with signs of a very specific directedness in human history. Because we have to do with God's freedom we cannot set arbitrary limits on what may or may not be a sacrament and there may well be properly unique sacraments within the engagement of God with individual stories which go beyond the sacraments of church practice: in this sense the 'seven, no more and no less' of Trent is an ecclesiastical impertinence. On the other hand, God gives himself to history, to the particular, to this nation, this group of disciples, in these signs and not others, and the 'no more and no less' is also an attempt to respond to this particularity. Trent itself pronounces an anathema on those who count all the sacraments as equal, and Luther's fixing on baptism and bread makes the same point that these two are the most clearly rooted in the particularity of Jesus' history.

The attempt to say very precisely what is a sacrament, and therefore what is not, is surely symptomatic of a theological and ecclesiastical attitude very unevangelically concerned with right doctrine rather than right practice. Other liturgical occasions which have, at the least, a sacramental quality are services such as those for the thanksgiving for the birth of a child, or for adoption, in the Alternative Service Book of the Church of England, or various forms of blessing. These can be rooted in scripture, and specifically in Jesus' story, as easily as many of the existing seven; they too relate to the community, and it is not clear what aspect of a 'full' or 'true' sacrament we might want to deny them. In any event it is certain that whether we are speaking of sacraments in the broader sense of Oman and Farmer, or whether more narrowly of liturgical acts, be they two, seven, or some greater number, we are speaking not simply of Christian community as such, but of the free community waiting upon the free God. To understand how scripture became the Word of God Barth proposed the model of the pool of Bethesda, which had healing power only when the angel stirred the waters. In the same way the promise of God, on which Luther based his account of the *ex opere operato* doctrine, cannot mean that we take God for granted. The engagement of God which we know in Word and sacrament presupposes faith on our part, as Luther also insisted, namely prayer in faith for God's forgiveness, for the ability to be still and listen, to know judgement and through judgement grace. The community of which we speak therefore is the attentive, waiting, listening, needy community. Sacraments are food for people on a journey, rather than banquets for those who have reached their journey's end.

The fundamental neediness of the community is emphasised by Segundo and other Liberation theologians who have been concerned to draw attention to those situations where class differences within a community make celebration of the sacraments difficult, if not impossible, a

question already raised by Paul in the earliest days of Christian community life. Paul faced a situation where factions within a community
accused each other of drunkenness on one side, and unseemly behaviour
on the other, and where some, evidently wealthy, members 'humiliated
those who had nothing' and so 'despised the church of God' (1 Cor.
11:22). In such a situation, Paul warned, the Lord's Supper might be an
occasion of judgement rather than blessing. This is the case where
sacraments are used as opiate by haves and have nots alike, used to
sanctify the injustice of class division on the grounds that all have access
to true 'eternal' food. At the same time the church cannot constitute a
small island of the perfectly reconciled within a deeply divided world: it
shares, necessarily, in the contradictions and inhumanities of that world.
In this situation sacraments can only be celebrated with integrity where
conflict is faced:

> In a Church that is alive, the seven sacraments constitute a fountain-
> head of conflicts, not some goal of security that is attained in spite of
> the divisory elements.[9]

In the exposition of the Word, and in the mutual celebration of sacraments, we must feel, says Segundo, the brush of our dominating demon,
named and identified through the Word, and drawn out of abstract
categories by that. The conflict that engenders is part of the struggle to
be and to stay human which is God's purpose in the world, as we see this
in Christ. In a community which can face and go through conflict we have
holy communion, real meeting between those who are called to be disciples, at a level beyond trivialities, and a sharing in things which pertain
to God's kingdom.

Affirming the material

To speak of sacraments is to speak of those rents in the opacity of history
where God's concrete engagement to change the world becomes visible.
It is therefore to speak of the Holy Spirit, which is to say of the awareness
of events which are wholly worldly, opaque and ordinary on the one hand
and wholly divine, radiant and mysterious on the other, for such a duality
is the mark of the Spirit. Sacraments are reminders, if we need reminders,
that matter and spirit, body and soul are not opposites, not temporarily
and unfortunately mismatched, but proper expressions of each other.
From a very early period the eucharist, and by extension other sacraments, have been understood as an affirmation of the created, material
order. Towards the end of the second century Irenaeus speaks of the
church making a 'pure offering' from creation 'with thanksgiving' because
Christ is 'the Word through whom the trees bear fruit, the springs flow,
and the earth yields "first the blade, then the ear, then the full corn in the

ear".'[10] We have here, therefore, an affirmation of earth and its possibilities, of its goodness and its character as gift. Extrapolating from this at the end of the patristic period, and summing up the sense of much patristic discussion, John of Damascus defends a theology of matter:

> I do not worship matter. I worship the God of matter; who became matter for my sake, and deigned to inhabit matter; who worked out my salvation through matter...Do not vilify matter, for it is not dishonourable. Nothing is dishonourable that God has made. This is the Manichaean notion.[11]

Again, in the history of the church the use of physical elements in the sacraments, of water, and bread, wine and oil, has been understood as an affirmation of the material, as the assertion, consonant with the Incarnation, that you cannot go round, or beyond matter, but that you must go through it. Likewise the recognition of marriage as a sacrament has carried with it, albeit reluctantly, an affirmation of the bodily and the sexual as something we do not need redeeming from but which may properly be a means of grace. And in affirming creation, matter and the bodily, human work has also been affirmed: 'bread which you have given and human hands have made'. This fourfold affirmation is 'eucharist' – giving thanks for existence, for the concrete, for the creation which makes redemption possible. Like Marx, Christians are concerned with people 'in their actually empirical process of development under definite conditions' – a fundamental rule of sacramental theology. There are three points we can take from this. The first concerns the nature of the Christian affirmation of the material world. Speaking of this affirmation Paget invoked Wordsworth's 'obstinate questionings/Of sense and outward things' which

> Uphold us, cherish, and have power to make
> Our noisy years seem moments in the being
> Of the eternal Silence.

The point of this is not the relegation of sense and outward things to secondary importance but rather of discerning mystery not behind but in the appearances, reality transfigured. Sacraments do not, as some followers of Feuerbach would have it, give us a more imaginative insight into the everyday than crude materialism allows; they unmask the triviality of crude materialism. For if Christianity is, as Maritain suggested, true humanism, sacraments represent true materialism, a materialism not constrained by the loss of depth of the rationalism we associate with capitalist development, but open to the delight, surprise and inventiveness of the triune engagement.

It was partly as a response to this delight, surprise and inventiveness, surely, that language about transubstantiation developed. What this language points towards, albeit with philosophical clumsiness, are those situations where the material, the concrete, the bodily become patent of divinity. It says that there are moments when persons, things, 'work of human hands' are so transfigured by the story of the openness, generosity and self-giving of God, which with infinite temerity we label 'love', that they become transfigured, as music transfigures air, refracting the silence, making known the divinity already there. In fixing on seven or two sacraments the church pointed to occasions where there was, paradoxically, a regular pattern of surprise. But by definition surprise cannot be contained and there are moments, events, things in each life story which are properly sacramental, in which the engagement of God we sometimes call 'grace' is known through the transfiguration of this or that material circumstance.

Whilst we must defend the attempt to speak of transfiguration as language of the utmost sobriety it remains necessary to beware of what Marx scorned as mystification, which is allowing legitimate awareness of mystery to tip over into giving it an illegitimate priority, to the detriment of persons 'in their actually empirical process of development'. This is the point of the famous protest of the prophet in the Isaianic tradition:

> Is not this the fast that I chose:
> to loose the bonds of wickedness,
> to undo the thongs of the yoke,
> to let the oppressed go free,
> and to break every yoke?
> Is it not to share your bread with the hungry,
> and bring the homeless poor into your house;
> when you see the naked, to cover him,
> and not to hide yourself from your own flesh?
> (Isa. 58:6-7)

On this understanding the 'sacrament that God chooses' has to be a sign of the requirement that the one earth's resources be shared, and not hoarded or exploited in the interests of one class or group; that the fundamental equality of all human beings as expressed in every sacramental practice be given concrete economic and physical expression; that all forms of human labour are equally affirmed and that therefore distinctions of value between, for instance, mental and physical work cannot ultimately be countenanced. What would be the meaning of fifty-two masses celebrated in a year, asks the Sri Lankan theologian Tissa Balasuriyea, if it had not made concrete differences to the poor in their shanties? This question applies to every liturgical sacrament, and if the answer is that they make no difference whatsoever then clearly they come under the prophetic judgement.

Once again we have to insist that this does not imply a purely instrumental or moralistic view of the sacraments. In his exegesis of Job, Gutierrez has beautifully illustrated how the search for justice leads to celebration, and prophecy to contemplation, which then feeds back to the hunger for righteousness. Grace, he says, 'is not opposed to the quest of justice nor does it play it down; on the contrary, it gives it its full meaning. God's love, like all true love, operates in a world not of cause and effect but of freedom and gratuitousness...the issue is not to discover gratuitousness and forget the demands of justice, but to situate justice within the framework of God's gratuitous love.'[12] It is precisely this that the sacraments do.

Fashioning the future

The church exists not for itself, as William Temple said, but for others. The sacraments are extroverted, which is the beautiful meaning preserved in the term 'mass', from the last words of the Latin rite: *Ite, missa est*, 'Go, it is the dismissal.' Having gathered for a short while you are sent out again. The sacraments, like the gospel, are not about religious satisfaction but about changing reality, about the realisation of the kingdom, and this happens only 'amongst the bulks of actual things'. Neither can they be understood, in contemporary terms, as extensions of leisure activities, as a time for 're-charging batteries'. Great art can be known, says Lucien Freud, because it surprises, instructs, questions and converts. This applies also to the gospels, to the sacraments, as to some kinds of human relationship. Such surprise and questioning goes far deeper than the refreshment of mind we gain through leisure which is more analogous to second-rate art, which is merely decorative and makes no real demands upon us.

We have seen that the sacraments contain an affirmation, and as the obverse of that they also structure a protest. Like prophetic signs they not only signify but help to effect what they signify. Thus they represent an opting out of unequal and unjust structures, bringing persons into situations where such differences are seen to be unjust. They represent a realistic dreaming of the new society where these equalities take flesh, and therefore mark the beginning of the creation of a counter-culture in the midst of the old. We have already seen how this element of challenge, protest and subversion can itself be subverted: baptism can become a sign of admission to an exclusive club instead of a branding for radical openness: marriage can become the acme of bourgeois respectability instead of the sign of an equal, liberating and sharing sexuality; the eucharist can be co-opted by a secular religion of power, administered as opiate, as a placebo to stave off rather than to encourage revolutionary intent. But the Word in which the sign inheres can be smothered but not extinguished, and sooner or later again bursts into flame catching the *verba visibilia* in the process. This, too, is the work of the Spirit of the new age, of the realisation of the gospel. For this reason Moltmann has spoken of the sending of the Spirit as the sacrament of the kingdom. He appeals to the second sense of 'mystery' in the New Testament, the mystery of the divine resolve made known in the signs of the end. A christological focus on the concept of mystery or sacrament must not be so concentrated on the Incarnation that it fails to embrace the messianically open history of the incarnate, crucified, exalted and coming Christ. Both Christ and the church have to be understood within the eschatology of world history:

> Not Christ for himself but Christ in the Holy Spirit, not the church for itself but Christ's church in the Holy Spirit, must be called the mystery or 'sacrament'... In the eschatological gift of the Holy Spirit 'word and sacrament', 'ministries and charismata' become comprehensible as the revelations and powers of Christ and his future. As the emblematic revelations of Christ they are messianic mediations of salvation. As glorifications of Christ they are actions of hope pointing towards the kingdom.[13]

The sacraments are, therefore, future creating: they contradict an unjust *status quo* and maintain hope for a different, more open and more just future. This future changing role can also be regarded as an essential part of what it is to be a sacrament. If this is the case then the well known refusal of Camillo Torres to continue to celebrate the eucharist until a new order of society was established is fundamentally misconceived. He practised, of course, in a situation where the sacraments had been more deeply subverted than in most places, but since his death the Latin American base communities have recovered a vision of how both Word and sacrament can be redeemed and play their proper role in the divine subversion of human subversion.

Grace and the political

'Grace' is theological shorthand for God's continuing engagement with us, for his refusal to let us go, for the judgement and forgiveness with which he re-makes us, for his opening up of closed and impossible situations, for his subversion of the constricting regularities of human history towards the openness of the kingdom. It is shorthand for the power of the presence of Jesus to make all things new. Sacraments are 'means' of this work and engagement, 'channels' of this grace, as they help enflesh the story, create community, affirm the material and hold open the future. They are sinews of that love which Barth described as 'absolute matter-of-factness towards the problematical character of existence'. This means that they are concerned with that making of all things new which is the special mark of the Spirit, the power by which the existing order not only exists, but is changed. To speak less coyly, as Barth expounded the love which is the fruit of faith in the twelfth and thirteenth chapter of Romans, he took up the political question, human response to God's engagement in conservation and revolution. Because the Spirit drives and subverts us towards the radically new the conservative, the person of the *status quo*, which has to be thrown down, stands condemned. And yet, said Barth, the revolutionary stands in far greater danger of obstructing God's purpose because the revolution which seeks to renew things stands closer to the divine direction. The revolutionary stands in danger of usurping the place of God, of mistaking a human, fallible programme for the kingdom. But does this leave us with nothing but a pious wringing of hands? Although Barth would doubtless repudiate the term it is still tempting to characterise his response to this question in terms of the Kierkegaardian irony by which he was much influenced at the time.

Barth's *Romans* continues Kierkegaard's attack on Christendom. Christendom escapes the demand of God, wrote Kierkegaard in his *Journals*, by turning God 'into a driveller snuffling something about salvation and grace and so on, in such a way that worldliness sees good sense in the words; and this is *lèse-majesté*...no pagan people has worshipped such a ridiculous and nauseating deity as "Christendom" which worships and adores – a driveller.'[14] The situation is highly ironic:

> If someone were to say 'Christianity is surely an irony of God towards us men' I should reply, 'No, my good man, but we men have it in our power to transform Christianity into irony, into biting irony.'
>
> The matter is quite simple. God in his majesty takes so high a tone that if a man is unwilling to let go of his finite good sense, to give up his flat self-indulgent mediocrity, then what God calls help, salvation, grace, and so on, is the most biting irony.

Precisely this irony has long invested both sacramental theory and practice, but if it is true that sacraments effectively signify the Triune engagement with all, and not simply pious, reality then we have in them the irony of God and not the irony of man. Barth understands the love which Paul expounds in Romans 12 following as that which 'transfigures the passion of revolution so that its promises may in truth be born', as that which frees the revolution for the practice of the truth in its cause.[15] And sacraments, properly understood, are the irony of revolution. They postulate both the seriousness and the fallibility of human political action.

They point to, and are part of, the triune making of all things new. They bear, therefore, on the concrete and material, which is to say the political. But they bring every human action under judgement at the same time, submitting every human and political act to the divine irony. Their celebration is the occasion to deflate revolutionary pomposity and challenge the dehumanising power of self-righteousness. They bear on the concrete: otherwise they are neither sacraments, as the church has properly understood them, nor gracious. But they illumine it with the divine humour and season it with forgiveness. They underline what Barth called the 'game like' quality of politics, whilst never for a moment failing to take them seriously. The eucharistic community is therefore, as Lehmann describes it, 'a laboratory of maturity in which by the operative (real) presence and power of the Messiah-Redeemer in the midst of his people, and through them of all people, the will to power is broken and displaced by the power to will what God wills...the power to be and to stay human, that is, to attain wholeness or maturity'.[16] This community is the sign that God is here and now doing what it takes to make and to keep human life human. It is this in virtue of its life from Word and sacrament. Word and sacrament in their indissoluble unity enable those who respond to Christ's call to fall in line with what Primo Levi, victim and chronicler of Auschwitz, still dared to call 'a slow progress to the messianic age'. In this way they further Christ's prayer that God's kingdom come on earth.

Notes

1. K. Barth, *Church Dogmatics* IV/I tr. Bromiley (Edinburgh 1956), p.296.
2. K. Barth, *Church Dogmatics* IV/2 tr. Bromiley (Edinburgh 1958), p.40.
3. Luther's Works, American Edition (Philadelphia 1960), vol. 36, p.92.
4. J.L. Segundo, *The Sacraments Today*, tr. Drury (Dublin 1980), pp.22 f.
5. P. Lehmann, *Ethics in a Christian Context* (London 1963).
6. K. Rahner *Theological Investigations*, vol. 14, tr. Bourke (London 1976), p.175.
7. J. Oman, *Grace and Personality* (London 1960), p.151.
8. H.R. Farmer, *The World and God* (London 1963), pp.72 f.
9. Segundo, *op. cit.* p. 60.
10. *Adversus Haereses* 4.18.4, Bettenson's translation.
11. In B.J. Kidd, *Documents Illustrative of the Christian Church History*, vol. 3 (London 1941), p.73.
12. G. Gutierrez, *On Job* (New York 1987), p. 87-8.
13. J. Moltmann, *The Church in the Power of the Spirit*, tr. Kohl (London 1977), pp. 205 f.
14. S. Kierkegaard, *The Last Years: Journals* 1853-5, ed. and trans. R. Gregor Smith (New York 1965) p. 280-1.
15. P. Lehmann, *op. cit.*, p. 47.
16. Lehmann, *op. cit.*, p.101.

CHRISTIANITY AND POLITICS

David Nicholls

'The State is sacred', wrote W.J.H. Campion in his *Lux Mundi* essay; it possesses, like the church, a 'divine sanction'.[1] The understanding of the relation between Christianity and politics set forth in *Lux Mundi* is one that has, over the past hundred years, gained in popularity among English churchpeople. I shall here examine its basic features, pointing to some of its weaknesses, and shall suggest alternative ways of looking at the relation of Christianity to politics.

There are three theses common to the *Lux Mundi* position. First that the state is God's creation, possessing authority derived ultimately from him. Secondly that it is the state's purpose to effect the common good. Thirdly that the lineaments of this common good and the limits of the state's legitimate authority are determined by moral principles and ideals, deduced from Christian faith and prior to any political order. The principal link between theology and politics – between God and the state – is believed to be ethics.

The political realm, and in particular that collection of institutions known as the state, is thought to receive legitimacy from its role in a divine plan. Both church and state are ordained by God as part of his creative or redemptive purpose. Whether the state is a result of the Fall – a remedy for sin – as Augustine appears to have believed, or a part of the created order, as Aquinas taught, it is seen in both traditions as divinely ordained. The leading Protestant reformers of the sixteenth century did nothing to challenge this position and it has continued to dominate mainstream Christian thinking on the subject since that time.

The most elementary task of the state is, according to Campion, to secure the conditions of an ordered and civilized life. Its successful performance will, however, involve a recognition that many citizens are susceptible only to the lowest motive, a fear of punishment. Coercive force is therefore one of the state's chief instruments; but this inhibits its appeal to higher motives and at this point 'the Church steps in to supplement the moral action of the State'.[2] The other principal role of the church in its relations with the state is, in the words of Charles Gore's Preface to *Lux Mundi*, 'to throw herself into the sanctification of each new social order'. This 'sanctification' of the secular order, urged by Gore and his colleagues, may be traced to the influence of F.D. Maurice, who taught that 'the State is as much God's creation as the Church'. I believe that the attempt to Christianize or sanctify the secular order, breaking down any distinction between sacred and secular, has totalitarian implications, particularly in a situation of cultural and social pluralism.[3]

Although the state is viewed as ordained by God, wielding authority derived ultimately from him, any idea of the divine right of kings or of absolute non-resistance is firmly excluded. Campion saw, in good Whig tradition, a struggle in seventeenth century England between the forces of darkness and light, and regretted that the Caroline divines had allied themselves with the former against a growing tide of liberalism and democracy. They failed to acknowledge the limits of state authority and the ultimate right of resistance to unjust commands. 'In the great battle which was being fought out in England between arbitrary power and freedom, they threw the whole weight of the English Church on the side of the former.'[4] They thereby betrayed a tradition going back from Hooker, through the medieval theorists to the early church. Tyrannical governments, except when subsequently legitimized by 'consent', may properly be resisted.

A Christian view of the state, according to Campion, requires that it should not merely secure peace and order, but also must realize 'the common good'[5] – a substantive condition under which the good of all citizens is subsumed. Thomas Hill Green, the influential Oxford philosopher, had made this conception central to his political theory and many of the *Lux Mundi* contributors had come under his pervasive influence. A government which has as its aim anything other than this common good is not a true government at all. Welfare is thus built into the very conception of the state.

I have argued elsewhere[6] that in the late nineteenth century the liberal image of a benevolent but omnipotent God became a pattern for a bureaucratic and omnicompetent welfare state. The fatherhood of God was for many Christians the model for a paternal state, which would mitigate some of the harsher consequences of a capitalist economy and avoid, in England, the violent conflicts which led in Russia, Italy and Germany to overt totalitarianism. The influence worked both ways and the popularity of 'the fatherhood of God' among liberal theologians of this time, especially in Germany and in Britain, may partly be ascribed to the analogy with the paternal state. God was seen as performing more perfectly the welfare role which the state found it increasingly necessary to assume.

In the view I am here criticizing, a legitimate state 'rests upon and gives expression to a group of moral principles and ideals'[7] which are postulated as prior to political institutions and derived from theology. Later thinkers in this tradition have argued that these general principles or rules are applied to practical political issues with the aid of 'middle axioms'. It is the church's role to enunciate moral rules and encourage those of its members who are appropriately qualified to examine how these can properly be 'applied' to concrete issues. The experts state the 'facts', the theologians bring their principles, and together – with the aid of middle axioms – they relate the two. As William Temple once put it: 'Christian industrialists and business men should get together, along with some economists and one or two theologians, to work out what is really involved for their own part of the nation's life.'[8]

In contrast to this belief in the divine origin of political authority and the presumption that the Christian's duty towards the state is 'first and foremost, the duty of obedience', a duty 'invested with the same sanctions as the most sacred claims',[9] biblical writers are much more ambivalent about political matters. The early life of the people of Israel manifested a notion of authority as dispersed among the different tribes and among certain national institutions cutting across these tribal divisions. There was no conception of a sovereign state; ultimate authority was found in Yahweh. The idea of a strong centralized system of political domination, which characterized some of the neighbouring states, was indeed seen as endangering the traditions and liberties of the people. James Barr has contrasted their situation with that of certain Mesopotamian peoples: 'Kingship was not lowered from heaven in the beginning, on the contrary there had been a long time in Israel before kingship began...The idea of having a human king was a revolt against God.'[10] Under Saul and his successors an ideology of kingship developed, in terms of 'the Lord's anointed', but the king's powers were severely restricted and after the fall of Jerusalem and end of the monarchy authority passed to prophet and priest.

The New Testament writings, too, are equivocal about systems of political domination. In the Johannine tradition, the 'kingship' of Jesus plays a crucial role and calls into question all earthly claims to sovereignty. The cry of the chief priests, 'We have no king but Caesar' (John 19:15), is seen as the ultimate betrayal of their divine calling. In the book of Revelation, Babylon – which symbolizes the kingdoms of this world (Rome) – is doomed to destruction and has no claim on Christian loyalty. Some critics see, in the Pauline writings, a close connection between earthly, political, authorities and the 'principalities and powers', rulers of darkness in the heavenly spheres. They point out that every time the term *exousiai* (authorities) is used in these writings, it refers, with one exception, to heavenly (demonic) powers. That exception is when Paul uses the term with explicit reference to civil authorities in Romans 13:1-7. It is thus unlikely that, in this passage, the spiritual, demonic, connotation of the term is absent.[11]

Much debate has taken place on the interpretation of Romans 13, particularly in Germany, where it had been used by some Christians to justify obedience to Hitler. Most modern commentators argue that the statements made there, urging Christians to be 'subject' to the powers that be, must be read as advocating a response to specific historical circumstances, rather than as setting out general rules or providing a theology of the state. 'Paul is not advancing any theoretical considerations', writes Ernst Käsemann, 'He is certainly not making exhaustive statements about the relation to authorities. Thus he is silent about possible conflicts and the limits of earthly authority.'[12] The apostle's advice to Christians in Rome has illegitimately been erected into the foundation of an ideology of political domination, alien to the spirit of the New Testament, with its suspicion of 'the rulers of this age' who – ignorant of God's hidden wisdom – had 'crucified the Lord of glory' (1 Cor 2:8). Paul may not rightfully be seen as here supplying Christians with a political theory, nor may it be claimed that there is a single 'biblical' doctrine of the state.

I am not, of course, arguing that the biblical writings provide justification for an alternative system of government to that of kingship, such as populism, democracy, or republicanism. Far from it. As Barr notes, it was *the people*, in the days of Samuel, who clamoured for a king. There is nothing in scripture or in the history of the early church to suggest that consent of the governed in some way bestows authority on a person or body of persons. Consent is seen neither as a necessary nor a sufficient condition of moral obligation, and political theories which base authority on contract can make no claim to a specifically Christian foundation. Apart from their need to rely upon grossly deceptive ideas such as 'tacit consent', the very basis of their position is unsound.[13] The idea of a covenant between God and his people did, however, in the seventeenth century serve as an analogy to the social contract which some opponents of royal absolutism developed out of medieval sources.[14] Any such attempt to derive political or constitutional principles or models from scripture involves a selective and slanted reading.

Parliamentary or 'representative' government may possibly be justified in terms of its consequences – 'we agree to try strength by counting heads instead of breaking heads', as one nineteenth century writer put it[15] – but it cannot, from a Christian standpoint, claim divine sanction. Representation is indeed a phantom. Perhaps Rousseau's most valuable contribution to political thinking was his critique of representation – of the idea that one will can be represented by another.[16] A person may will something *instead* of me or on my behalf and may act in a way conceived to be in my interest, but this is different. Theories of representation claim more.

In a sophisticated but vain attempt to rescue the concept of representation, Hanna Pitkin acknowledges that it is impossible to represent another person's will or desire. She suggests rather that representation involves acting in the interests of the public represented. But, recognizing that benevolent despotism may claim to do this, she adds that representative government must also remain 'responsive to the people'.[17] She thus assumes there is such a thing as a public interest, or a common good – a matter to which I shall return – and that 'the people' is an entity having wishes to which a government may respond. The population of a modern state cannot, however, legitimately be said to have the kind of coherence and organic structure that is assumed in talking about its wishes. I am not asserting that only individual persons can properly be said to have wishes, or make decisions. Certain voluntary human groups may develop sufficient of a common life and purpose to make it possible to speak of their wishes or decisions, but the modern state is not one of them, and the attempt to make it into such will succeed only at the cost of freedom, individual and corporate. Rousseau's assault on group life within his state was integral to his totalitarian aims. The kind of unity he sought, where 'the will of all' is replaced by a 'general will', is possible only when intermediate groups are eliminated and individuals identify themselves unambiguously and totally with the state.

Furthermore, representative government may be seen to encourage a subtle form of irresponsibility. Millions of adults hand over to a few hundred so-called representatives the right to make decisions on their behalf, while for the following five years these millions pursue in good conscience their own interests and pleasures. In any case, serious attempts to challenge decisions of the elected mandarins is denounced as undemocratic. 'Representative government' is perhaps the most effective disincentive there is to constructive social action at the local, regional or functional levels.

If talk of representation is nonsense, proportional representation is (to borrow a phrase of Bentham) 'rhetorical nonsense, nonsense upon stilts'. Such a system would merely give counterfeit validity to a regime on the grounds that it fully embodies 'the will of the people'. Depriving electors of any say in the person who is to 'represent' them, it removes the last vestige of power from local parties, handing it over to huge centralized party machines. This is the system of government which in 1976 the Church of England General Synod thought fit to urge as desirable for introduction in this country.[18] Like many Christian pronouncements on political issues it assumes (and in assuming gives a kind of approval to) a whole set of institutions and principles which are, to say the least, of questionable validity. In advocating proportional representation the Synod assumed that the notion of representation itself is meaningful and practicable.

When similarly challenged on controversial issues of the moment, Jesus – as portrayed in the gospels – frequently refused to answer in the terms proposed; rather he contested the assumptions of the questioner. Asked to adjudicate in a dispute between brothers about property, Luke has him calling into question the covetousness which constituted the basis of the whole property system and of the acquisitive society of his day (Luke 12:13-20).[19] When asked whether taxes should be paid to the state, Jesus challenged his questioners with the absolute claims of God: 'Render to Caesar the things that are Caesar's and to God the things that are God's' (Matt. 22:21). His reply carefully avoids giving a general legitimacy to the state.

Christianity does not, then, provide justification for the claim that obedience to rulers is the first duty of citizens, nor does it supply principles and ideals which limit the authority of the state or legitimize resistance. Behind the model of Christian politics I have been examining lies the belief that 'principles' can be derived from theological propositions in some kind of a political vacuum and subsequently be 'applied' to concrete situations. All we need to do is to get our theology straight, deduce our moral principles and, by means of middle axioms, apply them to the political world. The relationship between Christianity and politics is that of 'implication'. The report *Faith in the City* is rightly critical of an excessively 'deductive and academic' tendency in theology. Yet in its discussion of the connection between Christianity and politics, it assumes this very model, referring to the 'social and political implications' of a gospel which is essentially concerned with 'personal relationships and individual responses'.[20] On this assumption the cosmic and social dimensions of Christian faith become matters of secondary importance, being deduced from the individual and personal kernel of the gospel. Enoch Powell, in contrast, has rightly maintained that 'The Gospel is indeed a social gospel...The good news of the Gospel is imparted to the individual only as a member of a society...The most fundamental heresy of all is to imagine that the Gospel is given to individuals or received by individuals or apprehended by individuals'.[21]

In response to the view of the relation between Christianity and politics that I am considering, it must be insisted that theology is always developed in a particular cultural, economic and political situation and that the very terms and images used in theological discourse are influenced by these social factors. How Christians think of God's authority – his 'government of the universe', to use a phrase popular in the eighteenth century – will inevitably be affected by their experience of earthly structures of domination. Either consciously or sub-consciously they will draw from this experience in their theological endeavours. If their only experience of human authority has been autocratic they are likely to conceive of God's relation to his people in similar terms – sometimes as reinforcing the claims of earthly rulers, as in the thinking of King James I, or as challenging these claims, as in that of his parliamentary opponents.[22] Thinking about God cannot therefore be done in a political vacuum. Hebrew beliefs about Yahweh were evolved in the midst of social – and specifically political – conflicts as were those of the early Christian church.

Images of God as father and shepherd and the idea of the Holy Spirit as feminine, which were salient in the very early church, and remained influential in the Syriac tradition for a long time, were gradually replaced as predominant by images drawn from the rhetoric of political domination.[23] When churches became politically powerful and Christians were no longer an embattled and persecuted minority the picture of Christ the *pantocrator* became popular. These images of God strengthened in turn the claims of earthly rulers to absolute power.

Today the Church of England is similarly involved in a political system and this involvement cannot but affect its beliefs and practices. It may, in the form of archiepiscopal edicts or synodical resolutions, adopt a patrician pose of standing above the waterflood of political conflict, but it is in fact deeply involved. With much of its income deriving from investments and property managed by the Church Commissioners, its officials enjoying a comfortable standard of living and a degree of job security unknown among most fellow citizens, the general endorsement given by the Church of England to the current political system is not surprising. 'Where your treasure is there will your heart be also' (Matt. 6:21). Indeed many of the (frequently justified) criticisms made of the Thatcher regime by establishment figures – in the churches, civil service or professions – are made from the standpoint of a deep commitment to the *status quo*. Her assailants see the radical policies pursued by the government in certain areas as threatening a situation in which traditional elites have been able to manipulate a welfare state to their own advantage. The high-minded tone of episcopal pronouncements, from as far north as Durham, is less convincing when viewed in this light.

The state is seen as a powerful and benevolent agency for achieving the common good. The more power it has, the more good it can do. The left-of-centre liberalism which marks most church pronouncements on political issues is unashamedly statist in its assumptions. Though critical of the Thatcher regime it shares this basic standpoint. For the present government, despite lip-service paid to individual freedom and local initiative, has systematically undermined the power of functional and regional institutions and, as one of Thatcher's former cabinet colleagues has observed, manifests profound centralist and authoritarian tendencies.

Not only are the political statements of church bodies patently influenced by the social position of the churches in contemporary England but the theological liberalism, which has characterized Anglican thought over the past hundred years, is also directly related to this position. The image of God as powerful, benevolent and bureaucratic is related to beliefs about the state. Punishment, human and divine, has come to be seen as less concerned with past offenses, than with future conditioning and manipulation of 'deviants', so they may better conform to the requirements of the social order. God is interested less in righteousness than in mercy and forgiveness; though in fact mercy and forgiveness make sense only within a righteous structure.

It is perhaps of some significance that the English term 'righteousness' has almost dropped out of current usage. This is partly because the term unfortunately acquired an individualist flavour, due to its being employed in reformation controversies on justification. It has, however, been revived among the Ras Tafari of Jamaica, where it signifies the divine judgement of evil and oppressive social conditions of the earthly city, 'Babylon'. We tend to use the term 'justice' when the translators of the Authorized Version of the Bible used 'righteousness', but the connotation is different. Righteousness has a prophetic and uncompromising tone, justice is a question of balance, a nicely calculated less or more. Moderates may call for justice, only extremists talk of righteousness. To use Péguy's language, righteousness is a matter of *mystique*, while justice is an aspect of *politique*. Official church pronouncements on social issues ought to be more in the mode of *mystique* than *politique*. Regrettably today official statements generally reflect the well-balanced and sensible opinions of the average *Guardian* reader and do little to challenge the assumptions prevailing in the secular world.[24]

The God of British Christianity in the twentieth century is a God of conciliation and of peace at any price, who never takes sides. An article in the *Oxford Diocesan Magazine* stated that at a recent clerical conference in a large midland diocese, the SDP-Liberal Alliance (as it then was) had 120 supporters, against 80 Conservatives and 42 for Labour. 'This is not surprising', commented Sir James Cobban. 'There is much in its policy, much more in its approach to politics and in the outlook of its leaders, that makes it attractive to a Church that is dedicated to reconciliation.'[25] But the kind of reconciliation which Christianity preaches is reconciliation through a cross. 'Without the shedding of blood there is no remission of sins' (Hebrews 9:22). It is the very 'incarnationalist' emphasis, characteristic of the *Lux Mundi* theologians, that has led many Anglicans to ignore or underestimate the significance of social conflict and political struggle.

I have here been arguing that the connection between Christianity and politics is a dialectical one. There is no possibility of simply working out the political implications of a 'neutral' theological understanding enjoying immunity from political taint. Even for those of us who hold a 'high' doctrine of revelation, truth is revealed in a specific political context, in language and images which are influenced by this fact, and it is apprehended in the present day by churches which similarly exist in such a context. Neither theology nor moral principles, then, are immune from political influence. But nor are the so-called 'facts' that the experts are thought to supply.

In much contemporary debate among Christians on social issues there is an exaggerated respect for experts, particularly economists, who are believed simply to be technicians providing factual data which is ideologically neutral. In truth the analysis of the situation presented by economists and other social scientists is fundamentally influenced by presuppositions and assumptions that in turn are related to their social and political experience. While the quality of reports on social issues from the Church of England has markedly improved in recent years, their authors frequently suffer from the positivist illusion that they are engaged in an exercise of applying general moral principles, derived from theology, to a set of facts supplied by neutral experts.

A further aspect of the model I am discussing that needs questioning is the role played by 'principles' in the process of political judgment. I believe W.G. Ward was right in his insistence that Christian moral judgement is made in the particular case rather than in the general principle. We do not judge the rightness of actions by referring upwards to principles, rather we assess the adequacy of principles by examining the moral status of the particular consequences they entail. As Ward argued, a man does not first come to see that murder is wrong and then deduce that the murder he has just committed must have been bad. 'It is,' he maintained, 'with indefinitely more keenness manifest to me that my past act was base, than that those general propositions are true.'[27]

In trying to discover what is right in a particular situation, rather than referring upwards to general principles, it is perhaps better to look sideways to situations which are similar in relevant respects. Much legal argument, particularly when appealing to the common law, proceeds by looking for close analogies rather than by invoking general rules. The appeal 'sideways' will not assuredly solve all problems, for there remains the vexed question of which cases are relevant. This difficulty is, however, shared by those who attempt to make such judgements by subsuming particular cases under general rules.

A misconceived belief in the priority of moral principles is partly responsible for the insistence by many that Christian pronouncements on political issues should be restricted to the enunciation of generalities rather than the making of particular judgements. 'The main task of the Church,' wrote William Temple, 'is to inculcate Christian principles.'[28] Particulars, however, ever toucheth closer than generals.

It should be clear that I am by no means suggesting that general rules have no legitimate role. They may be useful guides to action, but are merely summaries of moral experience on the issue in question. Logically the experience and the particular judgements made on the basis of this experience are prior to the general rule, whose truth rests on the validity of the experience and the soundness of the judgement. But how are such validity and soundness to be found and recognized? Ward looked to the life and traditions of a community within which was cultivated a respect for holiness. It is in this environment that human character may develop and conscience become sensitive. Living in such a community may lead Christians to act in ways that sometimes scandalize the secular world, whose citizens cry 'why this waste?' It is, however, easier to recognize a group dedicated to righteousness than to formulate adequate principles and axioms, and Ward rightly insisted that, 'It is a far better test of a man's real sentiments that he joins the right *party*, than that he professes the right *opinions*.'[29]

A final inadequacy of the model under consideration is a comfortable belief in 'the common good' – that there is some substantive state of affairs which is in the interests of all – and that there is no conflict of interests that cannot be resolved with a little give and take. It is thought to be the duty of governments to bring this state of affairs into being with assistance from the churches. There may truly be some structural arrangement within which the various individuals and groups composing the state may freely be able to pursue their several substantive ends, but this is quite different from envisaging the government's task as the pursuit of a single substantive end.

How far the coercive institutions of the modern state are calculated to maintain even such a formal structure is questionable. The power and patronage at a government's disposal are likely to be exploited by groups in power to advance their sectional interest and oppress the weak. The degree of protection and benefit afforded to the rich minority by the modern western state is greatly in excess of their contribution to its costs. It is the mass of the people who pay the bulk of the taxes and, as numerous studies have shown,[30] it is the better-off who have benefited most from the welfare state. Even at the cultural level it is remarkable how the poor pay tax on football pools in order to subsidize opera and other entertainments of the *nouveaux riches*. The state has indeed become a huge engine for the transfer of wealth from the poor to the rich.

It may in many instances be expedient, wise or right for Christians to obey the laws of the state in which they live, but the important question to ask is always not *who* made the law, but *what* does the law enjoin and what the consequences of obedience or disobedience are. Hobbes spoke of laws as artificial chains, but they are nothing of the sort. They are penal in form, not unconditional commands issued by a body which can validly bind its subjects and which therefore ought to be obeyed. It is in fact the role of the churches to remove from the state that aura of divinity with which it has been invested. The civil rituals which mark legislative and legal proceedings are in need of urgent desacralizing, and the churches should be among the principal critics of what may be called 'the wig conception of politics'. Christians must also be prepared to expose the bogus ideology of a social contract by which citizens are said to have bound themselves to obedience, conditional or otherwise, reminding us that we 'must obey God rather than men'.

I am not arguing that scripture and tradition provide anything like a theological justification for anarchism as a positive theory, but rather that they cannot properly be used as a basis for theories of political obligation. It may, however, be worth bearing in mind the perceptive observation of Pierre-Joseph Proudhon that 'Government is either of divine right or it is nothing'.[31]

As they look at a world of conflict, violence, poverty and famine, Christians naturally ask, What can we do? Surely it is the job of Christians to help those less fortunate than they are and, from the riches of their own experience and resources, to answer the problems which face the modern world. The churches, we are told, must speak out on political issues condemning the guilty and outlining principles which governments should follow. I remember attending a conference on the Caribbean some years ago, composed almost entirely of European and North American politicians and academics. The question was continually asked, what can we do to help the region? It became necessary at a certain point to ask of ourselves the further question, who are 'we'?

Christians generally assume that they are, and somehow ought naturally to be, in the role of the priest, levite, or (optimistically) the Samaritan, called on to offer aid. Yet some forms of intervention and aid are harmful, leading to a debilitating dependence and to the strengthening of oppressive systems of domination. There are times when we ought to do nothing – to keep out. It is a mistake to assume that we are always 'called to serve', despite the emphasis on 'service' in the Alternative Service Book. Service has for the Christian its dangers. 'The privileged, unambiguous access to God is through service to the poor', writes a Latin American theologian.[32] Yet in the gospels it is the poor who are blessed, and not necessarily the clergy who 'serve' them. The concept of service too often covers a desire to dominate and change those among whom one is working.

Christians often assume that wealth is in itself a good thing – or at least morally neutral – and that the important question is how wealth is spent. 'The spiritual dimension', Margaret Thatcher told the General Assembly of the Church of Scotland, 'comes in deciding in what one does with the wealth.'[33] In a party so deeply committed to the doctrine of original sin – the Chancellor of the Exchequer practically defines conservatism in terms of this doctrine [34] – it is remarkable to find such naive ideas about 'freedom of choice'. Thatcherism, as set forth in this speech, is indeed pure political Pelagianism. The Bishop of Durham agrees that industry exists to increase wealth. As wealth is good, poverty is bad. It is 'morally as well as divinely offensive'.[35]

For New Testament writers precisely the reverse is true, wealth is offensive and poverty is blessed. 'Lay not up treasures on earth' (Matt. 6:19); 'A man's life does not consist in the abundance of his possessions' (Luke 12:15); 'The rich he has sent empty away' (Luke 1:53); 'Those who desire to be rich fall into temptation' (1 Tim. 6:9); 'Has not God chosen the poor?' (James 2:5); 'Come now, you rich, weep and howl for the miseries that are coming upon you' (James 5:1).

Charles Péguy distinguished between poverty and destitution.[36] A situation which leads to exploitation and exclusion, Bishop Jenkins rightly argues, is evil. Destitution is degrading. But not all poverty is degrading, and the poor *need not* be powerless. Many cases can be cited where the poor have successfully united to resist the impositions of the rich, securing justice for themselves and preserving their way of life. Solidarity is indeed more characteristic of the poor than of the rich. Frequently it is the poor who conserve and transform what appears useless in a country which regards everything as disposable. I vividly remember trying to convince an incredulous politician in Washington that money can actually do harm, disrupting the life of communities, and that the problems of a country like Haiti would not be solved and might be exacerbated by increased US aid. Small co-operative projects among the poor can be ruined totally by a large influx of foreign cash.

Jenkins indeed recognises elsewhere that unlimited economic growth will rapidly deplete the world's resources and lead to serious ecological problems for future generations. The aim of social policy, then, ought not to be raising the life-style of the poor to that of the rich, but reducing the life-style of the rich to something more like that of the poor, thereby giving them more than a camel's chance of entering God's commonwealth.

Christians thus speak much of grace in their *theology*, but their political assumptions are Pelagian or worse. They issue high-minded statements, from Rome, Geneva or from Church House Westminster, about what should be done in the world, but who listens? They speak from positions of wealth and privilege and recommend good works. 'Incarnationalists' of the *Lux Mundi* tradition and many liberation theologians, armed with a *kenotic* Christology, urge Christians to 'identify' with the poor and outcast, to follow in the footsteps of Christ who 'though he was rich, yet for your sake became poor' (2 Cor 8:9). Yet this true identification is impossible for us to achieve by a mere act of will. Many have tried and may be respected for having done so. Yet even Father Lowder in the slums of east London enjoyed privileges unknown to those living around him. As is the case with most liberation theologians in Latin America today, the safety net of family or religious community cushions against the insecurity which true poverty involves, and numerous foreign holidays or lecture tours relieve the boredom. Conrad Noel did his best to identify with the humble villagers of Thaxted, but also valued the 'breakfast in a luxurious canopied bed with logs blazing on an open hearth, and then slippers and dressing gown provided', at the home of Lady Warwick![37]

True identification with the poor is by grace not works. A stock market crash which reduces the income and increases the insecurity of the young broker to the level of that experienced by the working class family whose house he has recently purchased, is a more effective cause of identification than his helping in a local youth club each week. Unexpected early redundancy for a moderately successful business executive and a period on the dole is a better way for him to understand the problems of the unemployed than years of voluntary work in a legal aid centre. Hundreds of highly motivated liberals going to work in 'third world' countries to serve the local population, are likely to have less effect than a basically conservative priest who finds himself propelled into the position of archbishop of San Salvador, and who feels compelled to speak and act on the concrete issues which he finds confronting him. Oscar Romero was outspoken and his words were quite explicit. Addressing the armed forces he declared: 'In the name of God...I plead with you, I beg you, I order you in the name of God: stop the repression.'[38] To the US government he spoke in equally precise terms. His position is in stark contrast to most episcopal statements on the British miners' strike of 1984-5. Like the impartial God of modern western religion, they spoke from above the battle, and conscientiously refused to take sides.[39]

'There is a time to speak and a time to keep silence.' In England today Christians should be less concerned to say *what ought to be done* than to find out and take to heart *what is going on*. The logic of Christian political action and commitment should neither be that of applying general principles, derived from theological propositions, to concrete cases, nor should it normally be by a misconceived attempt to 'identify' with or 'serve' the poor.[40] If only we could, with a measure of humility and humour, be more sensitive to the position in which we find ourselves! At least we would then be open to the movement of the Holy Spirit, who questions and subverts the structures of domination and oppression which characterize Babylon – the earthly city – for, 'Where the Spirit of the Lord is there is liberty' (2 Cor 3:17). While we might find modest ways to facilitate this movement of the Spirit, we will beware of thinking, for example, that the 'massive transfers of wealth' recommended by the Brandt Commission will solve the world's problems, or that a donation of 'one per cent' of our income will bring justice to the world's poor.[41]

Never in human history has the condition of the poor and oppressed been significantly improved by action from the rich; why should we assume that things will be different in our day? We can indeed pray that they may become powerful enough to improve their own position. We might also prepare ourselves and our neighbours for a time when the mighty are being put down from their seat and the rich being sent empty away, and subvert, wherever possible, the efforts of the powerful to resist such changes. For, as Thomas Hobbes observed, 'The power of the mighty hath no foundation but in the opinion and belief of the people.'[42]

Notes

1. W.J.H. Campion in Charles Gore, ed., *Lux Mundi: A Series of Studies in the Religion of the Incarnation*, 5th. ed. (London 1890), p.444.

2. Campion in Gore, ed. *Lux Mundi*, p.444.

3. Gore, 'Preface', *Lux Mundi*, p.ix; F.D. Maurice, *The Kingdom of Christ* (London 1838), 3, p.103; see also David Nicholls and Rowan Williams, *Politics and Theological Identity* (London 1984), pp.31-2; Nicholls, 'The Totalitarianism of Thomas Arnold', *The Review of Politics*, 29:1, 1967, pp.518f.; and Nicholls, *The Pluralist State* (London 1975).

4. Campion in Gore, ed. *Lux Mundi*, p.448.

5. Campion in Gore, ed. *Lux Mundi*, p.449.

6. David Nicholls, *Deity and Domination: I, Images of God and the State in the 19th and 20th Centuries* (London 1989), chs. 2 and 3. Some passages in the present chapter are taken from the introduction to this book, where these ideas are more fully developed.

7. Campion in Gore, ed. *Lux Mundi*, p.445. In certain contexts it is useful to distinguish between *principles*, as formal axioms ('do as you would be done by'), and *rules* as substantive axioms ('killing is wrong'), but in the text I use the terms indiscriminately.

8. William Temple, *The Hope of a New World* (London 1940), p.66. See David Nicholls, 'William Temple and the Welfare State', *Crucible* (October-December 1984), pp.161-8.

9. Campion in Gore, ed. *Lux Mundi*, p.450.

10. James Barr, 'The Bible as a Political Document', *Bulletin of the John Rylands University Library of Manchester*, 62:2, 1980, p.273.

11. For a discussion of the extensive literature see Clinton D. Morrison, *The Powers That Be: Earthly Rulers and Demonic Powers in Romans 13: 1-7* (London 1960), and Oscar Cullmann, *The State in the New Testament* (London 1957), pp.95-114.

12. Ernst Käsemann, *Commentary on Romans* (London 1980), p.354. See also his classic discussion of the question in 'Römer 13, 1-7 in unserer Generation', *Zeitschrift für Theologie und Kirche* 56 (1959), pp. 316ff.

13. See the excellent work of Carole Pateman, *The Problem of Political Obligation: a Critique of Liberal Theory* (New York 1979); also David Nicholls, 'A Comment on "Consent"', *Political Studies*, 27:1, 1979, pp.120f.

14. The classical treatment of this may be found in Otto von Gierke's massive *Das deutsche Genossenschaftsrecht* (Berlin 1868-1913), part of which has been translated into English by Ernest Barker under the title *Natural Law and the Theory of Society, 1500-1800* (Cambridge 1934). See also Gierke's, *The Development of Political Theory* (London 1939). For a criticism of Gierke see H. Höpfl and M.P. Thompson, 'The History of Contract as a Motif in Political Thought', *American Historical Review*, 84:4, 1979. See also J.W. Gough, *Social Contract* (Oxford 1957 ed.). A recent discussion of the issues can be found in Michael Lessnoff, *Social Contract* (London 1986). On the analogy between federal theology and contract theory in the American colonies, see Perry Miller, *Errand into the Wilderness* (Boston 1956) and *The New England Mind: the Seventeenth Century* (Boston 1939).

15. James Fitzjames Stephen, *Liberty Equality Fraternity* (London 1874 ed.), p.31.

16. J.-J. Rousseau, *Du contrat social*, 3:15; in C.E. Vaughan, ed., *The Political Writings of Jean Jacques Rousseau* (Oxford 1962 ed.), i, pp.95ff.

17. Hanna Pitkin, *The Concept of Representation* (Berkeley and Los Angeles 1972 ed.), p.232.

18. In February 1976 the Synod passed a resolution that 'urges all political parties to adopt a preferential system of proportional representation as a policy commitment for future elections', Church of England, *Proceedings of the General Synod* (London 1976), 7:2, p.335.

19. For a consideration of early Christian attitudes to property see Martin Hengel, *Property and Riches in the Early Church* (London 1974), and Luke T. Johnson, *Sharing Possessions: Mandate and Symbol of Faith* (Philadelphia 1981).

20. *Faith in the City: a Call for Action by Church and Nation* (London 1985), pp.63 and 48. Duncan Forrester also refers more than once to the social 'implications' of the gospel, in *Christianity and the Future of Welfare* (London 1985), see pp.33, 39 &c.; this work contains some acute observations and criticisms.

21. J. Enoch Powell, *Wrestling with the Angel* (London 1977), p.28. But compare a later statement of Powell's, 'Man...is born as an individual, he dies as an individual, and if there is forgiveness and redemption, he is forgiven and redeemed as an individual. It is to man the individual that the Gospel speaks.' (*Theology*, no 85 (1982), p.476; quoted in D. Forrester, *Christianity*, p.96.) Powell would seem here to be less consistent than his admirers claim.

22. See David Nicholls, 'Deity and Domination', *New Blackfriars*, nos. 775 and 776 (January and February 1985).

23. On the way this operated among Syriac Christians see Sebastian Brock, *The Holy Spirit in the Syriac Baptismal Tradition* (Poona 1979). While the image of Jesus as the good shepherd is a frequent theme of mosaics in the Roman catacombs, it is impossible to find a traditional ikon of that picture. There is one ikon carrying the words 'I am the good shepherd', but the *picture* is of Christ the high priest. See Dionysius of Fourna, *The Painter's Manual* (London 1981 ed.), p.88.

24. This point was well made by E.R. Norman in his Reith Lectures, *Christianity and the World Order* (Oxford 1979). For my criticism of his general position see 'The Politics of Dr Norman', in K. Leech, ed., *Christianity Reinterpreted?* (London 1982 ed.), pp.8f.

25. *Oxford Diocesan Magazine*, July 1983, p.13.

26. Nicholls and Williams, *Politics and Theological Identity*, pp.27-44.

27. W.G. Ward, *Essays on the Philosophy of Theism* (London 1884), ii, p.90. See David Nicholls, 'Conscience and Authority in the Thought of W.G. Ward', *The Heythrop Journal*, 26:4, 1985, pp.420f.

28. William Temple, *Christianity and Social Order* (Harmondsworth 1942), p.23.

29. W.G. Ward, *The Ideal of a Christian Church* (London 1844 ed.), p.519.

30. Julien Le Grand, *The Strategy of Equality* (London 1982); Frank Field, *Inequality in Britain* (London 1981); Rhodes Boyson, ed., *Down with the Poor* (London 1971); Church of England Board for Social Responsibility, *Not Just for the Poor: Christian Perspectives on the Welfare State* (London 1986).

31. P-J. Proudhon, *Idée générale de la révolution*, in *Œuvres complètes de P-J. Proudhon* (Paris 1923), iv, p.208.

32. Leonardo Boff, *La fe en la periferia del mundo* (Salamanca 1981), p.36. The rich tend indeed to be more exacting and less appreciative of the services of the clergy than the poor!

33. 'Text of a Speech given by the Prime Minister...on Saturday 21 May 1988' (Press release), p.17. The letter of the Chairman and Secretary of the Church of England Board for Social Responsibility, addressed to the Prime Minister, points to the ambiguities of wealth. For an exposition of the Thatcher ideology on this matter see Brian Griffiths, *The Creation of Wealth.*

34. Cited in John Atherton, *Faith in the Nation: a Christian Vision for Britain* (London 1988), p.61

35. David E. Jenkins, *God, Politics and the Future* (London 1988), p.23. An old-fashioned view is that industry exists not to create wealth (or even worse to create jobs) but to satisfy human needs.

36. *Cahiers de la Quinzaine*, 4:3, 1902, in Péguy, *Basic Verities* (London 1943), pp.58f.

37. L.E. Ellsworth, *Charles Lowder and the Ritualist Movement* (London 1982), esp. pp.88, 131f., 164f.; Conrad Noel, *An Autobiography* (London 1945), p.114.

38. Catholic Institute for International Relations, *Romero: Martyr for Liberation* (London 1982), p.65.

39. The Bishop of Durham, for example, insisted that there must be no victors, *God, Politics and the Future,* pp.8f. Viewed against the background of a government policy dedicated to destroying the power of organized labour in Britain, the strike was of wider significance than was immediately apparent.

40. I am far from suggesting that Christians should not work in poor parts of the country or in poor countries overseas. I worked in the Caribbean for eight years myself, but am fully aware of the relatively privileged position I enjoyed there. Many European missionaries, technical assistants and field officers live, with servants performing their domestic work, in a style which is unknown in their home country. They are not necessarily wrong in this, but they should be under no illusion that they are 'identifying with the poor'.

41. The Brandt Report is published as *North-South: a Programme for Survival* (London 1980), see esp. pp.241f. A pamphlet circulated in 1987 by the Oxford Diocesan Stewardship Council makes the fraudulent suggestion that such a donation of 1% by Christians would 'bring justice to the poor'.

42. Thomas Hobbes, *Behemoth*, in William Molesworth, ed., *The English Works of Thomas Hobbes*, vi (London 1840), p.184.

CHRISTIAN ETHICS

Alister McGrath

The moral seriousness of Anglicanism has been one of its chief glories. The contribution to *Lux Mundi* entitled 'Christian Ethics' (pp.467-520) emphasized that moral earnestness required an equally great *theological* seriousness, if the moral dimension of the Christian faith was not to be lost. Its author, Robert Ottley,[1] later to become Regius Professor of Pastoral Theology, argued forcefully that a 'Christian ethics' worthy of the name was potentially, if not actually, distinct from other ethical systems on account of its presuppositions and methods. A Christian ethics was inextricably linked with certain understandings of God and human nature, and focussed on the person of Jesus Christ.[2] 'Morality', he stressed, 'finds its starting point in theology' (5th ed. p.470). An inadequate theology does not merely fail to preserve, but utterly dissipates, the moral potency of Christianity.

Every period has witnessed the origins and propagation of a 'modern' form of Christianity, allegedly free from the defects of its traditional antecedents and capable of meeting the needs of the modern period. The anonymous *Gospel of the Nineteenth Century* (London 1880[4]) reacting against what it derivatively regarded as an abstract and irrelevant orthodox dogma of Christ, affirmed that 'Christianity consists in the imitation of Christ'. The contemporary ethical relevance of Jesus of Nazareth, and hence the Christian faith, was to be grounded in an appeal to his moral personality, rather than in 'the cold empyrean of theology'.[3] In this paper, I propose to develop the agenda set by our Victorian predecessors, arguing that 'Christian ethics' both presupposes and expresses Christian theology. More specifically, I propose to argue that any relevance which the narrative of Jesus of Nazareth may possess for Christianity and the world is, in the first place *secured*, and in the second *interpreted*, through an incarnational christology.

The question concerns the manner in which Jesus Christ can be regarded as normative in relation to Christian ethics.[4] In what way may the contours of the history of Jesus Christ be allowed to shape our own moral existences? In what way is it authoritative? According to some (such as Bultmann and Kant), Christianity enunciates no distinctive moral insights.[5] Christians are free to (and expected to) echo prevailing secular ethical standards. A similar devaluation of the moral example of Jesus is the effect, if not necessarily the intention, of liberal Anglicanism. Jesus' example is approached through a filter of antecedent values and principles, derived from other sources (such as prevailing liberal middle-class values). It is these antecedent values and principles which are finally normative if the example of Jesus is marginalized where he appears to contradict them, and appropriated where he appears to endorse them. It is not the moral example of Jesus which is important, but those pre-selected contemporary moral values which appeal to his liberal inter-preters.

The origins of the modern discussion of this question may be traced back to the Renaissance, with the rise of the humanist idea of *philosophia Christi*. The words and actions of Jesus, it was suggested, embodied an authentically Christian lifestyle, lent dignity and authority through his divinity, but firmly anchored in his humanity. Christ was to be imitated as embodying the perfection of humanity. The moral authority of *this* specific human existence was grounded in his divinity, whereas the historical existence thus designated as authoritative was totally human and thus equally amenable to imitation.

The Enlightenment, drawing upon such insights, suggested that Jesus of Nazareth was to be imitated as a supreme example of humanity, whose authority resided in the force of his moral personality, which earlier generations had needlessly extrapolated into his divinity. The superiority of Jesus over other religious teachers and moral examples, such as Socrates, was not maintained without some difficulty, however, in that the rationalist dismantling of the orthodox framework of Incarnation and resurrection was found to leave the moral authority of Jesus of Nazareth apparently suspended in mid-air, without visible or credible means of support, seemingly maintained as an axiom or dogma ill-suited to the critical spirit of the age. Jesus might be permitted to endorse the insights of culture and reason – but to suggest that he established them in the first place, or added to them, was to compromise the autonomy of human reason. While the influence of the Enlightenment continues to diminish, part of its intellectual heritage remains remarkably forceful within west-ern Christianity: the concept of Jesus as a human moral example, com-monly designated 'exemplarism'. This essay suggests that we are obliged to re-examine, but not to abandon, the concept of exemplarism if we are to sustain the moral credibility of Christianity in an age still influenced by the critical spirit of the Enlightenment.

I

At the heart of any ethics of imitation, such as Enlightenment exemplarism, lies the very general human tendency to hold up one single life-history as a paradigm, and turn an historical person into an archetype. An individual is isolated, and identified as an example, shaping the contours and defining the horizon of our moral vision. Example, however, is contagious, influencing by proximity, inspiring those in its immediate neighbourhood. The influence of example depends upon conditions of time and space, in that it is inherently difficult to to feel some bond of sympathy with one who lived 'far, far away and long, long ago'. The problem of historical distance diminishes both the force of this example, and the *spontaneity* of an individual's response to it. The authority of that historical example comes to reside, not in a spontaneous and uncoerced individual response to that person, but in a normative transmitted pattern of response which ultimately *derives* from that original historical person, but lacks its historical substance. My response to that individual becomes mediated, rather than immediate, in that I am confronted with the response of another to the example, rather than the example itself. I am required to simulate the response of an intermediate, rather than respond to the original example.

The moral example of Christ is thus transmitted to us indirectly. We cannot stand alongside him and marvel at his personality. We cannot share the personal impressions which he created in the brief flux of his historical existence in Palestine. What we can experience, what is mediated to us, is a series of accounts of that impact, a narrative – an attempt to trap in words something which ultimately defies capture. By its very nature, genius is incommunicable. If the gospels were concerned to mediate to posterity the moral character of Christ, the problem of cultural and historical distance must be judged to place formidable obstacles in their path. Christ's life appears to have been lived under conditions, both internal and external, as unlike those of modern Europeans or North Americans as any human life yet lived. In what way may we realistically ask such a modern person to 'imitate Christ'? What authority do we have for identifying certain aspects of Christ's existence as morally normative, and others as not? How are we to distinguish the historically conditioned elements from the permanently valid moral components – the superfluous from the essential, the husk from the kernel – of the life of Christ?

There are now signs developing, in both academic and popular moral theology, of a new 'quest for the historical moral example of Christ', similar to that of the late Victorian period. Perhaps as a reaction against a perceived incoherence and confusion in contemporary Christian ethics, a search for moral certitude has gained momentum. Searching for a

fundamentum inconcussum, an unshakeable foundation upon which to
ground Christian ethics,[6] a return to the simple morality of Jesus of
Nazareth is advocated. This moral existence, it is suggested, is itself an
adequate foundation of a Christian ethics. This 'historical moral example', we are told, may function as the basis of a new Christian morality,
adequate to challenge prevailing social and political norms.

Harnessed to the service of this end, the gospels are treated as
biographies of Jesus, recording for posterity incidents in the life of their
subject which might prove morally illuminating. The synoptic gospels are
sifted in the hope that some trace of acceptable contemporary moral
norms may be uncovered, and thence lent added dominical weight, setting
aside critical questions in order that such 'dominical' weight might not be
lessened. The suggestion that such norms might be imposed upon, rather
than discerned within, the narrative of Jesus of Nazareth by the pre-
committed gospel reader is occasionally treated as being unworthy of
serious response, thus neatly converting the absence of such a response
into a moral virtue rather than a fatal theological flaw.

But is there any suggestion in the New Testament that such a process
is legitimate? The portrait of Christ as the 'teacher of common sense'
(Pelikan)[7] is an eighteenth-century invention which continues to find
service in the twentieth, even though rendered obselete through subsequent developments. Common sense, as an inherited amalgam of past
clarities and confusions, has limited moral potential, save for the
preservation of what past generations, through intuition as much as
through critical insight, regarded as morally self-evident. And is there
really any persuasive reason for suggesting that the gospels are
fundamentally moral, rather than theological documents? The attempt to
penetrate beneath the New Testament portrait of Christ in order to
uncover a normative historical moral example for posterity is as
unrealistic as the nineteenth-century quest for the historical Jesus, to
which it is methodologically wedded. For the New Testament, however,
the real Christ is not a moral example *tout simple*, but the crucified and
risen redeemer of humanity and transformer of the human situation.[8]

To suggest that Jesus is a moral exemplar in any significant sense is
to raise with acute force the question of how the ethically quintessential
element of this specific historical existence may be distinguished from the
peripheral. For such a distinction must be made, unless we are to drag
the entire cultural context of that existence into the twentieth century as
perennially normative. In the simplest version of the *imitatio Christi* moral
vision, we are given to understand that the ethical torch kindled by Jesus
of Nazareth, and so nearly dropped by the New Testament writers, was
skilfully caught and carried on by his successors in the Enlightenment.

This neat ethical lampadophory leaves one crucial issue unresolved: what *authority* is to be attached to the specific historical example of Jesus of Nazareth?

In part, this question raises the problem of ethical creativity. More seriously, it forces us to address the question of what permits us to identify this specific historical existence as being charged with a supreme ethical significance? Perhaps it is the sheer intractability of this question which moves some to suggest that we might do well to look elsewhere, to the more recent specific historical existences which each and every age admires (however briefly), in which the problem of temporal and cultural distance is mitigated. Exercising the right to choose a moral exemplar may seem to permit the circumvention of historical difficulties – yet, on closer examination, the problem proves to have been postponed, rather than resolved.One cannot overlook the insistence of the Christian tradition that the historical existence of Jesus of Nazareth has been pre-selected for us in this respect. It is something given, rather than chosen, something imposed rather than selected. If we are to select an alternative individual as an exemplar, we are constrained to demonstrate that some essential and ethically normative continuity with the historical existence of Jesus of Nazareth – thereby presupposing knowledge of *both* the ethically normative parameters of the historical existence of Jesus *and* the adequate and authentic reflection, echo or embodiment of these parameters in that alternative existence.

Similar problems, of course, arise in other fields of thought. For example, consider Shakespeare's *Romeo and Juliet*, in the French translations of Pierre Letourneur (1778), Emile Montégut (1870) and Georges Duval (1908). Each translation attempts to convey to its contemporaries the literary and dramatic sense, the rhythm, the cadences of the original – in short, all that goes to make up the 'Shakespearian' character of the narrative. Any evaluation of the extent to which they succeed in this task is dependent upon a knowledge of the original English text, in that we are forced to ask how effectively and faithfully they mediate, echo and embody the *literary* (not *literal*) meaning of their original. We are forced to inquire concerning the authoritative character of their translation, in that these translators are not the sole masters and makers of their literary creations. Their possibilities are limited. They are under authority. There is a certain element in their work which is imposed upon them, in that we seek to encounter Shakespeare (rather than, shall we say, Montégut) as we read. Creative reinterpretation distances us from him, setting Montégut in his place. And this is precisely the point – creative reinterpretation may be identified and evaluated through a comparison with the original in its totality, allowing us to interrogate the translator concerning his intentions and achievements. We are enabled to judge whether the thread of continuity between Shakespeare and Montégut holds firm, or whether it has snapped altogether. Unfortunately, however, we cannot set out the totality of the historical existence of Jesus of Nazareth for inspection and moral analysis, in order to establish how authentically, how *authoritatively*, its essential and normative moral characteristics are echoed in the historical existences of his imitators. The moral Jesus of history remains elusive and mysterious, open to the perennial threat of being naively reconstructed by well-meaning enthusiasts, and passively echoing their ethical axioms across the 'dreadful gulf of history' (Lessing).

To be alert to these enormous difficulties, however, is not to invalidate an appeal to the narrative of Jesus Christ as having a referential function to Christian existence and conduct. It is not to discredit the idea of 'exemplarism', even if it is to expose the Enlightenment understanding of the concept (and its ethical progeny) as truncated and inadequate. It is to use the story of Jesus Christ as a basis for contemporary ethical reflection and action, avoiding the understandably seductive attraction of the simplistic rationalist ethics of the 'imitation of Christ'.[9] 'The exploration of Christian moral concepts must always, in the first place, be the work of theology'.[10]

Christian ethics is specifically formed by this very definite story, which the Christian church recapitulates in its worship and liturgy, and which cannot be divorced from the actions of that church. An ethic which dispenses with reference to Jesus Christ in order to derive its insights from elsewhere cannot be judged 'right' or 'wrong' for that reason: it may, however, not be described as 'Christian'. Morality may not require religion;[11] but Christian faith demands a morality. The exploration of the shape and scope of that morality is an integral and essential part of the task of the Christian church and believer as they reflect upon the implications of the Christian gospel for humanity. Nevertheless, in undertaking this process of reflection, the church must not be permitted to adopt a naive ethical fundamentalism, either by insisting that Christ is our moral example *tout simple*, or by projecting contemporary ethical concerns and their culturally-acceptable solutions onto his person.

II

The fundamental theological difficulty associated with such an ethic of the imitation of Christ is not, however, simply that it is methodologically questionable (in that it almost certainly cannot be, and anyway probably ought not to be, done), but that it is also deficient in both its christological and soteriological dimensions. This form of exemplarism invites us to believe in Jesus Christ as an exemplar whose influence is ostensive rather than effectual – who shows us, as one who is outside us and historically distant from us, what *ought* to be done, but is unable to transform the tragic situation of humanity in order that it *can* be done. Human moral action is taken to be an extension of Christ's actions, a continuation or repetition of his lifestyle. But what, it may reasonably be asked, are the consequences for this exemplarism if there is some fundamental deficiency, some fatal flaw, in human nature itself, which inhibits or totally prevents such imitation in the first place? *Video meliora, proboque; deteriora sequor* (I see the better and approve; I do the worse: Ovid, *Metamorphoses* vii, 20).

The effect, if not the intention, of such an exemplarist approach to the human situation is to portray it as suffering from ignorance, from a sad lack of understanding of its moral obligations – which, once remedied, leads to true morality and the common good. Is this not an inadequate view of the tragedy of the human situation? Perhaps our Victorian forebears could be excused for adopting such an attitude – but for the modern period, steeped in the dreadful knowledge of Auschwitz and Hiroshima, such an approach to human nature must be reckoned as belonging to the dreams of a past and gone age. In a world come of age, we must learn of the sheer tragedy of the human predicament.

In his Bampton Lectures of 1915, Hastings Rashdall developed a strongly exemplarist view of the moral and soteriological relevance of Jesus Christ, as educating and extending the moral vision of humanity.[12] Yet he seemed almost unaware of the war then raging on Europe, reducing both the number of students available to hear his lectures and perhaps their receptivity towards their content. For how, it must be asked, could two Christian nations, steeped in centuries of Christian culture and values, initiate and propagate such a war? Had they not learned from the example of Christ, in the manner in which Rashdall suggests?[13] If Christ's mission was to educate humanity, how could he have so signally failed within cultures allegedly receptive to his instruction? And does not the history of the Christian church itself suggest that it shares the frailty of its common stock of human nature? Christ may indeed be the great moral educator of mankind – but the human capacity for moral education gives every indication of being limited,[14] conditioned and restricted by forces over which we have little control (Rom. 7:15-24).

This exemplarist view of Christ as a moral example is inextricably linked with a deficient view of human nature, which does not – or *will* not – come to terms with human sin, and the tragic history of humanity in general, and the Christian church in particular. As Charles Gore pointed out a century ago:[15]

> Inadequate conceptions of Christ's person go hand in hand with inadequate conceptions of what human nature wants. The Nestorian conception of Christ...qualifies Christ for being an example of what man can do, and into what wonderful union with God he can be assumed if he is holy enough; but Christ remains one man among many, shut in within the limits of a single human personality, and influencing man only from outside. He can be a Redeemer of man if man can be saved from outside by bright example, but not otherwise. The Nestorian Christ is logically associated with the Pelagian man... The Nestorian Christ is the fitting Saviour of the Pelagian man.

An exemplarist soteriology, with its associated understanding of the nature and role of the moral example of Jesus Christ, is ultimately the correlative of a Pelagian view of the situation and abilities of humanity. The ontological gap between Christ and ourselves is contracted, in order to minimize the discontinuity between his moral personality and ours. Christ is the supreme human example, who evinces an authentically human life-style which we are alleged to be capable of imitating. Such a view is not merely inadequate as an exposition of the significance of Jesus Christ,[16] but is unrealistic in its estimation of the capacities and inclinations of human nature.[17] It is an ethic addressed to an idealized humanity, which does not correspond to humanity as we empirically know it, and as we have been taught to view it by the Christian tradition, trapped in its predicament. Perhaps the most characteristic feature of sin is self-deception,[18] a reluctance to accept the tragedy of our situation. Perhaps the first step in the reconstruction of an authentically Christian ethic must be the elimination of the 'perfectionist illusions' (Niebuhr) which have so hindered liberal Christian ethical reflections during the present century. An inability to lodge the moral life in the realities of historical human existence results in utopianism.[19]

This 'moral example' theory also appears to rest upon a deficient view of the person of Christ. This view of his significance ultimately grounds his continuing ethical relevance in his exemplification of allegedly universal moral values. The death of Socrates in 399 BC directs our attention to virtues, such as courage and integrity, which are not limited to one particular time and place. In that the narrative of Socrates' death exemplifies these virtues, it may be said to be charged with moral authority. Socrates is of moral importance in that he witnesses to these virtues. They are prior to his existence, and were not established through his death, although they are conveyed through it. In principle, these and other virtues could be conveyed through the narrative of the life and death of other humans: the moral authority of such a narrative is interchangeable, in that it can be predicated of other subjects – such as, in the view of exemplarism, Jesus Christ. Exemplarism locates the moral authority of the narrative of Jesus of Nazareth in its reflection of previously recognized universal moral values, the validity of which is independent of him. Other witnesses, preferably more recent, might function considerably better in this respect. On this view, the moral authority of Jesus rests in his pointing to the moral order, as a mediator – only to retreat into obscurity as the observer's attention is held by that universal moral order, rather than the contingent historical means by which it was disclosed. If the idea of Incarnation is taken seriously, however, the adequacy of this understanding of the identity and significance of Jesus must be called into question. For latent within the very idea of Incarnation, is the suggestion that the history of Jesus Christ may shape and transform our understanding of the moral order in a qualitatively distinct manner.

What, then, can Christian ethics say concerning the significance of Jesus Christ, and his referential role in relation to Christian existence?

III

The concept of Incarnation, rightly understood, is of central importance to any attempt to unfold the significance of Jesus for human moral conduct. For the very idea of God assuming human nature carries with it the suggestion that Christian ethics is concerned with the perfection of humanity. In that God entered the world in the form of a man, Christian ethics must be orientated towards the fulfilment of humanity. Christian ethics does not abrogate the created order, but fulfils it. The very fact that Christian ethics is orientated towards this world, engaging creatively with it, is grounded in the belief that the Incarnation itself legitimates this engagement. In that God lodged himself firmly in human history, Christian ethics may address itself to that same history, contrary to the view that it ought to be other-worldly, purely spiritual in character. To abandon the doctrine of the Incarnation, returning to a purely transcendent view of God, is to abandon a christological insight which anchors Christian ethical reflection firmly in the realities of the present age.

The New Testament itself clearly presupposes that ethical exhortations are grounded in christological insights, in that christology provides both the presuppositions of the Christian's existential situation and the pattern for his conduct.[20] This is especially true of Paul's writings, which frequently suggest that Paul's personal existence is a recapitulation of the life-pattern embodied in Jesus Christ,[21] and further that Paul's experience is paradigmatic for Christian experience in general. Paul's narration of his personal history, interpreted in the light of that of Jesus Christ, is understood as sketching the contours of a model Christian existence.[22] For the Christian to live *ek pisteos* is to live in accordance with the structure of existence defined by the history of Jesus Christ, and reflected in that of Paul.[23]

In the earlier part of this century, the failure of the 'quest for the historical Jesus' appeared to compromise fatally any attempt to base Christian theology upon Jesus of Nazareth. That dilemma has now been resolved, through the realization that the *kergyma* – the New Testament proclamation of the perceived quintessential *significance* of Jesus – itself transmitted a picture of Jesus which could function as the basis of a coherent Christian theology, eventually leading to the development of narrative Trinitarian theology, focussing on the death of Jesus. A parallel process has been taking place within Christian ethics, through the recognition that the Enlightenment suggestion that Jesus of Nazareth is simply a moral example we are required to imitate is no longer a viable option. The New Testament transmits to us an interpretation of the moral significance of the historical existence of Jesus – an ethical *kerygma*, in effect, grounded in the narrative of Jesus.[24]

Christian ethics, therefore, may make an appeal to the historical example of Jesus. The New Testament, however, does not identify all aspects of that historical existence as possessing equal importance. Jesus' diet, his form of clothing, the language he spoke, the cultural values of his environment – none of these is treated as normative, or even as necessarily morally illuminating, by the New Testament writers. Rather, Jesus is understood to map out a way of living, a form of existence, whose contours believers are expected to echo through the work of the Holy Spirit as they are 'conformed to Christ'. We are not presented with a set of rules,[25] which we must absolutely obey, irrespective of context, but rather with the scriptural narrative of Jesus Christ,[26] and the subjective guidance of the Holy Spirit, as the external and internal means of grace. This is no new set of rules for conduct: it is a vision of a new humanity, with the demand for a new obedience. What shape might this new obedience take?

The starting point for Christian ethics is the church – the community which bears and transmits, in word and sacrament, the narrative of God's involvement with the creation, culminating in the story of Jesus Christ, and which shapes its identity and expectations in accordance with it.[27] Indeed, the very term 'Christian' carries with it a reference to a pervasive community tradition, defined in terms of the narrative of God's redeeming action, culminating in the death and resurrection of Jesus Christ. This narrative is retold in the worship of the church, supremely in the eucharistic narrative of death and resurrection. Exemplarism, as it ought to be conceived, locates the moral authority of Jesus in his history, as viewed through the paschal symbol of death and resurrection, grounded in his cross and resurrection.

The cross and resurrection constitute an *authoritative* reality within the believing community, which challenges our ethical pre-under-standings, demands a response, and generates a new outlook upon life. The narrative of Jesus Christ is retold, with the emphasis falling upon the paschal mystery of life coming through death, gain through loss. As the church worships, its corporate character is shaped by reflection upon this story. That corporate character includes the way in which the world is viewed: Christian theology and ethics alike are shaped by reflection within a community called into existence by, and nourished through the *anamnesis* of, this paschal mystery.[28] *Lex orandi, lex credendi.*

This paschal narrative serves two fundamental purposes: it lays a foundation for our understanding of the various concepts which Christian theology is obliged to deal with, and it shapes our outlook on life, illuminating our existential situation, and assisting in the formulation of moral judgements. The doctrine of the Trinity, for example, is perhaps most helpfully regarded as a summary of the history of God, of the narrative of God's dealings with the creation, as understood and expressed by scripture and the Christian tradition.[29] Who God is, and what God is like, are defined by the narrative which concerns God as its subject – just as who we are, and what we are like, is defined by the same narrative. We learn to see ourselves as sinners, as the characters in a tragedy. The prerequisite of Christian ethics is a vision of the world, deriving from the scripturally-mediated story of God's dealings with us, distilled into and interpreted by the eucharistic narrative, disclosing both the reality of human sin and the possibility of divine redemption.

In that Christian ethics presupposes the existence of a Christian community, whose understanding of its origins and destiny are formed by the narrative of the death and resurrection of Jesus Christ,[30] it is obvious that such an ethics both presupposes and expresses Christian faith. We do not imitate Christ in an external manner, as if it were through recap-itulating and imitating his existence that we are saved.[31] The Christian church must re-echo the emphasis of the New Testament – that through the death and resurrection of Jesus Christ, God has intervened in, has altered or transformed, the human dilemma. The doctrine of justification by faith declares that God makes available as a gift a new mode of existence, a new lifestyle, and enables believers to act in such a way that their actions correspond to those of Jesus. In no way does this suggestion compromise the ontological distinction between Christ and the believer: the significance of Jesus in this respect is ultimately dependent upon the identity of Jesus and God as articulated by the doctrine of the Incarnation. This process of establishing the conformity of the structure of existence of the believer to that of Jesus is already clearly evident in the New

Testament itself. Particularly in the Pauline writings, participation in Christ points to a conformity of one's existence to his.[32] Through faith, the believer is caught up in a new outlook on life, a new structure of existence, embodied paradigmatically in Jesus Christ – and both in their proclamation and person, believers reveal this story of Jesus Christ.[33]

The narrative of Jesus is thus interpreted as a story which grounds Christian existence, which gives some shape and specification to what human outlooks on life, what form of actions, what moral motivations, are appropriate expressions of our own sharing in the life of Christ. 'It is because we all live out narratives in our lives and because we understand our own lives in terms of narratives that we live out that the form of narrative is appropriate for understanding the actions of others.'[34] Narratives are grounded in history, in actions, enabling us to avoid thinking of Christian ethics in terms of universal abstractions, and instead to ground ethics in the contingencies of our historical existence. Our moral vision is shaped and informed by the story of Jesus of Nazareth, recalled in the eucharistic celebration of his death and resurrection and the benefits which these are understood to bring us, which we recognize as embodying the shape or pattern of our lives as Christians.[35]

This point is given added force through Jesus' use of narratives, such as parables, which were orientated towards an audience which could identify with those narratives. Jesus' narratives spoke of sheep wandering from their flock, of the hazards of sowing seeds, of yeast at work in dough, of things which happened when fishing. The narratives projected the world of their audience, not simply as an unpretentious and memorable way of conveying universal truths, but as a way of identifying with their horizons as a rural Galilean community. It is addressed to its hearers in terms which actively engage with their horizons of experience and understanding, in order to transform them. It is a point of contact for the transforming power of the gospel.

Hearers are drawn into this narrative world, as a story is told with which they can identify, only to be confronted with a twist to that tale which disturbs and puzzles them. It is not the righteous Pharisee, but the dishonest publican, who is justified. Those who work for one hour are paid the same as those who laboured a full working day. The narratives challenge, and force a re-evaluation of, natural human concepts of justice and rights. Jesus must be allowed to surprise the church, by pointing to something different from what was expected. The narrative of Jesus Christ himself, as retold and interpreted in the New Testament, points to a fundamental challenge being laid down to our natural ways of thinking. Life comes through death. The first are last. The poor shall inherit the earth. Power lies in powerlessness. Our status is something given, not something earned. The humble shall be exalted. Throughout the narrative, there is an implicit lifestyle, an outlook upon existence, which is being evaluated and criticized, as the better way is commended. The story of Jesus Christ embodies that better way, which we are in turn expected to reflect.

Perhaps that story has no obvious direct bearing upon the social and political realities of the present day. We have moved far beyond the rural Galilean community, unconcerned by the threat of nuclear war and the possible self-extermination of humanity. Perhaps that story will not enable the Christian church to function as the guardians of the morals of nations – but where in the New Testament is this role to be found? The primary function of the Christian church is the exposure and overthrow of the standards of the world, evident in the conducts of governments, corporations and individuals: 'eat, drink and be merry, for tomorrow we die'; the dedicated quest for power and wealth is acceptable and legitimate; status is something earned; self-preservation is a virtue; the powerful shall inherit the earth.

The gospel story of Jesus Christ, thrown into sharp focus through the paschal narrative of the liturgy, judges and exposes these as false, as un-Christian, and calls the church to repent of these attitudes herself before she applies this criticism to others. Christian ethics is interrogative as much as it is prescriptive, challenging the presuppositions underlying secular values. It is a demand for faith as much as for obedience. It is an invitation to adopt a different framework for understanding the world and our role within it. For, in the end, the most powerful and permanent contribution which a Christian ethics has to offer the world is not specific prescriptions, but a challenge to human attitudes, to the presuppositions which underlie secular society. Actions and judgements presuppose values, which are in turn grounded in an understanding of our situation. The story of Jesus is and remains an irritant to secular moral values, exposing the delusions of humanity, pointing to a better way, to an alternative attitude to life, embodied in the narrative of Jesus of Nazareth and echoed in the scriptural witness and the life of believers. How we see ourselves determines our conduct in relation to others, to the world and to God – and if we cannot grasp the relevance of the story of Jesus Christ for us, we shall have little option save to act in the ways that the fashions of this world legitimate and dictate.

Notes

1. 1856-1933. Details in *The Oxford Dictionary of the Christian Church*, 1974[2].
2. Gore had himself demonstrated his concern for the same question

somewhat earlier in his famous essay 'Our Lord's Human Example', *Church Quarterly Review* 16 (1883), pp.282-313.

3. F.W. Farrar, *Life of Christ* (London 1874) p.57. The curious phrase derives from de Pressensé's *Jesus Christ: His Times, Life and Work*.

4. In using the term 'norm', we do well to note its dual sense (especially in the natural sciences): norm as *median or average*, and as *final or critical limit*. The former suggests that Jesus reflects average human morality (perhaps echoing Thomas Aquinas' curious suggestion that Jesus is the golden mean of humanity, *habuit decentem et mediocrem quantitatem*: *Summa Theologiae* IIIa q. 33 a. 2 ad 2um), the latter that he embodies the ultimate limit to which we may tend, even if its achievement ultimately lies beyond us. The second sense governs our discussion in this essay.

5. Bultmann and Betz both argue that Christian obedience entails no particular type of moral conduct which is visibly different from than of an unbeliever: R. Bultmann, *Theology of the New Testament* 2 vols: (New York 1951), vol.1, p.138; H.D. Betz, *Galatians* (Philadelphia 1979), p.292. For Kant, the autonomy of morality is compromised through basing ethical norms on the historical person of Jesus Christ: K. Ward, *The Development of Kant's View of Ethics* (Oxford, 1972).

6. In view of the widespread confusion concerning various types of 'relativism', in which epistemological and ethical theories tend to become confused or coalesce, it is perhaps important to note that moral and epistemological relativism are independent, at least at the logical level. See Stephen Lukes, 'Relativism: Cognitive and Moral', *Aristotelian Society Proceedings, Supplement* 48 (1974), pp.165-89, who points out that the absence of any 'Archimedean point' from which absolute moral value may be established is not in any way logically dependent upon an *epistemological*, or (to use his term) 'cognitive', relativism.

7. Jaroslav Pelikan, *Jesus through the Centuries: His Place in the History of Culture* (New York 1987), pp.182-93.

8. 'The result of [Christ's] life and teaching was that [the disciples] all forsook him and fled; but the result of his Cross, resurrection and glory was to rally them and create the Church in which he dwells.' P.T. Forsyth, *The Person and Place of Jesus Christ* (London 1930[4]), p.326. The same point was repeatedly made by Scott Holland.

9. See E.J. Tinsley, *The Imitation of God in Christ* (Philadelphia 1960); John B. Webster, 'Christology, Imitability and Ethics', *Scottish Journal of Theology* 39 (1986), pp.309-26.

10. Oliver O'Donovan, *Resurrection and Moral Order: An Outline for Evangelical Ethics* (Leicester 1986), p.8.

11. See the well-rehearsed views of W.D. Falk, 'Moral Perplexity', *Ethics* 66 (1956), pp.125-9; Kai Nielsen, 'God and the Good: Does Morality need Religion?', *Theology Today* 21 (1964), pp.47-58. For a much more penetrating discussion, see Stanley Hauerwas, 'On Keeping Theological Ethics Theological', in S. Hauerwas, and A. MacIntyre, (eds.), *Revisions: Changing Perspectives in Moral Philosophy* (Notre Dame 1983) pp.16-42.

12. Hastings Rashdall, *The Idea of the Atonement in Christian Thought* (London 1921).

13. At the time of the Reformation, it was the Anabaptists who were supremely committed to the idea of *imitatio Christi* - and their pacifism was a direct result of this.

14. C.S. Lewis' words summarize the dilemma: 'We never have followed the advice of great teachers. Why are we likely to begin now? Why are we more likely to follow Christ than any of the others? Because he's the best moral teacher? But that makes it even less likely that we shall follow him. If we can't take the elementary lessons, is it likely that we're going to take the more advanced one? If Christianity only means one more bit of good advice, then Christianity is of no importance. There's been no lack of good advice over the last four thousand years. A bit more makes no difference.' *Beyond Personality: The Christian Idea of God* (London 1944), p.11.

15. Gore, 'Our Lord's Human Example', p.298. Gore, of course, employs the term 'Nestorian' prior to the twentieth-century re-evaluation of the nature of Nestorius' christology.

16. The manner in which the authority of Jesus Christ is ultimately grounded in soteriology is explored by Hans W. Frei, *The Identity of Jesus Christ: The Hermeneutical Bases of Dogmatic Theology* (Philadelphia 1975). Cf. p.82: 'The very distinctiveness of the gospel story as a story of salvation rests wholly upon the claim that the Savior is completely identical with the specific man Jesus of Nazareth.'

17. Compare the incisive epigram of Reinhold Niebuhr: 'Man's capacity for justice makes democracy possible; but man's inclination towards injustice makes democracy necessary.' *The Children of Light and the Children of Darkness* (New York 1944), p.ix.

18. Stanley Hauerwas, *The Peaceable Kingdom: A Primer in Christian Ethics* (London 1983), pp.46-9.

19. A charge frequently levelled against Christian socialism: see Ronald Preston, 'Christian Socialism Becalmed', *Theology* 91 (1988), pp. 24-32.

20. See H. D. Betz, *Nachfolge und Nachahmung Jesu Christi im Neuen Testament* (Tübingen 1967).

21. E.g. 1 Corinthians 11:1; Galatians 2:19-20; 1 Thessalonians 1:6. See Heinz Schürmann, 'Das "Gesetz des Christus" [Gal. 6,2]: Jesu Verhalten und Wort als sittliche Norm nach Paulus', in J. Gnilka, (ed.), *Neues Testament und Kirche* (Freiburg 1974), pp.282-300. For a penetrating theological analysis, see Eberhard Jüngel, 'Erwägungen zur Grundlegung evangelischer Ethik im Anschluss an die Theologie Paulus. Eine biblische Meditation', *Zeitschrift für Theologie und Kirche* 63 (1966), pp.379-90. Betz suggests that Paul understands the existence of the Christian as 'Mimesis Christi': *Nachfolge und Nachahmung*, p.186.

22. Most recently, see Beverly Gaventa, 'Galatians 1 and 2: Autobiography as Paradigm', *Novum Testamentum* 28 (1986), pp.309-26. The older study of W.P. DeBoer, *The Imitation of Paul* (Kampen 1962), repays study in this connection. The best general study of the relation between Paul's ethics and his theology remains V.P. Furnish, *Theology and Ethics in Paul* (Nashville 1968).

23. Cf. Furnish, *Theology and Ethics*, p.223. The narrative structure of Pauline theology and paranesis, of particular relevance in this connection, is analyzed by Richard B. Hays, *The Faith of Jesus Christ: An Investigation of the Narrative Substructure of Galatians 3:1-4:11* (Chico 1983), pp.193-246.

24. See the important study of Gene Outka, 'Following at a Distance: Ethics and the Identity of Jesus', in G. Green (ed.) *Scriptural Authority and Narrative Interpretation* (Philadelphia 1987).

25. Cf. Karl Barth, *The Humanity of God* (London 1961), p.85: 'The question of good and evil is never answered by man's pointing to the authoritative Word of God in terms of a set of rules...Holy Scripture defies being forced into a set of rules; it is a mistake to use it as such.'

26. For an excellent analysis of the role of narrative in Christian decision-making, see Luke Johnson, *Decision Making in the Church: A Biblical Model* (Philadelphia 1983).

27. The narrative character of Christian ethics has been explored with particular insight by Stanley Hauerwas: *The Peacable Kingdom*, pp. 17-49.

28. This point is developed by Paul Ramsey, 'Liturgy and Ethics', *Journal of Religious Ethics* 7 (1979), pp.139-71.

29. See Robert Jenson, *The Triune Identity: God according to the Gospel* (Philadelphia 1982).

30. This is linked with the concept of 'symbolic' authority: see Rowan Williams, 'Authority and the Bishop in the Church', in M. Santer, (ed.), *Their Lord and Ours* (London 1982), pp.90-112; Alister McGrath, 'The General Synod and Authority', in P. Moore, (ed.), *The Synod of Westminster*, (London 1986), pp.73-94. For the ethical dimensions of this concept, see Timothy Sedgwick, *Sacramental Ethics: Paschal Identity and the Christian Life* (Philadelphia 1987).

31. The basic point at issue - whether one becomes righteous through performing righteous acts - lies at the centre of Luther's misgivings concerning the concept of *imitatio Christi*, and points to the notion of *conformitas Christi* as being more appropriate for the distinctively Christian articulation of the relation of the lifestyle of the believer and that of Jesus Christ: see E.J. Tinsley, 'Some Principles for Reconstructing a Doctrine of the Imitation of Christ', *Scottish Journal of Theology* 25 (1972), pp.45-57, especially pp.45-7, and more recently (and fully) Eberhard Jüngel, 'Die Welt als Möglichkeit und Wirklichkeit: Zum ontologischem Ansatz der Rechtfertigungslehre', in *Unterwegs zur Sache: Theologische Bemerkungen* (Munich 1972), pp.206-33.

32. James Gustafson, *Christ and the Moral Life* (New York 1968), pp. 171-6. Cf. J.C. Beker, *Paul the Apostle* (Philadelphia 1980), p.130 'It is...not the teachings of Jesus but the crucified and risen Christ himself who constitutes the new Torah for Paul.'

33. We use the phrase 'structure of existence' in the sense suggested by Leander Keck, 'The Law and "The Law of Sin and Death" (Rom. 8:1-4): Reflections upon the Spirit and Ethics in Paul', in J. Crenshaw and S. Sandmel (eds.), *The Divine Helmsman* (New York 1980), pp. 41-57.

34. Alasdair MacIntyre, *After Virtue* (Notre Dame 1981), p.197.

35. The importance of 'foundational narratives' in shaping individual or corporate identity has been emphasized recently: Amos N. Wilder, *Early Christian Rhetoric: The Language of the Gospel* (London 1964), pp. 63-78; David B. Harned, *Creed and Personal Identity* (Edinburgh 1981); Michael Goldberg, *Theology and Narrative: A Critical Introduction* (Nashville 1982).

HISTORICAL RETROSPECT: LUX MUNDI 1889

Geoffrey Rowell

1989 marks the centenary of one of the theological works of the last century, which has been seen as a significant turning point or shift of emphasis in Anglican theology. In November of that year a volume appeared with the title *Lux Mundi*, 'the Light of the World', with the subtitle, 'a series of studies in the religion of the Incarnation'. The editor was Charles Gore, a young Oxford priest and don, who had recently been appointed as Principal of the newly established Pusey House – the house of sacred study built around Dr Pusey's Library, as a memorial to the great Oxford Movement leader after his death in 1882.

The contributors were all relatively young priests and teachers, either at Oxford or recently there, whose sacramental spirituality and theological outlook placed them in succession to the Tractarians, but who equally saw the need for a new theological expression of the great Christian themes. There were eleven contributors: Henry Scott Holland, Aubrey Lackington Moore, John Richardson Illingworth, Edward Stuart Talbot, Robert Campbell Moberly, Arthur Temple Lyttelton, Walter Lock, Francis Paget, William James Campion, Robert Ottley and the editor, Charles Gore. Holland was a Canon of St. Paul's; Illingworth, a former Fellow of Jesus and Tutor of Keble, was rector of the country parish of Longworth between Oxford and Faringdon. Talbot was Warden of Keble, and his brother-in-law, Arthur Lyttelton (who had also for a time been a tutor at Keble) was Master of Selwyn College, Cambridge. Walter Lock was another tutor of Keble, as were Moore and Campion. (Both of the latter were to die young shortly after the publication of *Lux Mundi*, Moore in January 1890 and Campion in April, 1892). Ottley had again spent a brief time as a Keble tutor, but was Vice-Principal of Cuddesdon at the time of *Lux Mundi*. He subsequently became Regius Professor of Moral and Pastoral Theology. Only Francis Paget (subsequently Dean of Christ Church and Bishop of Oxford) the son-in-law of Dean Church, R.C. Moberly (later Regius Professor of Pastoral Theology) and Gore himself had no direct link with Keble College.

The contributors were almost all identical with the group that Scott Holland had christened 'the Holy Party'. In the Easter Vacation of 1873 Illingworth had participated in a reading party at St. David's. During the following year, according to Wilfrid Richmond (later to be Warden of Trinity College, Glenalmond), 'there grew in our minds the idea, the dream, of a brotherhood life, a fellowship of those who were devoted to the Truth. It was inspired to some extent by what we knew of the Oratorians.'[1] The Oratorian reference is a significant comment in view both of John Henry Newman's choice of the Oratorian community as the one he entered following his conversion to the Church of Rome, and of Gore's later foundation of the Community of the Resurrection in which Oratorian ideals played a significant part.

In August 1875 Henry Scott Holland organised the first of the 'Holy Party' gatherings at Brighstone in the Isle of Wight. Holland characterised this and subsequent meetings as being 'simply the habit of a gang of us young donlets to occupy some small country parish for a month, do the duty, read, discuss, say the offices, and keep our hours together... We would work, and play, and talk over the possibilities of an Anglican Oratorian Community, and be exceedingly happy.'[2] Richmond suggests that part of the inspiration came from a retreat given by Alexander Penrose Forbes, the Tractarian Bishop of Brechin, a retreat which Illingworth remembered, as he also recalled the man: 'the great Bishop of Brechin was one of the attractive figures of one's youth – a kind of mysterious romantic figure, with the halo of courtliness and sanctity mixed – and he took a wonderful retreat for us – which we have never forgotten – urging us to Christian philosophy – when we were at the beginning of our Oxford time.'[3] Forbes pointed his retreatants towards Leibnitz 'as suggesting a direction for Christian philosophy'. Richmond, who had been reading the works of Lotze, wrote that it was then 'that the word "Personality" became magical to us as symbolising a Christian philosophy of the future.'[4]

The pattern of the Brighstone meeting – 7 a.m. Holy Communion or Meditation; 8 a.m. breakfast; silence and study from then until the midday Office and lunch at 1.00; an afternoon walk; tea at 4.30 followed by a discussion of some selected book – plotted the course of future summer meetings of the Holy Party. Interestingly Richmond questions the extent to which the Holy Party was identical with the *Lux Mundi* group, citing Moberly's judgement that 'the source of the *Lux Mundi* party was in the gathering of friends and spiritual forces, of which Dr. Talbot, then Warden of Keble, was the centre.' Noting the close involvement of almost all the *Lux Mundi* contributors with Keble, this is certainly true, but it was very much the same people who comprised the Holy Party.

Charles Gore, the editor of *Lux Mundi*, had been born in 1853, the son of a civil servant. In the family home at Wimbledon they were neighbours of the Holland family, and although Henry Scott Holland was a few years older than Gore they were already closely acquainted by the time Gore came to Oxford in 1871. Three years earlier, in 1868, Scott Holland had begun his undergraduate career at Balliol having been at school at Eton. Gore came from Harrow, where Brooke Foss Westcott, then an assistant master at Harrow, was one of those who influenced him.

Scott Holland had an enthusiasm and a genius for friendship, which soon showed itself at Balliol. He was particularly close to R.L. Nettleship, later to make his name as a philosopher, and Stephen Fremantle, an Etonian contemporary and the youngest son of Lord Cottesloe. Fremantle's tragically early death in 1874 (from typhoid caught on a reading party at Newquay) left a deep mark on Holland. But it was Thomas Hill Green, idealist philosopher and Fellow of Balliol, who was the most significant shaper of Holland's thought. In reaction against the utilitarianism of John Stuart Mill, Green inculcated an idealism with social and political consequences which proved powerful and attractive to the young High Churchmen who came under his influence (despite the fact that Green himself was suspicious of dogmatic religion). Green taught that 'a Church unconnected with its effect upon the political justice and social welfare of its society cannot be said to be the bearer of the Gospel taught by Jesus'.[5] Life, he stressed, was for action. Whereas, David Newsome points out, for an F.D. Maurice faith was merely recognition, for Holland faith was 'an active principle, a source of energy, a spring of movement' verifying itself only in actions: 'its reality can only be made evident through experience of its living work.' Green's idealism, influenced by Hegel, which saw the world as 'the realisation of a spiritual principle', consorted well with a Logos theology, and a stress (also of course to be found in Westcott) on *Christus consummator*, Christ the fulfiller of all human truth. The words which Mrs Humphrey Ward in her novel, *Robert Elsmere*, puts into the mouth of Mr Grey (a thinly disguised T.H. Green), illustrate this stance:

> (God) is in all life, in all thought. The thought of man as it has shaped itself in institutions, in philosophies, in science, in patient critical work, or in the life of charity is the one continuous revelation of God.[6]

Green's influence was powerful and readily acknowledged, even though Richmond observed that Green was 'cruelly inarticulate...tough and tangled' and full of 'teeth-breaking and head-splitting' Hegelian jargon. He was appreciative of Illingworth's achievement, for Illingworth had, he believed, translated Green into a more intelligible style.[7] Holland readily acknowledged his own debt to Green, who had, he claimed, taught him everything of importance that he had learnt at Oxford.[8] When he was ordained as deacon in 1872 he reiterated his debt to Green: 'I still feel to myself at least (that I must) trace all the strongest and clearest threads of my life to you.' He hoped that his ordination would not prove a barrier between them, believing that their only major difference was what he believed to be Green's stated preference for morality to sanctity.[9] Green in his reply was quick to point out that he had never meant to oppose religion and morality. Rather he held all morality to be religious for it rested upon the consciousness of God. What Green found objectionable was the supposed sanctity of those who made religion their God instead of God their religion. Dogmatic theology, he continued, was grounded on the theory 'that true ideas about God and things spiritual are derived from miraculous events'. The underlying truth of the ideas Green did not wish to dispute; what he queried was their grounding in miracle.

> It is the derivation from miraculous events that I reject, holding that the belief in the events was derived from the ideas (of which philosophy is the true intellectual expression) not the ideas from the real happening of the events. The result is that from orthodox Christianity, as expressed in prayer, and in the ordinances of Protestant worship, I find no alienation, while I could not subscribe to one of the creeds.[10]

Green argued that the Christian understanding of God was prior to and not constituted by belief in miracle. He disliked evidence theology, which seemed to him to contradict 'the philosophic condition of Theism' that 'there is nothing real apart from thought, whereas the doctrine of miracles implies that there is something real apart from thought, viz. "nature", but that thought has once or twice miraculously interfered with it.' Green claimed Holland as an ally in the company of those for whom the revelation of God did not rest on miracle, though he saw him as liable to fall prey to 'sacerdotalism' and 'sacramentalism' which in Green's book were the substitution of 'a miraculous and mystical' presence of God in the Church for a moral one.[11] Green's influence was significant not only on Holland and Illingworth but also on Gore. One who was neither an Anglican nor a member of the Holy Party, the Methodist, Hugh Price Hughes, could describe Green as 'the most splendid Christian I ever knew...the philosophical expression of the good old Methodist doctrine of entire sanctification'.[12]

By contrast Benjamin Jowett did not have the same impact on Holland and his circle. Holland tartly commented on a Jowett sermon he heard in Balliol Chapel in 1869 that 'it was just Platonism flavoured with a little Christian charity: Christianity is gutted by him: it becomes perfectly meaningless...There is not an atom of the feeling of prayer, of communication with God, of reliance on any one but self...I admire the Symposium with all my heart and soul; but I must have something more to have brought God down to death to procure [salvation] for me.'[13]

Jowett's religion was too thin and intellectualised for Holland who need-ed a religion of grace and salvation, with a cutting social edge.

The 'Holy Party' met regularly each year from 1875, though the attendance varied. In 1884 Holland moved from Oxford to a canonry at St. Paul's. H.P. Liddon, Pusey's disciple and biographer, already a fellow-canon, welcomed the appointment, but expressed in a letter to Holland his growing concern about the theological stance of the younger Oxford churchmen. These were to become much sharper when *Lux Mundi* was published five years later. Liddon wrote:

> I have feared sometimes that the younger Churchmanship of Oxford was undergoing a silent but very serious change – through its eagerness to meet modern difficulties and its facile adoption of new intellectual methods, without fully considering the use to which they might be put by others...There is a difference betwen the new and the old Churchmanship. The new cares less for authority, and relies more on subjective considerations and expects more from fallen humanity, and attaches less importance to the Divine organisation and function of the Church, than did the old. We live here (in London) on terms of easy intercourse with so many to whom Catholic doctrine, and indeed the whole Creed of Christianity go for nothing, that this new estimate may well have grown up without being noticed. But to yield to such influences means sooner or later some essentially Pantheistic sub-situte for the Ancient Faith.[14]

In 1887 the meeting of the Holy Party had determined on the pub-lication of a volume of essays. The essays were to express the common view of Christian doctrine and its moral application that was shared by those who for more than ten years had not only met together each Long Vacation for study and discussion, but had also been closely bound together by a common churchmanship and work, mostly in Oxford. Gore, by now Principal of Pusey House, became informally the editor of the collection. A year later they met at Holland's house in Amen Court to consider the essays that had been produced. Arthur Lyttelton, the Master of Selwyn, was asked to re-cast his essay on the atonement. Gore was commissioned to write on the Holy Spirit and inspiration to fill what was thought to be an obvious gap. Ironically it was this essay which was to prove the centre of controversy when the book was published. In June 1889 the Holy Party gathered at the Westminster Arms at Malvern and the essays were finally revised and approved for publication. The book had originally been offered to the Oxford University Press under the title *The Religion of the Incarnation*, but had narrowly been turned down. 'The orthodox voted against, I shd. gather on the ground that it would open flood gates,' Gore told Holland.[15] The book was offered to another publisher, John Murray, who accepted it. The title, *Lux Mundi*, was supplied by Illingworth.

The concerns of the writers were set out in the preface, which was written by Gore as editor. *Lux Mundi*, he said, endeavoured to 'put the Catholic faith into its right relation with modern intellectual and moral problems' and arose out of a common understanding of the Christian faith evolved over the ten years of meeting and discussion between 1875 and 1885. It was an exercise in the reinterpretation of the Creed. 'We have written,' Gore continued, 'not as "guessers at truth" (an allusion to the volume *Guesses at Truth* published earlier in the century by Julius and Augustus Hare), but as servants of the Catholic Creed and Church, aiming only at interpreting the faith we have received.' Theology had to give expression to development, which did not mean either innovation or heresy on the one hand, nor 'a narrowing and hardening of theology by simply giving it great definiteness or multiplying its dogmas' on the other.

The real development of theology, Gore maintained, was rather the process in which the Church, standing firm in her old truths, enters into the apprehension of the new social and intellectual movements of each age: and because 'the truth makes her free' is able 'to assimilate all new material, to welcome and give its place to all new knowledge, to throw herself into the sanctification of each new social order, bringing forth out of her treasures things new and old, and shewing again and again her power of witnessing under changed conditions to the catholic capacity of her faith and life.' As Newman would have said in a different context, 'it changes always in order to remain the same'.

Gore was conscious that there were omissions, such as an essay on sin, a discussion of historical evidences, and miracles. On miracles he commented:

> If we have not found room for a treatment of miracles, at least we hope that the Church's conception of God, as He manifests Himself in nature and in grace, which we have endeavoured to express, will at once acquit us of any belief in capricious 'violations of law'; and will also suggest a view of the world as disordered by sin and crying out for redemption which will make it intelligible that 'miracles' should appear, not as violating law, but as a necessary element in its restoration, as well as its completer exhibition; contrary, not to the fundamental order of the Divine working, but only to a superficial or mechanical view of it, or to a view which sin has distorted or preoccupation with physical science has unduly narrowed. [16]

In the first essay Holland wrestles with the nature of faith. He is concerned with faith in the sense of the subjective act of believing rather than, initially, what is believed. Faith, he suggests, is 'a primary intuition' like love or will. 'It is, essentially, an active principle, a source of energy, a spring of movement: and, as such, its verification can never take place through passive introspection. It verifies itself only in actions: its reality can only be made evident through experience of its living work.' It is rooted in the inner reality of relationship to God, and is 'the spiritual temper and attitude' which belongs inherently to that fact. 'No one can escape such a claim: for his existence constitutes the claim.' Christ, as the supreme revelation of that relationship to God, the perfect expression of Sonship, is the touchstone of faith and that to which all credal and dogmatic statements refer. Christian dogmas 'are simply careful rehearsals of those inherent necessities which inevitably are involved in the rational construction of Christ's living character.' If, as the Christian creed maintains, Christ is the final and definitive revelation of God, then, writes Holland, 'we have touched in Him...the ultimate stage of all development.' 'It is this finality which justifies dogma. If Christianity is final, it can afford to be dogmatic.' Faith does indeed call on feeling, reason and imagination, as well as proof and argument, but in the end it must go beyond all of these. To be 'like birds on a bough, who...refuse to fly until they have fully known that they can' is not to have faith.[17]

In the essay on the Christian doctrine of God, Aubrey Moore poses the problem that after Feuerbach we are left in the dilemma that 'an anthropomorphic God is the only God whom men can worship, and also the God whom modern thought finds it increasingly difficult to believe in.' Moore counters this by a renewed emphasis on the doctrine of the Trinity; by an underlining of the importance of the Logos doctrine in the formative period of Christian theology; and by a stress on the need for a proper awareness of divine immanence in response to an over-emphasis on divine transcendence. In the deism of the eighteenth century 'God "was throned in magnificant inactivity in a remote corner of the universe", and a machinery of "second causes" had practically taken His place.' Now, Moore proclaims:

> the one absolutely impossible conception of God, in the present day, is that which represents Him as an occasional Visitor...We must frankly return to the Christian view of direct Divine agency, the immanence of Divine power in nature from end to end, the belief in a God in Whom not only we, but all things have their being, or we must banish Him altogether. It seems as if, in the providence of God, the mission of modern science was to bring home to our unmetaphysical ways of thinking the great truth of the Divine immanence in creation, which is not less essential to the Christian idea of God than to a philosophical view of nature.

That having been said, the conception of God as personal, Moore concludes, is necessary and vital to prevent the doctrine of the Divine immanence being expressed only as a pantheism that is less than personal.[18]

Illingworth's essay, 'The Incarnation and Development', begins with a recognition of the impact of the theory of evolution far beyond its original scientific context. 'Evolution is in the air. It is the category of the age...We cannot place ourselves outside it, or limit the scope of its operation...In the face of the historical spirit of the age, the study of past theology can never again be regarded as merely a piece of religious antiquarianism.' Illingworth criticises Reformation and post-Reformation thought for narrowing the religion of the Incarnation into the religion of the atonement, with a consequent sharp division between sacred and secular, and a subjectivising of religion. He contrasts this with the cosmic perspective of the patristic period. 'They realized that redemption was a means to an end, and that end the reconsecration of the whole universe to God.' He quotes with approval from Aquinas: 'the incarnation is the exaltation of human nature and consummation of the universe' – a theme that Bishop Westcott set out in his appendix headed 'The Gospel of Creation' in his commentary *The Epistles of St. John*.[19] The recognition of evolution and development in nature is for Illingworth a providential opportunity to recognise in that development the presence and activity of the Logos who is Life. The religion of the Incarnation as opposed to one exclusively emphasising the atonement, enables, Illingworth suggests, an appropriate appreciation of the material world and the whole range of human life and activity. The religion of the Incarnation:

> welcomes the discoveries of science, as ultimately due to Divine revelation, and part of the providential education of the world. It recalls to art the days when in catacomb and cloister she learned her noblest mission to be the service of the Word made Flesh. It appeals to democracy as the religion of the fishermen who gathered round the carpenter's son. It points the social reformer to the pattern of a perfect man, laying down His life alike for enemy and friend. While it crowns all earthly aims with a hope full of immortality, as prophetic of eternal occupations elsewhere.'[20]

It was Gore's essay 'The Holy Spirit and Inspiration' which was to prove the most controversial in *Lux Mundi*. Christianity he maintains is 'a manifested life' – first in Christ and then in the church. The Christian church is 'the Spiritbearing body', and in that body four aspects of the Spirit's activity may be recognised: the *social*, which is seen in the sacraments as social ceremonies, and the order and structure of the church, and the apostolic tradition binding the church together; the *individual*, the differentiation of gifts and the transfiguration of personality enabled by the Spirit, and included within this the educative function of a guiding authority within the church; the *consecration of the whole of nature* – the overcoming of the false dualism between nature and grace, Spirit and matter; and, finally, *the gradualness of the Spirit's operation*. Under this last heading Gore discusses the imperfection of the Old Testament. He goes on to look more particularly at the doctrine of the inspiration of scripture. That belief, Gore maintains, must spring out of a more general belief in the presence and activity of the Holy Spirit in the Church and in the world. Gore argues that the doctrine of the inspiration of scripture is not 'among the *bases* of Christian belief'.

The Christian creed asserts the reality of certain historical facts. 'To these facts, in the Church's name, we claim assent: but we do so on grounds which, so far, are quite independent of the *inspiration* of the evangelic records.' To speak of the inspiration of scripture is to speak of the writers of scripture as being 'subjects of a movement of the Holy Ghost, so shaping, controlling, quickening their minds, thoughts and aspirations, as to make them the instruments through which was imparted 'the knowledge of God and of the spiritual life'. But the supernatural does not override the natural. Inspiration does not mean something mechanical or ecstatic. The primary point of reference for a doctrine of inspiration is, Gore maintains, the fact that what is written is written with the concern to see all in relation to the judgement of God. This leaves Gore free to argue that the acknowledgement of the historicity of the Old Testament is not demanded in every detail. 'The recorders of Israel's history were subject to the ordinary laws of the estimate of evidence...their inspiration did not consist in a miraculous communication to them of facts as they originally happened.' Spiritual illumination does not override natural conditions of knowledge. Finally, Gore maintains, in what was seen, perhaps, by his critics as the place where he came closest to an abandonment of the older orthodoxy, that the words of Jesus cannot be taken as foreclosing critical questions about the character of the Old Testament, giving as an example the story of Jonah. It is because the 'Incarnation was a self-emptying of God to reveal Himself under the conditions of human nature and from the human point of view' that we are able to draw a distinction between what Christ revealed and what He used. 'He *used* human nature, its relation to God, its conditions of experience, its growth in knowledge, its limitations of knowledge...He willed so to restrain the beams of His Deity as to observe the limits of the science of His age.'[21] So Gore concluded, but we should note the criticism that the thrust of the essay deals mainly with the inspiration of the *Old*

Testament, and assumes that the New Testament is not so threatened by sharp, historical criticism.

Lux Mundi went through ten editions in its first year of publication and excited considerable interest. As is well known, one of those who felt Gore's essay to be a betrayal was Liddon, who had supported Gore as the first Principal of Pusey House. He questioned Gore's critical assumptions as being psychological, whereas Liddon wished to stand with Pusey for whom criticism was, he said, 'the bringing of all that learning and thought could bring to illustrate the mind of Christian Antiquity'. He told D.C. Lathbury that he had been deeply distressed by the concluding section of Gore's essay:

> which has come upon me like a thunderbolt out of a clear sky. It is practically a capitulation at the feet of the young Rationalistic Professors, by which the main positions which the old Apologists of Holy Scripture have maintained are conceded to the enemy, in deference to the 'literary' judgment of our time. Not only could Dr Pusey not have written these pages, it would have been difficult to have written anything more opposed to his convictions.' [22]

'I did not suspect,' he told Lord Halifax, that Gore 'had constructed a private kennel for liberalising ideas in Theology within the precincts of the Old Testament, and so much of the New as bears upon it.' *Lux Mundi* appeared to Liddon as having 'a naturalistic and Pelagianising tone'. 'The writers seem to think it a gain when they can prune away, or economise the Supernatural, or the great and awful doctrines of Grace, which are the heart of Christianity.'[23] Newman, now at the very end of his life, seemed to give an uncertain comment on the book. On the one hand he told a correspondent, who had asked him whether he agreed with Gore, that he was content to leave it for the Holy See to decide. 'I wait until the Holy Church has given its answer, and am not impatient if she delays.' As to whether it was the end of the Tractarian counter-offensive against Liberalism, he replied that 'it is the finale, because we are bound to go not by mere Reason, but by Faith, which will be the safer in the long run.' This was confirmed by a message Newman sent to Ward through Neville that he thought the argument of *Lux Mundi* was 'the old one of private judgement.' But Wilfrid Ward himself recorded in his reminiscences that although Newman was said to condemn *Lux Mundi*:

> but I found in conversation that he was still in the same position as he held in the days of Acton and Simpson's effort in the *Home and Foreign*. His sympathies were divided. He sympathised strongly with the desire to keep thought among Christians open-minded and up to date. But he dreaded the liberalism and rationalism which he knew would introduce themselves under cover of this laudable endeavour.

He desired to open a door to increased life and freedom in the Catholic schools but to do it very cautiously. He certainly thought that *Lux Mundi* as a whole was too liberal. But to myself he did not speak of it with unmixed reprobation. He rather treated it as an indication to be taken very seriously of the necessity of a strong plea within the Catholic Church for a frank recognition of the sober conclusions of biblical science, and a view of biblical inspiration compatible with complete frankness as to facts.'[24]

Various reviews commented on *Lux Mundi*. The *British Weekly* discerned a parallel between Gore and R.W. Dale, but said the book was enough to make Dr Pusey turn in his grave. The Evangelical *Rock* thought it indicative of the complexity, or sinuosity of minds warped by Ritualism, and saw Ritualism and Agnosticism were going to join hands as Romanism and Infidelity did before the French Revolution. *The Speaker* generally welcomed it but declared it to be better as literature than theology. The *Record* admitted that the book was 'stimulating' but disagreed with Gore's essay in particular. Archdeacon Denison issued a rallying cry to the defence of 'the integral and absolute Authority of "Holy Scripture" as delivered to us of GOD and committed to our keeping by the Church.' *Lux Mundi* was 'a most unhappy and dangerous book'. A later issue of the *Record* called the writers the 'Neo-Rits'.[25]

The authors replied to their critics in a substantial preface appended to the tenth edition (1890), signed by Gore but discussed in common. Exception was taken to the disproportionate attention concentrated on one section of Gore's essay on inspiration. Gore pleaded that he had wished to free Anglicans from an 'obscurantist fear of historical enquiry' and to convince his readers that critical enquiry could only be met with true assurance if it were seen that the critical positions were in fact compatible with 'the real *inspiration* of Holy Scripture'. The aim had been to give anxious enquirers 'a freedom in regard to Old Testament problems as wide as the Catholic faith seemed to warrant'. Gore argued that, as far as Jesus' own use of the Old Testament was concerned, nothing depended on questions of authorship or date. 'He appeals to them in that spiritual aspect which abides through all changes of literary theory – their testimony to the Christ.' Furthermore, Gore continues, the self-limitation involved in the Incarnation meant that Jesus must have referred to the Old Testament scriptures in the manner used by his hearers. 'Unless He had violated the whole principle of the Incarnation, by anticipating the slow development of natural knowledge, He must have spoken of the Deuteronomist as "Moses", as naturally as He spoke of the sun "rising".' The omission of an essay on sin was met by the inclusion of a Cambridge University sermon Gore had preached on the subject.

The writers hoped that the discussion to which *Lux Mundi* had given rise might lead to two good results – first, an emphasis on the fact that Christian faith is faith in a Person, not a book; and, secondly, that a clear line was drawn in regard to development between the Old and the New Testament. 'For us the Old Testament depends upon the New, not the New upon the Old.' Such a drawing of the line between Old Testament development and a critical analysis of it and the New Testament did not prove a possible line to maintain. But *Lux Mundi* as a whole was about more than that, and about more than Gore's essay. It marked the recasting of Anglican theology in an incarnational mould, *Christus consummator* rather than *Christus redemptor*, inductive rather than deductive in character, and welcoming of historical criticism, scientific advance, and an awareness of development. It was a church theology, a prayed theology, and a theology with clear social implications. Not for nothing were Gore and Scott Holland founders of the Christian Social Union, as other contributors were involved with East End settlements, and as Gore himself was the founder of the Community of the Resurrection.

Notes

1. A.L. Illingworth (ed.) *The Life and Work of John Richardson Illingworth, MA, DD* (1917), p.33.
2. S. Paget: *Henry Scott Holland, Memoir and Letters* (1921), pp.85-6n.
3. *Life of Illingworth,* p.187.
4. *Ibid.,* p.33.
5. D. Newsome: *Two Classes of Men: Platonism and English Romantic Thought* (1974), p.119.
6. Mrs Humphry Ward, *Robert Elsmere* (1952 ed.), p.345.
7. *Life of Illingworth*, pp.316-7.
8. *Life of Holland*, p.47.
9. *Ibid.,* p.64.
10. *Ibid.,* p.66.
11. *Ibid.,* pp. 67-8.
12. D.P. Hughes, *Life of Hugh Price Hughes* (1905³), p.134.
13. *Life of Holland*, pp.33-4.
14. *lbid.,* p.114.
15. G.L. Prestige, *The Life of Charles Gore: a great Englishman*, (1935), pp.98-9.
16. C. Gore (ed.), *Lux Mundi: a series of studies in the religion of the Incarnation* (1904¹⁵), p.ix.
17. H.S. Holland, 'Faith', *Lux Mundi*, pp.1-39.
18. A. Moore, 'The Christian Doctrine of God', *Lux Mundi*, pp.41-81.
19. B.F. Westcott, *The Epistles of St. John: the Greek Text with notes and essays* (1883), pp.273-315.
20. J.R. Illingworth, 'The Problem of Pain: its bearing on faith in God', *Lux Mundi*, p.156.
21. C. Gore, 'The Holy Spirit and Inspiration', *Lux Mundi*, pp.230-266.

22. J.O. Johnston, *Life and Letters of Henry Parry Liddon, DD, DCL, LLD* (1904), pp.367-8.

23. *Ibid.*, pp.371-2.

24. C.S. Dessain and T. Gornall (eds.), *The Letters and Diaries of John Henry Newman*, XXXI (1977), p.294 & n. (I am indebted to Dr Hilary Jenkins for this reference).

25. MS volume of correspondence and press cuttings on *Lux Mundi*, Pusey House archive, Oxford.

26. Preface to the tenth edition of *Lux Mundi* (1890), *Lux Mundi*, ed. cit., pp.x-xxx. Gore had also re-written some sentences in his essays for the fourth edition to prevent misunderstanding.